ARGUMENT FOR ACTION: ETHICS AND PROFESSIONAL CONDUCT

John Lawrence has taught social policy for thirty years, taking a special interest in the ethical justification of policy and of professional intervention. He is a graduate of the Universities of Adelaide and Oxford, and of the Australian National University. Australia's first Professor of Social Work, he headed the School of Social Work at the University of New South Wales for fourteen years, chaired the University's Faculty of Professional Studies, was a member of the University Council, and was centrally involved in the development of its Social Policy Research Centre, a national centre directly funded by the Australian Government. A former federal president and life member of the Australian Association of Social Workers, he has served on its National Ethics Committee. For eight years, he was an elected member of the Executive Board of the International Association of Schools of Social Work. He has had membership of the governing bodies of community agencies, including a vice-presidency of ACOSS (Australian Council of Social Service). He is a firm advocate of international experience, and has spent almost seven years away from his native Australia, studying, researching, teaching and acting as a consultant in England, the United States, Canada, Thailand and Sweden. This has been assisted by various awards - a Rhodes scholarship, Fulbright senior awards, the Moses Distinguished Professorship at Hunter College in New York, and a Canadian Commonwealth Fellowship - and university study leave and exchange arrangements. He is a Member of the Order of Australia.

Argument for Action: Ethics and Professional Conduct

JOHN LAWRENCE
Emeritus Professor
The University of New South Wales

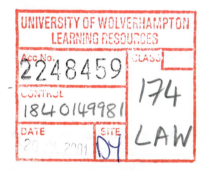
Ashgate

Aldershot • Brookfield USA • Singapore • Sydney

Published by
Ashgate Publishing Ltd
Gower House
Croft Road
Aldershot
Hants GU11 3HR
England

Ashgate Publishing Company
Old Post Road
Brookfield
Vermont 05036
USA

British Library Cataloguing in Publication Data
Lawrence, John
    Argument for action : ethics and professional conduct
    1. Professional ethics
    I. Title
    174

Library of Congress Catalog Card Number: 98-74840

ISBN 1 84014 998 1

Printed in Great Britain

Contents

Figures

Acknowledgements

The intrinsic interest and worth of much of professionals' work can keep them going, but without expressions of genuine gratitude both given and received, professional life can become impersonal and sterile. Clearly, for this kind of book, I owe a very wide debt of gratitude - to my parents, my teachers, my professional colleagues, my students, and particularly to those whose writing has contributed to my understanding of ethics and the professions.

I have been working on this book since 1983 - at first spasmodically, and then consistently in more recent years. Six months at the Social Welfare (now Social Policy) Research Centre at The University of New South Wales, and twelve months as the Moses Professor at Hunter College, City University of New York, gave me invaluable clear time and stimulating colleagues, to get on with the highly ambitious task I had set myself.

It seems invidious to mention particular people, but I must mention and thank at least some. Damian Grace, Jim Lawrence, Peter Linklater, Jill Roe, and Tony Vinson, all willingly read the completed manuscript and provided helpful comment. Tony Vinson played an additional special role in providing comments on work-in-progress for Part 2 of the book. I also owe a special debt to Harold Lewis, Dean Emeritus, Hunter College School of Social Work, who performed a similar role for the first two chapters of Part 1, and who made possible my time at Hunter. Others who have been of assistance in a variety of ways include: Mimi Abramovitz, Diane Barnes, Werner Boehm, Natalie Bolzan, Guido Calabresi, Miriam Dinerman, Howard Goldstein, Charles Guzzetta, Virginia Held, Terry Hokenstad, Austin Hukins, Adam Jamrozik, Ruth Lawrence Karski and Pierre Karski, Paul Kurzman, Bruce Lagay, Peter Lawrence, Phyllida Parsloe, Florence and Joseph Vigilante, and Sylvia Wenston. Finally, the unfailing love, support, and intelligent criticism of my wife, Trish, have been essential to the completion of this and many other projects.

Introduction

Why is it especially important for professions and professionals to be able to justify morally their actions? The brief answer is - because their knowledge and their skills place them in positions of considerable trust and power in modern society. However, it is only reasonable to give them this trust and power if it is going to be used for morally justified purposes. A crucial feature of a profession is hence its so-called 'ethics' which supposedly guarantees that a profession serves rather than exploits the society in which it operates. Moral or ethical reasoning provides grounding argument for appropriate action.

Professional ethics has become the focus of a great deal of recent writing within individual occupations and, to some extent, more generally. What makes this particular book distinctive is the breadth and nature of its argument - that in the modern world ethical justification needs to be grounded in rational action for human well-being; and that justifiable professional conduct is not reasonably grounded unless and until it can be related to this basic value. It challenges and supplements the many narrower publications which concentrate on the 'ethics' of particular occupations. It helps each occupation to identify its contribution to society and to understand the argument in which it must engage if it is to provide adequate justification for its conduct. The specialized nature and power of professional occupations make this task both more difficult and more pressing. The book links the relatively recent rediscovery of 'ethics' with the continuing significance of the idea of professionalism in modern societies affected by Anglo-American traditions.

The work has been written for all who are interested in and affected by the Anglo-American traditions of professionalism and are willing to read and follow an extended argument. It should be of particular interest to people who are dealing with professions and professionals, to those who are developing, leading and educating professional occupations, to those who are engaged in professional practice and are members of professional associations, and to those increasing numbers who are teaching, and undertaking a course on professional ethics. It should also capture the interest of anyone who puzzles about the nature of ethics in the modern world.

The work is divided into two parts. Part 1 discusses the concepts of 'ethics' and 'professional conduct', indicating their dimensions and contested nature. In each case, following examination and analysis of relevant literature, a conceptual framework or model is proposed for locating instances of, in turn, 'ethics' and 'professional conduct'. The first chapter, for many, will serve as an introduction to ethics as a systematic subject for study and reflection. Chapter 2 provides an intellectual framework for addressing ethical issues if human well-being is accepted as the prime justificatory value for human conduct. These first two chapters suggest what might be seen as a reasonable basis for ethical choice in the modern world.

The rest of the book concentrates on a particular form of human conduct, professional conduct, which calls for justification because of the influence of professions and professionals on human well-being. Chapter 3 first examines the place of work in human society, and then more particularly the scope and nature of professional work in Anglo-American societies as this has been understood by serious writers on the subject. Chapter 4 builds on the previous chapter in providing an analytical model of what the term 'professional conduct' might refer to in any particular instance of individual or collective conduct.

A practically-oriented reader may become impatient with the conceptual discussion of Part 1. Each of the chapters, however, is part of the developing argument of the book which should become apparent as the reader proceeds. Each chapter has some inherent interest, as well as being part of a general argument.

In Part 2 of the book, the model developed in Chapter 2 - of ethical choice based on rational action for human well-being - is used to discuss the ethical justification of professional conduct in the various forms, locations, and stages, provided by its social setting. In this way, it provides grounding argument for relevant action by professionals and others dealing with professionals. Professional conduct is ethically assessed in relation to individual agenda-setting; then in relation to agenda-setting by collectivities - governments, families, commercial organizations, and non-profit organizations. Consideration of professionals as the relevant moral agents to deal with the agenda items is followed by discussion of professionals in policy, implementation, and evaluation stages of rational action. Each and all of the stages of rational action can come under ethical scrutiny by individual conscience or by outside observers.

The book concludes with a proposal for a national commission on the professions which could help in strengthening the ethical justification of professional conduct, provided certain conditions are met.

PART 1: THE BASIC CONCEPTS

Our task in Part 1 is to gain understanding of the two basic concepts 'ethics' and 'professional conduct'. We will then be in a position to tackle the ethical justification of professional conduct in Part 2.

1 What is Ethics?

Ethics or morality[1] is concerned with the evaluation of human conduct and human character. It is an activity in which every human being is inescapably involved - as an actor and on the receiving end of others' actions, and as a judge of one's own and others' conduct and character. Past, present and future conduct and character come within its ambit. It is a characteristically human activity dependent upon our rationality, our ability to seek and give reasons for our actions, to understand and seek alternatives, to weigh their merits, to make decisions and act accordingly. It is concerned with both description and prescription.

Descriptive Ethics

Nature and Convention[2]

Descriptive ethics tells us what criteria or standards have been, are, and will be used by people in deciding what to do and what kind of people they will be. Humans are essentially social and normative beings. We cannot exist, let alone flourish, in isolation from each other. Our capacity to think, to speak, and to reason - to learn, to be aware of ourselves and others, to understand, to calculate, to follow an argument, to plan, to reflect, to imagine, to have foresight, to remember, to aspire, to identify feelings - has made us essentially normative beings living in social orders of various kinds, families,

---

[1] In accordance with ordinary language and the practice of many philosophers, these terms will be used interchangeably. Although they are sometimes distinguished, there is no standard distinction between them. 'Ethics' comes from Greek, and 'morality' (or 'morals') from Latin. Both origins mean 'disposition' or 'custom'; the Latin giving more emphasis to social expectations, the Greek, to individual character. (Williams, 1985: 6.) Some philosophers describe ethics as the philosophical study of morality: others, especially in Britain, call this 'moral philosophy'.

[2] The important distinction between nature and convention is discussed in Popper, 1950, vol. 1, chap.1; and Benn and Peters, 1959: 15-18.

5

friendships, community groups, religious groups, societies, economies, polities, institutions of many kinds. In and through these we value certain things and avoid others, making and following rules to achieve our ends.

All of the norms in our social orders have obviously not been consciously thought out and instituted, but the norms or social conventions are expressive of human desires and aversions and are the sort of things which can be altered by human decision. This contrasts with the laws of nature or scientific laws which humans can discover and utilize but not change. Nature is what is the case, and what is the case is established by careful scientific procedures to establish the truth. Human beings as part of nature have certain natural ways of behaving. These set limits to every system of social order and are the subject of the various human and social sciences.

Predictability in Human Affairs

There are a number of quite fundamental reasons why generalizations in social science cannot have the same law-like character as generalizations in the natural sciences, no matter how much rigorous scientific work is done to develop them. Alasdair MacIntyre points out 'it is necessary, if life is to be meaningful, for us to be in possession of ourselves and not merely to be the creations of other people's projects, intentions and desires, and this requires unpredictability' (MacIntyre, 1981: 99).

MacIntyre identifies four sources of 'systematic unpredictability' in human affairs. First, is radical conceptual innovation. Second, unpredictability in the social world arises because each person cannot predict his or her future while contemplating a decision about alternative courses of action. As yet unmade decisions make our future unpredictable. A third source of unpredictability arises from the game-theoretic character of social life. This has a number of aspects. Trying to predict each other's predictions of each other can render an unpredictable outcome. A condition of success may be the successful misinformation of other actors in a situation and also of external observers. Players in the real world are often involved in many different transactions or games at one and the same time. Even when there is some certainty what game is being played, there may not be a determinate set of players and pieces or a determinate area in which the game is to take place. A retrospective standpoint may make these determinate, but a prospective view cannot. MacIntyre's final source of unpredictability is pure contingency. Trivial contingencies occur which cannot be foreseen, and yet they can powerfully influence the outcome of great events. (MacIntyre, 1981: 89-96.)

In contrast to the unpredictable elements in social life, MacIntyre identifies four kinds of predictable elements - the shared expectations in a culture which schedule and coordinate many of our social actions; statistical regularities in human behaviour, relatively independent of causal knowledge; the causal regularities of nature; and finally, knowledge of causal regularities in social life (MacIntyre, 1981: 97-8).

Convention or the Normative Structure of Social Order

It is impossible to describe a society or a social order of any kind without referring to the values and rules, or normative conventions, which sustain and shape it.

Values

Concepts and characteristics[3]   Values or 'goods' are primary in human existence. They are conceptions of the desirable (positive values) or of the undesirable (negative values) in life, in terms of which we make our choices and behave in characteristic ways. They help to keep our social environment orderly and predictable, and they also provide a person with an ordered and desired self from which he or she can operate. It is values which give point and purpose to the various rules which humans make, follow and resist.

Some values are highly abstract - the worth and dignity of every person; others at much lesser levels of abstraction - a good job, a particular friendship. Each value has a cognitive, feeling, and tendency-to-act component. Values tend to occur in systems and people build their lives around a whole constellation of values. They are not all held with equal intensity but can be arranged in a hierarchy of importance. A dominant value is determined by the extensiveness of the value in the total activity of the system (personal, group or societal), its duration, and the intensity with which it is sought and maintained. Values are inevitably related to the conditions people experience, and change through time as conditions change. The level and strength of people's value aspirations are to a great extent social products. The same value may be both an end in itself and also a means, or of instrumental value,

---

[3] See Barnsley, 1972; Feather, 1975; Howard, 1969; Kluckhohn and Strodbeck, 1961; National Education Association, 1976; Reich and Adcock, 1976; Rescher, 1969; and Rokeach, 1973.

to other valued ends. For example, education, health, or employment can be valued in their own right but also as instrumental values. People may support a common objective having different values in mind, just as many different objectives can be pursued in the name of a single value.

Conflicts Often only careful empirical analysis will reveal whether a conflict is actually about ends, usually seen as a genuine value conflict, or about means to attain particular ends, a conflict about technical and factual matters. Since people in practical situations must address both ends and means in relation to each other, many apparent value conflicts are not only or even primarily about ends, and similarly many apparent technical conflicts are not only or even primarily about means. To think of something as an 'end' implies at least some means that could be used to attain it, and the idea of a 'means' implies 'an end' of some sort. Value conflicts occur within individuals and between individuals, within groups and between groups, and between individuals and groups.

Operational values Declared values may or may not be the same as operational values. What values are actually operating in the behaviour of an individual, or group, or a society, can be verified by a number of complementary methods: by taking note of what people say their values are; by inferring values from the things which have a capacity to arouse emotions; by observing what people pay attention to; by studying what is left unsaid (what is taken for granted is often of fundamental importance); by systematically studying peoples' choices when they are confronted with alternatives; and finally, by observing the things that are rewarded and the things that are punished (Williams, 1960: 403-9).

Rules[4]

Values provide the rationale and motivation for human action. Rules of various kinds enable values, or goods, to be achieved or harm or evils to be avoided, in efficient and socially appropriate ways. Again empirical inquiry will reveal what norms or rules actually operate in any particular social order, how these have come into existence, what form they have taken, how they are

---

[4] See especially Warnock, 1971: 35-50; also, Solomon, in Reich, ed., 1978: 407-12; and Mayo, 1986: 57-73.

authorized and changed, what has been their content, and what and whose values they have reflected.

Principles, policies, and regulations Rules operate at different levels of generality. Principles are rules usually at a high level of generality and are intended to give rise to more specific rules and actions. Policies are often fairly specific rules although 'policy' may be used in a very broad way to cover a whole field of rule-making, as in 'social policy' or 'economic policy'. Regulations are usually specific rules, often derived from broader ones. What they all share, as rules, is that they are all intended to regulate human conduct, by prohibiting, requiring, or permitting some type of action in certain circumstances. They are standing guides in that they are intended to apply whenever the relevant circumstances occur. If this does not happen, then the 'existence' of the rule may be brought into question.

Character[5] Rules tend to be stated relatively simply so they can be understood and learned by those to whom they apply. Qualifications or exceptions may be built into rules, but if they become too complex they lose their general guidance function, and then people must constantly decide afresh what to do. The assumption behind having a rule is that the conduct in question is desirable and that having a rule will increase the likelihood of the conduct. There is no point in making a rule if the behaviour is going to occur anyway, and, indeed, sometimes making it a rule can undesirably change people's motivations for acting in this way.

A rule can coordinate actions for common purposes. It can provide predictability and reduce uncertainty where these are desired. It sometimes, in games, can deliberately make a task more difficult so that the game is more challenging and interesting. Many rules can be seen as an attempt to summarize existing perceptions of when certain actions are permitted, required, or prohibited. Other rules, however, create the possibility of new forms of action.

Existence The 'existence' of a rule is not always a simple matter. When there are people or institutions with clear and accepted authority to make rules, the rules within their area of authority are those derived from this source. This does not mean, however, the rules of even accepted authorities are always

---

[5] This section and the next draw heavily from Warnock, 1971.

complied with. Any rule is, of course, expected to be complied with by those to whom it applies, but in practice it may not be complied with on particular occasions. If it is never complied with, an 'official' rule can scarcely be described as still in 'existence'. It is still 'on the books', but that is all it is.

Where rules emanate from people and institutions whose authority is unaccepted or questioned, there may still be some level of compliance, because some rules may be preferred to none, or because of the sanctions attached to non-compliance. There are rules which no particular authoritative rule-making body or person has made. Unlike 'made' rules which can exist to a large extent independent of what people in general either think or do, unmade rules only exist when people think and believe in ways that indicate the presence of the rule. People cannot be unaware of such rules often described as conventions.

All rules can be deliberately changed. This is obviously the case when there are rule-making authorities, but 'unmade' rules can also be changed by general agreement to abandon them.

Rules often define what constitutes a particular activity, and similarly rules define what constitutes the performance of a social role. Depending on the activities and the roles, individuals can exercise various degrees of freedom within the defining rules. If, however, they go too far beyond the prevailing norms, they are no longer seen as engaged in that activity at all, or not engaged in it 'properly'.

Sanctions   The breaking of some rules, for example, health rules, will result in certain 'natural', not man-made consequences. The breaking of others, as has been mentioned, will result in non-recognition of particular activities or role performances. These are consequences not punishments or penalties as such. Many rules have deliberate sanctions attached to them to encourage their observance. Sanctions take a wide variety of forms of punishment and reward. The punishments can include eternal damnation, death, restriction of liberty, fines, withdrawal of cooperation, censure, or social ostracism; the rewards, eternal salvation, praise, social esteem, continuing membership of a group. Sanctions attached to rules may be formally designated and strictly applied by specified authorities, as in the legal system, or be much less formal and certain. Sanctions are attached to the type of action contained in a rule, but may be varied according to the existence of mitigating or exonerating circumstances in specific cases. People may conform to a rule primarily because of the sanctions attached to it, not because they necessarily agree with the purpose or content of the rule itself.

Scope The scope of rules depends upon the people to whom they have application, the aspects of their conduct being regulated, and where and when the rules apply. Legal, religious, and customary authorities all claim their rules have general applications within their respective systems, but their rules apply only to those who come under the relevant categories of conduct and the circumstances being regulated by their particular rules.

Systems Rules often operate as parts of systems, deriving their significance not only from the content of the rule, but from the location of the rule in a system of rules. This is obviously true of legal rules, and a deliberate effort is made to ensure that laws do not conflict. Similar efforts are made within religious traditions to provide consistent and coherent guidance to believers.

Rules can, however, be put in relation to each other to achieve some degree of 'system' according to any number of human purposes - the living of a particular person's life, the maintenance and development of informal human groups, the running of formal organizations, the development of human institutions in crucial areas of human need. Obviously, at best there can be a strain towards consistency in the various rules which shape conduct for these purposes, but especially in modern society with such a diversity of ends being sought, multiple means available, and potentially conflicting authorities, the degree to which individual rules strengthen or weaken various social systems requires complicated empirical observation. There are various parallel, overlapping and sometimes competing and conflicting rules and rule systems under which we now live our lives.

Four historically important rule systems A broad classification of rules which has been historically important has been in terms of four different ways in which the various rules have originated and been maintained. (Benn and Peters, 1959: 22-9.) Customs and traditions (including moral conventions) have originated in the past and have been passed on through customary authorities, legal rules have originated with legal authorities, and religious rules have originated with religious authorities, either through revelation or interpretation of scriptures held to be divinely inspired.

A fourth category of rules has emerged from the operation of what might be called individual rational criticism or judgment. This dates back to at least Socrates in ancient Greece, and has tended to emerge whenever people, through trade, travel, warfare, and communication of all kinds, become aware of customs, laws, and religions, different from their own; whenever authorities disagree; whenever rules conflict with individuals' own reasoned conviction about what they should be; and whenever new circumstances bring into question the relevance of existing rules. On this view, particular rules, whatever their endorsement by authority, can only be justified if they meet certain rational tests applied by an individual. It is this procedure, not authority which provides the primary moral justification for the course of action. What seems to be involved in being morally reasonable will be considered shortly, when we move on to discuss prescriptive ethics.

Since at least the seventeenth century, the growing importance of the state as a basic form of social organization has been paralleled by the growth in critical moral thinking by individuals. Custom and religious rules still operate, however, and are crucially important in many areas of life for many people.

Rights and duties Rights and duties exist only in the context of recognized rules. A person does not actually have a right unless there is a correlative duty on the part of someone else to recognize the right, or in other words, unless there is a rule which specifies the normative relationship between the two. (Benn and Peters, 1959: 88-9.) All rule systems entail both rights and duties, not just the legal system. Again, it is a matter of detailed empirical study to discover what rights and duties exist in any particular social group or for any particular individual.

Frequently in the modern political arena, rights are claimed to exist before the relevant necessary correlative duties are recognized. This may be based on a theory of natural law or natural rights - people have these rights, irrespective of their recognition or non-recognition by a particular society at a particular point in time. But such assertions are not descriptions; they are clearly prescriptions calling for justification in the particular circumstances, and unless the justification is convincing and a relevant rule is established under which the correlative duties are recognized, the rights in question will not be a reality. (Lawrence, 1978.)

The Extent of Cultural Diversity

While descriptive ethics makes people aware of the variety of practices in different cultural groups, it is easy to exaggerate the extent of cultural difference. All cultures are likely to have some underlying values in common, even though they may differ greatly in their factual or religious beliefs, or in their geographic circumstances. Such values as protection of the young, truth-telling, and security against killing, would seem to be necessary for any group to survive. (Rachels, 1986: 19-22.)

Descriptive ethics is, then, concerned with describing the various values and rules according to which people have conducted and do conduct their lives. It is the terrain of novelists, dramatists, historians, social anthropologists, psychologists, legal scholars, theologians, and in fact anyone with an interest in and curiosity about the scope and nature of human culture.

Prescriptive Ethics

Normative or prescriptive ethics goes beyond description to prescribing what ought to be the case in human conduct and character. This is the typical concern of moral, political and social philosophers, moral theologians, statesmen and politicians, and, in fact, any reflective person who thinks about human behaviour past, present or future, and who is trying to live responsibly. For the general reader, MacIntyre provides a very helpful brief history of moral philosophy from the Homeric age to the twentieth century (MacIntyre, 1967).

The Analysis of Language

Many moral philosophers earlier in this century have not tackled directly the increasingly formidable task of attempting to prescribe conduct for the troubled and complicated world in which we now live. Instead, they have turned to analyzing the language and the logic of normative discussion (Warnock, 1966; Thiroux, 1980: 4). But what is distinctive about ethics is its subject-matter, not the language in which it is expressed - 'the sorts of grounds that are stated or implied for the things that are said, the sorts of considerations that are taken to be relevant and why'. Words like 'good', 'bad', 'right', 'wrong', 'ought', and 'duty' are not used only in moral discourse. (Warnock, 1971: 125-6.) So what then is the subject-matter? What does it mean to say something is morally wrong or unethical, or a person is immoral, or something is non-moral?

The Exclusive Claims of the New Critical Morality

In the above discussion of descriptive ethics, all of the values and rules which actively guide human conduct and character were deliberately included, because generally they would not exist or prevail unless they are valued by someone. In this sense, the morality or ethics of a group or a person consists of the personal and cultural standards which guide their lives. As we have seen, it is when these are brought into question by critical reflection that a new morality emerges. Its adherents have claimed, however, that this is not just another morality, it is morality properly understood, or 'genuine' morality, against which all conventional 'moralities' must be measured if they are going to claim to be morally justified. This way of thinking, sometimes characterized as 'the moral point of view', has been prevalent in western societies in particular, and a long succession of philosophers have both reflected and contributed to the development of such a view of morality or ethics.

Some Important Examples

A brief look at a number of modern contributions will illustrate this tradition of thinking. All illustrate the Kantian synthesis of individualism with universalism grounded in rationality, although as will be seen there are some differences about what moral rationality entails.

Baier

Kurt Baier argues that a moral conviction is not arbitrary. It is true if it is acceptable from the moral point of view, and a person must adopt this point of view if he or she is to be moral. That point of view is the highest court of appeal for conflicts of interest. As such, it cannot be the same as the perspective of self-interest. It requires a commitment to principles that apply to everyone, without exception, and that are for the good of everyone alike.

We act for the good of everyone alike, if we do not treat others as we would not want them to treat us, and if we treat others as we would want them to treat us - the principle of 'reversibility'. Also 'being for the good of everyone alike' requires us not to violate rules whose violation by everyone would be undesirable. The moral point of view is that of 'an independent, unbiased, impartial, objective, dispassionate, disinterested observer' - 'a God's-eye point of view'.

Baier argues that because we and all others benefit from the general existence of morality, we have reason to conform to moral rules even when doing so will not benefit us, and will require genuine sacrifices from us. (Baier, in Sher, ed., 1987: 332-49.)

Benn and Peters

Stanley Benn and Richard Peters, after reviewing the contributions of the main schools of moral theory, take the following view of morality. A rule becomes moral by being critically accepted by the individual in the light of the needs and interests of people likely to be affected by it, with no partiality towards the claims of any of those whose needs and interests are at stake. They see the acceptance of such criteria as being implied by the notion of being reasonable. (Benn and Peters, 1959: 56.)

Gewirth

In his book *Reason and Morality*, Alan Gewirth, in a century of 'unparalleled extremes of human barbarism and tragedy', is aiming not only for philosophical certainty, but also to make coherent sense about the principles that should govern how people treat one another (Gewirth, 1978: ix).

After pointing to serious flaws in previous attempts to provide a non-relativist foundation for ethics, Gewirth's book attempts to derive a supreme moral principle from the nature of human action. According to Gewirth, 'morality' has a certain core meaning - 'a set of categorically obligatory requirements for action that are addressed at least in part to every actual or prospective agent; and that are concerned with furthering the interests, especially the most important interests, of persons or recipients other than or in addition to the agent or the speaker'. (Gewirth, 1978: 1.) Morality is seen to have a unique status in that its requirements take precedence over all other modes of guiding action. Gewirth argues that agents in making practical judgments must recognize the 'generic rights', that is, rights to freedom and well-being, of those with whom they interact, otherwise they would be contradicting themselves. (Gewirth, 1978: 64.)[6]

---

[6] Critics have pointed out that the possession of rights comes from concrete social institutions and not from conditions for rational action. (MacIntyre, 1981: 64-5; Wong, 1984: 80-3.)

Hare

Richard Hare's book *Moral Thinking: Its Levels, Method and Point,* like Gewirth's, was written with a sense of urgency to help resolve important practical issues (Hare, 1981: v, viii; see also Smart, 1984: 8-10). Hare distinguishes between three levels in moral thinking - the intuitive and the critical which are both concerned with moral questions of substance, and the metaethical, concerned with the meaning of moral words and the logic of moral reasoning (Hare, 1981: 25-6).

Relatively simple principles of action used at the intuitive level are necessary but not sufficient for moral thinking. They are necessary because without these, and the dispositions and intuitions arising from them, we could not cope with the world. We should have to meet each new situation entirely unprepared and perform an 'existential' choice or cost-benefit analysis on the spot. If principles become too long and complex they cannot be learnt for use on subsequent occasions. In addition, a useful principle needs to be unspecific enough to cover a variety of situations all of which have certain salient features in common. (Hare, 1981: 35-9.)

Such principles and dispositions are, however, not sufficient for moral thinking. In any new situation, they may well not apply or may be seen to be in conflict. Being the product of our upbringing and past experience of decision-making, they can always be questioned. We, then, need to engage in critical moral thinking to decide what to do - not only to resolve conflicts between *prima facie* principles, but to select the best set of *prima facie* principles for use in intuitive thinking. (Hare, 1981: 39-40, 49-50.)

According to Hare, critical moral thinking consists in making a choice under the constraints imposed by the logical properties of the words or concepts which are used in moral discourse and by the non-moral facts, and by nothing else. Hare identifies three logical properties - prescriptivity, universalizability and overridingness. It is only the third, however, that distinguishes moral from other evaluation judgments. An ethical statement is prescriptive in that if I sincerely assert that I ought to do something, I am also disposed to do it. Ethical prescriptions are universalizable in that we contradict ourselves if we make different moral judgments about situations which are identical in their universal descriptions, or in ways which are seen as relevant. Hare says that we must imaginatively put ourselves in other people's shoes, or in the position of other sentient beings, which involves having their preferences not ours. Like Gewirth, Hare sees ethical judgments as overriding other prescriptions. (Hare, 1981: 21-4, 40, 55-9.)

Rachels

A 1986 book on *The Elements of Moral Philosophy* by James Rachels acknowledges that there are many rival theories, each expounding a different conception of what it means to live morally. He asserts, however, that most theories agree on at least a 'minimum conception' of morality, seeing it as 'the effort to guide one's conduct by reason - that is, to do what there are reasons for doing - while giving equal weight to the interests of each individual who will be affected by one's conduct'. This implies, according to Rachels, that the conscientious moral agent is:

> someone who is concerned impartially with the interests of everyone affected by what he or she does; who carefully sifts facts and examines their implications; who accepts principles of conduct only after scrutinizing them to make sure they are sound; who is willing to "listen to reason" even when it means that his or her earlier convictions may have to be reversed; and who, finally, is willing to act on the results of this deliberation. (Rachels, 1986: 11.)

Rachels argues that there are good reasons why theories must share at least this minimum, and claims that most of the disagreement lies in how the minimum should be expanded, and perhaps modified to give a fully satisfying account. He admits at the outset, however, that 'competent' philosophers do disagree even about fundamental matters. (Rachels, 1986: vi.)

Ladd

In the overview article on ethics in the *Encyclopedia for Bioethics*, John Ladd states that ethics, by its very nature, is controversial; at the same time it must deal with issues that are both urgent and inescapable. There are, he says, those who believe no good reasons for human conduct can be given, that is, reasons that are objective or valid between people. Others just dogmatically assert no reasons need be given for one's ethical views. But Ladd points out that both these positions are self-defeating, for to defend either of them requires giving reasons.

Ladd refers to four methods used in argument about ethics. First, is an appeal to authority - to a person, a group, an institution, a set of writings, a fictitious person like an ideal observer, or a supernatural being. This needs to show why the authority is indeed an authority in ethical matters, and that the alleged pronouncements of the authority are authentic. Second, is an appeal to alleged consensus among people in general, or of particular groups, concerning a particular issue. Again, however, such an appeal needs to show why these people are ethically competent, and whether they in fact hold the position attributed to them. Third, is an appeal to what is self-evident, but what is self-evident to one person is not self-evident to another. Finally, says Ladd, one can engage in argument which seeks to find a position or positions which can be sustained by a process of reasoning. This is where what moral philosophers have to say should be helpful, but philosophers cannot be expected to provide definitive answers acceptable to any rational being at any possible time. (Ladd, 1978: 400-7.)

Dissident Views

Substantial books by Alasdair MacIntyre, *After Virtue*, and Bernard Williams, *Ethics and the Limits of Philosophy*, claim that the attempt by philosophers of the Enlightenment to find a rationally inescapable foundation for living ethically have failed.

MacIntyre

MacIntyre's book seeks to re-establish the Aristotelian concepts of virtue and the good life as central to ethics, linking these with the ideas of 'a practice' and of the unity of a life. The exercise of the virtues is seen as a crucial component of the good life. These are exhibited and defined in an arena of practice. 'Practice' here means:

> any coherent and complex form of socially established cooperative human activity through which goods internal to that form of activity are realized in the course of trying to achieve those standards of excellence which are appropriate to, and partially definitive of, that form of activity, with the result that human powers to achieve excellence, and human conceptions of the ends and goods involved, are systematically extended.

The range of such 'practices' is wide - arts, sciences, games, making and sustaining family life, the professions. (MacIntyre, 1981: 175.)

MacIntyre argues that justice, courage and honesty are necessary components of any practice with internal goods and standards of excellence. To engage in a practice, 'we have to learn and recognize what is due to whom; we have to be prepared to take whatever self-endangering risks are demanded along the way; and we have to listen carefully to what we are told about our own inadequacies and to reply with the same carefulness for the facts'. We may cheat and still get external goods like money, power and fame, but this will disbar us from achieving the standards of excellence or the goods internal to the practice. (MacIntyre, 1981, 178.)

An additional virtue emphasized by MacIntyre is having an adequate sense of the traditions to which one belongs or which confront one. This should not be confused with any form of 'conservative antiquarianism', but manifests in 'a grasp of those future possibilities which the past has made available to the present'. (MacIntyre, 1981: 207.)

MacIntyre emphasizes how difficult it is in the modern world to envisage each human life as a whole. Modernity, he says, 'partitions each human life into a variety of segments, each with its own norms and modes of behavior'. Sociological and existential theories lose sight of the unity of human life when they make a sharp separation between the individual and the roles he or she plays, and between the different role enactments of an individual life. (MacIntyre, 1981: 190.)

According to MacIntyre, there is no such thing as 'behaviour' to be identified prior to and independently of intentions, beliefs and settings. When we identify a particular action, we place the agent's intentions in causal and temporal order with reference to their role in his or her history; and we also place them with reference to their role in the history of the setting or settings to which they belong. Narrative history is basic for the characteristics of what we call human actions. MacIntyre suggests that we all live out narratives in our lives and understand our lives in terms of the narratives that we live out. This in turn makes the form of narrative appropriate for understanding the action of others. (MacIntyre, 1981: 194-7.) The notion of narrative is closely linked to the notions of intelligibility and accountability, and all these are integrally linked to the concept of personal identity (MacIntyre, 1981: 203).

For MacIntyre, the unity of a good life is the end that transcends specific practices and provides an overarching purpose. The virtues are dispositions which not only sustain practices and enable us to achieve the goods internal to practices, but which also sustain us in the quest for the good. The good life, says MacIntyre, 'is the life spent in seeking for the good life for man'. (MacIntyre, 1981: 204.) Charles Larmore comments, however, that so tentative a conclusion clearly allows differing views on what constitutes the good life, and reveals MacIntyre as a modernist, despite himself, unwilling to return to Aristotle's excessive desire for unity. (Larmore, 1987: 37-9.)

Williams

Bernard William's book has been reviewed under the heading 'The Deflation of Moral Philosophy', because he rejects the moral theories that have dominated contemporary moral philosophy, and challenges the very enterprise of searching for the right ethical theory (Wolf, 1987). According to Williams, what makes an inquiry a philosophical one is 'reflective generality and a style of argument that claims to be rationally persuasive'. But, Williams points out, philosophy is obviously not the only reflective activity in the modern world, and in any case how could a subject to be studied answer the basic questions of life when these need to be answered by the person living a life. (Williams, 1985: 1-3.)

Williams believes that meaningful, substantive ethical thought is grounded in the concrete ethical experience of a particular time and shaped by what he calls 'thick' concepts embedded in the circumstances and customs of that society (Williams, 1985: 129, 40). He distinguishes between two levels of ethical thought, the reflective and the unreflective. Reflection may actually destroy rather than create knowledge at the directly practical level. (Williams, 1985: 148.) Also, we remain members of our culture even when critically evaluating it. We should, therefore, hesitate to evaluate the values and practices of members of other cultures. Such appraisal is appropriate only insofar as it concerns cultures or aspects of them, whose practices constitute 'a real option for the appraiser and the appraiser's society'. (Williams, 1985: 160-2.)

Williams contrasts the scientific and the ethical. With scientific knowledge, an objective model is appropriate. Scientific judgments attempt to describe and explain an independent physical reality. In contrast, ethical judgments relate to many possible social worlds, 'since it is certain both that human beings cannot live without a culture and that there are many different cultures in which they can live'. (Williams, 1985: 150.) Williams does acknowledge that there are some things any viable society must try to achieve, but such considerations greatly underdetermine the kinds of institutions, practices, and concepts a society might have. Moral criticism should think in more concrete terms and argue less from alleged universal principles and more from recognized shared values. (See Wolf, 1987: 821-33.)

Modest Claims

In Williams' view, philosophical reflection cannot be expected to answer directly the general question how to live, or any less general, practical question. But it can make a contribution by considering what is involved in answering such questions - 'what part might be played by knowledge of the sciences; how far purely rational inquiry can take us; how far the answer... might be expected to be different if (the question) is asked in one society rather than another; how much, at the end of all that, must be left to personal decision'. (Williams, 1985: 3.)

A similarly fairly modest set of claims for moral philosophy is made by Fred Feldman in a 1978 ethics textbook. Careful study of it, he says, may help us to avoid holding inconsistent moral principles, to understand the principles we hold, to be clear about the consequences of our moral principles, and to evaluate and be sceptical about faddish moral doctrines. The most we can expect from moral philosophy, however, is that it may show us that some principles are false. (Feldman, 1978: 13-15.)

The State of Moral Theory

This brief review of some spokespersons of the modern development of what has been called rational, critical morality illustrates how slippery and essentially contested is the subject matter of ethics. It is difficult enough to obtain agreement on how to characterize human conduct and character as a matter of description in various places and times, past and present. It is even more difficult to obtain agreement on what ought to be the case in human conduct and character, past, present, and future.

Virginia Held comments:

To consider the disparity in the development of scientific theory and of moral theory since about the seventeenth century is to be both stunned and saddened ... In the territory that moral theory would occupy if we could decide what it is, we still look to writers of many centuries ago not out of historical interest... , but because we are not at all sure that what we now think on many aspects of moral theory is very much better. To say this reflects our acknowledgement that moral theory and moral inquiry are in a quite pathetic state. (Held, 1984: 5-6.)

Held recommends as a way to progress, the pursuit of separate moral inquiries in different domains, testing a variety of theories and not letting the lack of a unified theory impede progress. Understanding and insight for dealing with actual moral problems will come from beginning with the point of view of a sincere moral agent with experience of the problem in question, not the point of view of an ideal observer removed from our actual reality. (Held, 1984: 3.) The pressing reality of actual moral problems has led many philosophers to concentrate on these rather than theoretical and metaphysical disputes. (Held, 1984: 13.) Held argues that in any case, ethical theory can only develop adequately in the light of practice. (Held, 1984: 40-61.)

The Position Taken By This Book

This book has as its focus the ethical evaluation of the behaviour of particular sorts of practical people - professionals. It will be argued in Chapter 3, because these people have considerable power and influence in modern society, it is especially important that they conform to ethically justifiable standards. Yet obviously if no agreement can be reached on what constitutes such standards, the argument is futile.

   To provide some order out of what may seem hopeless theoretical and practical confusion, a model to identify and assess ethical conduct will be proposed in Chapter 2. This sees ethical conduct in terms of an effective, rational, ethical response to a challenging moral situation. It sees ethical conduct as a particular form of rational action, which uses certain important human values to define challenging situations that require response, to decide on the nature of the response, to carry out the response, and to assess the result of the response. Parallel to each stage is a judging function which assesses the ethical performance. This may be done by the agent or actors themselves, either at the time or later, or by outsiders - to improve future performance, or to allocate praise or blame. The model will be used in subsequent chapters to identify and discuss various concerns raised by the situation of the professions and professionals in contemporary society.

   It will not be argued that this is the only form that morality does take or can take - that this is the only form of 'genuine' morality. The most that can reasonably be argued is that the values built into the model have a claim to at least serious moral attention on the part of those making decisions and living their lives in the real world. Values and principles claiming moral or ethical status can be no more than guides to conduct and character without breaching the autonomy of these actual decision-makers. There will be people who do not recognize or accept these particular moral guides, there will be those who accept them to some extent but will not give them paramount importance, and there will be those who accept them but disagree on various aspects of their application. The conduct and character of humans cannot be matters for universal certainty and consensus. Neither can they be matters of complete uncertainty and disagreement. We do not and cannot live as isolates, and this is especially the case with the present generation of human beings.

Unprecedented Ethical Challenges

Members of each generation have to make up their own minds about the values and rules which will guide their conduct and character. It can be persuasively argued, however, that the circumstances of the present generation are unprecedented - the extent of global interdependence, the threat of nuclear annihilation, the power of modern weapons, the awareness of the prevalence of violence, the rampant technology, the effects on issues of life and death of new medical technology, the emergence of new viral diseases such as AIDS, the development of genetic engineering, the increasing dominance of commercial values in many aspects of life, the resurgence of fundamentalism in religious faith, the spread of multinational organizations not obviously accountable to anyone, the increasing concentrations of power over people's lives in the hands of particular individuals and organizations, the continuing dominance of the nation-state as the most important form of political organization, the relative weakness of international and other broader cooperation efforts, the loss of confidence in government, the world population explosion, the pollution of the natural environment, the rapid depletion of natural resources, the speed and character of modern communications, the speed and unpredictability of social change, the growing disparities between the living conditions of people in different nations and within nations, the loss of confidence in a better future. (Lawrence, 1984.)

The Rediscovery of 'Ethics'

Under such circumstances, explicit thoughtful attention to the dimensions of ethical choice and judgment would seem to be a central, inescapable task. After a long period of relative neglect, educational institutions have begun to respond to the need, but the task is obviously extraordinarily difficult not only because of the scale and complexity of the subject matter, but also because of the powerful, specialized, vested interests now entrenched in our educational and societal institutions.

Throughout most of the nineteenth century, the most important course in the college curriculum in the United States was moral philosophy, taught usually by the college president and required of all senior students.[7] Much of what we now recognize as the social sciences first appeared in the college curriculum in the moral philosophy course.

The attempted intellectual and social unity of the nineteenth century moral philosophy did not, however, survive the burgeoning growth of specialized disciplines most of them professing to be scientific in character. Both in the United States and elsewhere, instruction of ethics became intellectually isolated from both the social sciences and the growing number of professional disciplines, all of whom, one way or another, were dealing with issues which can be seen as ethical in character.

The retreat by philosophers into analytical philosophy in the earlier part of the twentieth century has substantially changed in recent years. The 1970s saw 'a remarkable resurgence of interest' in the teaching of ethics at both undergraduate and professional school levels, and the value of such teaching was strongly endorsed in a 1980 special project report.[8] This report recommended that the teaching of ethics in professional schools ought to prepare future professionals to understand the kinds of moral issues they are likely to confront, to introduce them to the moral ideals of their profession, and to assist them in understanding the relationship between their professional work and the broader values and needs of the society. The university was seen as offering a unique context for a careful examination of moral claims and moral purposes. Many forces were seen to be at work within the society, within the professions, and within the universities, to confront issues of ethics and morality more squarely.[9]

---

[7] Foreword by Callahan and Bok to each of the monographs on the teaching of ethics, the Hastings Center, 1980.

[8] This was a 2-year project undertaken by the Hastings Center and funded by the Carnegie Corporation of New York. It produced a 2-volume report - Callahan and Bok, eds, 1980 - and a number of monographs.

[9] Callahan and Bok, eds., 1980a: 79-83.   Derek Bok, the President of Harvard University has shown particular interest in this development. His *Beyond the Ivory*
(continued...)

There are signs that 'ethics' is a relatively new growth industry in a number of the western industrial countries, and at least in the area of bioethics, links have begun to be made internationally (Callahan, 1986).

Held welcomes the recent surge of interest in 'applied ethics', but warns against the serious danger that ethics might become a form of 'ideological public relations or institutional advertising', especially when the money to pay the 'applied ethicist' comes from a corporate interest or self-serving professional group. The development has demonstrated in her view, the urgent need for moral theories to fill the vast distance between highly abstract ideal moral theory and practice in the real world. (Held, 1984: 1, 11.)

The Need for a General Approach to Professional Ethics

The renewed interest in ethics as a general field of study, and the growing awareness of a need for each professional occupation to produce a much more coherent and justifiable account of its professional ethics, has led to a burgeoning literature. Almost by definition, this seems to be an eminently justifiable set of developments, especially when contrasted to the previous levels of fragmentation and unexamined assumptions. There is, however, still an important and significant neglect. Amid the plethora of books on the ethics of one or other of the specific professional occupations, there are as yet not many general books on professional ethics.

Goldman

A book by Alan Goldman, *The Moral Foundations of Professional Ethics*, published in 1980, argues that the most fundamental question for professional ethics is whether those in professional roles require special norms and principles to guide their well-intentioned conduct, or whether ordinary moral categories and principles should apply. He sees a professional role as strongly differentiated if it requires unique principles, or if it requires its norms to be weighted more heavily than they would be against other principles in other

---

[9](...continued)
Tower: Social Responsibilities of the Modern University argues for educational institutions 'to consider how they might use their strategic position to encourage students to think more deeply about ethical issues and strengthen their powers of ethical reasoning'. Harvard subsequently introduced a university-wide Program in Ethics and the Professions.

contexts. In this case the professional must elevate certain values or goals, those central to his or her profession, such as health, or legal autonomy of clients, to the status of overriding considerations. (Goldman, 1980: 1-3.) Goldman argues that the burden of proof must lie with those who would have professionals defer to special norms. His impression is that professionals themselves assume that it is met, while moral philosophers tend to assume that a single moral framework must prevail directly. (Goldman, 1980: 31-2.) Goldman himself specifies a common moral framework, and then examines in turn the justification for strongly differentiated professional roles in the judiciary, in politics, in the law, in medicine, and in business.

Bayles

Another general book on professional ethics was produced in 1981 by Michael Bayles and revised, with a greatly enlarged bibliography from recent writing, in 1989. (Bayles, 1981, 1989.) He wrote it to fill what he called 'the void of an overview of ethical issues in several professions'. The original emphasis was on law and medicine, but it was claimed that the book's principles applied to all professionals in a consulting role, and many also applied to professionals in non-consulting roles. Employee professionals are fully included in the new edition. The book aims to examine professions from the viewpoint of the average citizen in society, in contrast to most of the literature on professional ethics which is written from the professional's point of view. (Bayles, 1989: ix.)

Bayles sees professional ethics as involving significant value choices confronting professionals and society. He attempts to identify the main areas of choice and the kinds of arguments which may be used in making morally justifiable decisions. Introductory chapters discuss the scope of professional ethics and the justification of professional norms in relation to other ethical norms (Bayles, 1989, 1-16: 17-30). Five chapters examine the obligations of professions and professionals - for the availability of professional services; between professionals and clients; to third parties; between professionals and employers; and to the profession. (Bayles, 1989: 32-181.) The final chapter discusses methods for ensuring compliance of professionals with ethical norms. (Bayles, 1989: 183-207.)

Bayles points out that historically the professions have controlled admission to their ranks, regulated the conduct of their members, and defined their role in society. In the twentieth century, the number of professions and their members has grown dramatically. As society has become more complex and dependent upon technology, the professions have become increasingly central to its functioning. Bayles refers to a new emphasis upon consumer rights in relation to professional services, but sees this as part of a broader struggle to redefine the professions' role in society so as to preserve and promote freedom, welfare, and other values. Professional ethics, he argues, must be concerned about the proper roles of professions in society. Prescription by professionals of their own roles cannot be simply accepted any longer. Although the responsibilities and situations of individual professionals vary, Bayles sees common elements stemming from their role as professionals. He argues that professional ethics can be properly analyzed only against a set of social values and a conception of the general role of professions in society. The chief values relevant to professional ethics are freedom, protection from injury, equality of opportunity, privacy, and minimum well-being. (Bayles, 1989: 4-7.)

The present book shares the concerns of Bayles's book and hopes to make some contribution towards stimulating the more general debate about the scope and nature of professional ethics.[10]

---

[10] Other general books on professional ethics include Camenish (1983), Callahan, ed., (1988), Kultgen (1988), and Mount (1990).

2 Dimensions of Ethical Conduct

The essentially normative nature of human conduct, both individual and collective, has been emphasized in the opening chapter. Like it or not, we cannot live without being consistently engaged in decisions about ends and means. And again, like it or not, this means that our conduct both individual and collective, can be evaluated by ourselves and others - in terms of the ends being sought and the effectiveness and efficiency of the means used to achieve the ends.

Before setting out a model suggesting the dimensions of ethical conduct and its assessment in contemporary society, this chapter briefly comments on a number of developments which are of relevance in the construction and application of such a model. One set of developments is the tremendous growth in all industrial societies of formal collective planning, including social planning which aims directly at the well-being of people. Planning has produced a common model of rational action to guide and evaluate such activity. A parallel and related development has been the demand for a moral or welfare justification of all human institutions, the world-wide spread of the 'democratic' ideal, and the ever-widening circle of moral concern focused on the recognition of 'persons'. Paradoxically, however, while 'scientific' developments have greatly increased human knowledge and technology, they have also apparently undermined ideas of human responsibility, with human behaviour being explained in terms of physical causes, or psychological or sociological conditioning, rather than in terms of values, means and ends.

The Modern Development of Formal Planning

The achievements of earlier civilizations clearly required foresight and organization, but it is only in this century that 'planning' has been formally established and professionalized. This has reflected the problems and possibilities of industrial societies and their political ideologies - the attempts to improve the built environment especially of industrial cities, to control modern economies, to plan economic activities at various levels, to develop effective large-scale organization, to win wars, to deliver mass services. The professionalization of planning has been fostered, in turn, by training courses

28

and professional planning associations. Planning procedures in the various fields have become increasingly sophisticated, whether in the hands of people called 'planners', or not. (Midgley, 1984: 11-12.)

Fields of 'Social Planning'

While all planning has social implications, social planning is seen by its advocates as dealing directly with social issues and problems, and 'the application of the ideals of planning to the direction of social events' (Midgley, 1984: 15). At least five different fields of social planning have been identified by James Midgley. First, with a somewhat uncertain status within sociology, is 'applied sociology', claiming to direct and guide social change, but without a clear role and location for sociologists as professional planners (Midgley, 1984: 16-18). Second, is the 'community organization planning' developed initially and most extensively by professional social workers in the United States, focused mainly on local communities, and increasingly concerned with promoting the interests of disadvantaged people (Midgley, 1984: 19-23). Third, is 'urban planning'. This originated in concern about the living conditions in the industrial cities of Europe and North America, but became dominated by engineers and architects with a focus on design, land use, and physical factors. After World War II, social problems associated with slum clearance and public housing construction gradually stimulated a greater interest in the social, economic and political dimensions of urban planning. Since the 1960s, urban planning has included social planning as a specialist activity. (Midgley, 1984: 23-5.)

A fourth field of social planning is what Midgley calls 'social policy and social service planning'. Public social services to meet educational, health, housing and other social needs have expanded considerably in western countries during the post-war years and these require planning and administration. In Britain, such planning has been fostered largely by central government, and university departments of social policy and administration undertake research and teaching relevant to it. (Midgley, 1984: 25-8.)

Finally, there is the social planning field of 'development planning in third world countries'. The initial exclusive emphasis on economic growth gave way in the later 1960s to an emphasis on 'balanced and integrated economic and social development', and then in the 1970s to 'overall development strategy' aimed at social objectives, but with continuing argument about the respective roles of economists, cultural anthropologists, and other disciplines in the planning process. (Midgley, 1984: 28-31.)

A feature of the modern world is, then, a far greater awareness of the need for, and possibilities of conscious planning to achieve ends, not only by individuals but collectively as well. We just cannot function, either as individuals or collectively, without some degree of planning. Particularly in a highly specialized, interdependent, technology-based, industrial society, operating through a multitude of organizations, the question is not whether to plan, but what form the planning should take, how it should be undertaken, and what and whose values it should reflect. (Kahn, 1969: 52-3.)

Planning Models of Rational Action

All planning can be assessed within a model of rational action, that is, a model relating means to ends. Many theorists have identified similar phases in what they variously call 'the planning process', 'the problem-solving process', 'the policy development process', or 'the process of policy formulation' (Gilbert and Specht, 1974: 14-15). Roughly the process is seen to consist of: identification of the problem; examining alternative solutions in terms of their cost effectiveness and adopting policies to address it; the development of a program to implement the policies; and monitoring, evaluation and feedback. This sequence is seen to be applicable generally, whatever the planning task, its scope and complexity, and its time period. (Gilbert and Specht, 1974: 14-15; Midgley, 1984: 14-15.) It is recognized, however, that in reality the various stages are in a state of 'dynamic readjustment' to each other, and diagrams of planning in action are typically drawn with feedback loops and spirals between the stages (Kahn, 1969: 62, 330).

At each stage of rational action, there are policy choices to be made between alternatives based on factual and normative considerations. These are the product of the socio-political processes, and increasingly are expected to be informed by comparative policy studies.[1]

The monitoring and outcome phase of planning, or the study of performance, has received special attention in relation to government social programs since the early 1970s, and has produced a burgeoning program

---

[1] In the field of social policy scholarship, growing interest in comparative work is an indication of its development (Lawrence, 1986). The main policy choices in social welfare have been analyzed by scholars such as Burns, 1956; Titmuss, 1968: 130-6; Rein, 1970; Kahn, 1969:192-213; and Gilbert and Specht, 1974.

evaluation literature. The usefulness of much of this has, however, been questioned because the findings have often not influenced subsequent policy-making (Cronbach and Associates, 1980).

How does the modern development of planning, including the various forms of 'social planning', and associated models of collective rational action, relate to ethics? They obviously indicate attempts by humans to achieve outcomes which they assumedly value. An ethos of deliberate collective planning is a feature of modern society, but what and whose ends are being furthered?

A 'Welfare Evaluation' of All Social Institutions?

Thirty years ago, a well-known book on industrial society and social welfare predicted that distinctions between welfare and other types of social institutions would become more and more blurred, and that all institutions would be oriented toward and evaluated in terms of social welfare aims (Wilensky and Lebeaux, 1958, 1965: 147). Put simply, every institution and not just 'welfare' would be assessed in terms of its contribution to the general welfare of the population. For a time, in the 1960s and early 1970s, it seemed as if this prediction was coming to pass. Few social institutions, in at least western countries, escaped the critical challenge to show how they contributed to the general welfare, and not just to sectional interests. In effect these were moral or ethical challenges, based on assumptions of a universal critical morality, but they were often not identified as such, partly because various narrow views of morality had made moral concepts pre-empted and suspect in modern thinking.

Those challenges can be seen as part of the continuing struggle to justify morally the institutions of modernity, and especially its economic and political institutions. Amongst the targeted institutions were the professions, particularly the long established, high-status ones like medicine and law, but also targeted were the multitude of newer occupations aspiring to professional status.

The ensuing period, however, witnessed a remarkable change in the economic, political, and social climate. In times of economic recession, unemployment, inflation, budget deficits, and uncertainty, economic values re-asserted their dominance, and 'market solutions', deregulation, decentralization, and privatization, found renewed support politically and amongst at least some theoreticians. Conservative governments prevailed and 'welfare state' programs came under attack for their alleged cost, ineffectiveness, inefficiency, and undermining of self-reliance. (Mishra, 1984.)

A newer generation of social policy scholars, building on the seminal work of especially Richard Titmuss, has provided a more sophisticated understanding of the role played by so-called 'welfare' institutions in contemporary industrial societies, but has also emphasized the complexities of moral critique of such institutions, let alone other activities. For example, Ramesh Mishra identifies five different approaches to the study of social policy in contemporary societies. The first is the social reform, piece-meal approach, which focuses on particular social problems and ways of dealing with them. Second, is a citizenship approach which focuses on the development of rights of citizenship for members of a society, and has shifted historically from a main concentration on civil and political rights to include social and economic rights. Third, is a 'convergence' theory which points to the development of increasingly similar social policies and services as functional to the needs of a modern industrial society. Fourth, is a more general functionalist approach which sees social institutions as interdependent and contributing to the efficient working of society as a whole. Finally, Marxist and neo-Marxist theory draws attention to the relationship between those with economic power and those with political power. (Mishra, 1981.)

There is now a greater awareness of the multiple purposes and functions served by state and voluntary welfare activities (Briggs, 1965, 37-70; Donnison, 1965, 15-30); of the political uses of different definitions of 'welfare'; of the different class-based systems of welfare, especially in relation to occupational welfare (Titmuss, 1963: 34-55; Piven and Cloward, 1971); and of gender and racial aspects of 'welfare' systems (Abramovitz, 1988; Dale and Foster, 1986). 'Collective action for social welfare' is a central feature of modern society. Such action relies on conscious goal-setting and planning and it makes continuing direct assumptions about human well-being. It must decide who? shall get what? how shall this be delivered? how financed? and under whose auspices? (Gilbert and Specht, 1974.) Because these questions bear so directly on human well-being, they are reasonably seen as questions of ethical choice. A careful examination of so-called 'welfare' activities can reveal that the ostensive 'welfare' purpose may not, in fact, be the primary purpose being pursued by the 'welfare' providers; or that when it is, it is the providers' version of welfare that is being pursued not the 'beneficiary's', and that often the focus remains on the providers' good intentions, rather than on results (Lawrence, 1968).

In addition to welfare institutions, however, there are all the other social arrangements in which we live our lives - our economic institutions, our governmental institutions, our families, our professions, our multitude of voluntary associations. Any and all of these can come under critical moral scrutiny, depending upon how important they are in contributing to, or harming human well-being.

The 'Democratic' Ideal and the Expanding Circle of Moral Concern

The first part of this chapter has briefly described the great extension of conscious collective planning in modern society, whatever its political ideology. It is a feature of almost every contemporary society, whatever its stage of economic development.

A parallel and often associated development has been the dramatic extension in this century of the 'democratic' ideal. 'The general welfare', or 'the well-being of the people' is now claimed to be the over-all purpose of the social, political, and economic systems of modern society. The United States is described as a 'liberal democracy' and Sweden as a 'social democracy'; the former East Germany was a 'socialist' or 'people's democracy'. Despite some degree of convergence, these and other societies continue to have differing views on the role of government in the achievement of human well-being, but each justifies its arrangements in terms of a democratic ideal, and the ideal has been firmly declared internationally, at least since World War II.

After the most destructive war in human history - between so-called civilized nations - the Preamble to the Charter of the United Nations reaffirmed 'faith in fundamental human rights, in the dignity and worth of the human person, (and) in the equal rights of men and women'. This was followed in 1948 by the Universal Declaration of Human Rights which declared 'a common standard of achievement for all peoples and all nations'. (Benn and Peters, 1959: 99, 101.)

By 1983, about half of the member states of the United Nations had ratified the two separate Covenants developed from the 1948 Declaration. The Covenant on Civil and Political Rights covers - legal protection against cruel, inhuman or degrading treatment; right to a fair trial and protection against arbitrary arrest or detention; freedom of thought, conscience and religion; freedom of opinion and expression; right of peaceful assembly and of emigration; and freedom of association. The Covenant on Economic, Social and Cultural Rights covers - right to work, to fair wages, to social security, to adequate standards of living and freedom from hunger, to health, to education, and to form and join trade unions. Both Covenants include the right of all peoples to self-determination and the use of their natural resources. (United Nations, 1983; United Nations, 1978.) The two groups of rights have been seen as interdependent, but the groups were separated because the second group could only be implemented progressively in accordance with the resources available. (United Nations Background Paper, 1976.)

It is, of course, easy to exaggerate the significance of these developments. In many instances they represent more rhetoric than active ideals, and the rights are stated so generally that there can be a great deal of disagreement on how they should be implemented, but they do represent principles in terms of which discussion can proceed and decisions defended (Benn and Peters, 1959: 101). Despite the diversity of peoples, religions, cultures and ideologies in the United Nations, they do indicate some movement in the direction of a universal shared morality - the idea that every person has moral claims and responsibilities, and that there are a number of important values which any society should respect for its members. And the expanding circle of moral concern has not stopped there. The claims of all sentient creatures, not just human beings, have been cogently argued by philosophers in recent years (Singer, 1977; 1979: 48-71), and an active 'animal liberation' political movement has emerged in western countries.

Peter Singer's *The Expanding Circle* (Singer, 1981) opens with a quotation from Lecky's *The History of European Morals*:

> The moral unity to be expected in different ages is not a unity of standard, or of acts, but a unity of tendency... At one time the benevolent affections embrace merely the family, soon the circle expanding includes first a class, then a nation, then a coalition of nations, then all humanity, and finally, its influence is felt in the dealings of man with the animal world.

According to Singer, what is eternal and universal in ethics is the process of reasoning. Any rational, social being can come to see that one's own interests are among many sets of interests, no more important than the similar interests of others - in other words one should be impartial in justifying one's conduct within a group. What has happened historically is that ethical thinking first shifted to a point of view that is disinterested between individuals within a group, and then pushed toward a universal point of view covering all the human species, and beyond into the animal kingdom. The idea that the concern we ordinarily feel only for our kin should be extended to all mankind is a tremendous change - an idea, which, according to Singer is only just beginning to be accepted on the level of ethical reasoning and is still a long way from acceptance on the level of practice. But, he insists, that is the direction in which critical moral thought has been going since ancient times. (Singer, 1981: 87-124.)

Geoffrey Warnock argues that the point of moral evaluation is for humans as rational beings, to ameliorate what he calls 'the human predicament'. Things are inherently likely to go badly for people - because resources are limited; knowledge, skills, information and intelligence are limited; people are often not rational either in the management of their own affairs or in the adjustment of their own affairs in relation to others; they are vulnerable to others, and dependent on others, and yet inevitably in competition with others; and, to put it mildly, human sympathies are limited. (Warnock, 1971: 23.)

The general object of ethics is to mitigate the ill effects that flow from the indifference or hostility of persons to other persons. Its scope cannot be confined within groups because people encounter and are vulnerable to members of groups that are not their own, and hostility and conflict between groups can be extremely damaging. Warnock suggests that this is the reason for the widely felt idea that the essence of morality is 'respect for persons', and perhaps for the idea that there are 'natural' rights. (Warnock, 1971: 149-50.)

The Moral Claim of 'Persons'

It has been said that the only universal right is the right for persons to equal consideration (Benn and Peters, 1959: 110). If we are going to justify a particular course of action - to ourselves and to others - we need relevant reasons for treating people differently, otherwise we will be accused of being 'unreasonable', 'unfair', or 'unjust'. The only reasonable ground for treating people differently is that they or their circumstances differ in some way that is relevant to the difference in treatment. To establish this we need to give impartial consideration to the claims of everyone involved. But this means listening to arguments about age, ethnicity, sex and gender, family, friendship, nation, social class, handicaps, disadvantages, attainments, size, strength, and so on - and deciding when these are morally relevant or irrelevant. In our modern complex society this is substantially what the moral debate is about. Yet clearly a person is more than just a collection of attributes and circumstances, and the person's own view of their well-being cannot morally be ignored.

Equal consideration requires discriminating thinking (Barrow, 1982),[2] the ability to think in terms of clear and specific concepts and to discriminate between matters that are superficially similar but nonetheless distinct. Our notions of justice, like Aristotle's, require that equals should be treated equally, and unequals unequally. Historically, egalitarians have been concerned about challenging the validity of particular existing criteria as a basis for discrimination, but new more justified distinctions are typically put in their stead. In the words of Benn and Peters, 'as fast as we eliminate distinctions, we create new ones - the difference being that the ones we discard we consider unjustifiable, while the ones we create seem reasonable.' (Benn and Peters, 1959: 115.)

The idea that each person has a right to equal consideration does not come from any descriptive equality shared by persons, because there is no human quality - physical or intellectual - in terms of which all humans are strictly equal (Benn and Peters, 1959: 108-10). We do, however, all have basic physiological needs, and a capacity to feel pain, to feel and desire affection, and to desire respect for us as persons. In at least these respects, we share a common humanity, but humans have also been seen to be strictly alike in that each is a rational moral agent. In Kant's view, humans are equally such agents and respect is owed equally to each as a member of the Kingdom of Ends, irrespective of any empirical characteristics we may possess. This parallels the Christian conception of the respect owed to all humans as equally children of God. (Williams, 1973: 232-35.)[3]

Downie and Telfer argue that 'respect for persons as ends' is morally basic; it is paramount and all other moral attitudes and principles flow from it. Respect requires taking into account in all one's dealings with another person that that person also is self-determining and rule-following. It requires an attitude of active sympathy and seriously considering that their reasons for their conduct may also apply to ourselves. This is a particular kind of love, the 'agape' of the Christian gospels. Downie and Telfer insist that 'persons' are more than the social roles they occupy, and that they leave their personal imprint on their roles. To the extent that children, human beings who are

---

[2] Barrow's preferred title for his book was *The Ethics of Discrimination*, but his publishers thought this too dull.

[3] Williams does, however, argue (pp. 235-6) that since actual people are seen as having different degrees of moral responsibility, there is not much left to their idea of their equality as moral agents.

senile or mentally incompetent, and animals, have characteristics of personality, the attitude of respect or 'agape' is proper, although in a suitably modified form. (Downie and Telfer, 1969: 13-37.)

'Respect for persons' must, of course, include respect for oneself. Each of us obviously has a unique responsibility for that particular person which cannot be assumed by anyone else. Others can tell us what to do and strongly influence our choices, but they cannot live our lives for us. Self-understanding and self-respect are basic in the moral justification of anything we do. This is why ideas of 'pure altruism' are difficult to sustain morally. On the other hand, the exaggerated or exclusive attention to self, which is typical in some parts of western society (Lasch, 1979) is impossible to sustain as an ethical position, because it treats all other people only as means to one's own ends.

The Age of Science and the Undermining of Persons

Modern society has often been described as the scientific society. Much of modern life has been shaped by scientific discoveries, and many of the cultural heroes are scientists. Scientific research is a major activity in universities, and a significant one in many commercial and government institutions. The intellectual fruits of scientific research occupy university and other courses; in almost every field seriously concerned with the development of knowledge, systematic inquiry based on proper regard for relevant evidence has revolutionized what is known about the world we inhabit. Every profession, based as it is on knowledge and knowledge claims, has its teaching/research arm. In addition, there are many scientific researchers who do not belong to any profession; there is no general profession of scientific researcher. All this research and educational activity can lead to modern society being better informed than its precursors, especially since information technology in now greatly contributing to the process. However, possession of knowledge is one thing, and using it - for good or ill - is another.

A striking paradox of modernity, highlighted by Evans, has been the parallel development of individual and collective action by responsible agents to further human well-being and other ends, and at the same time notions of scientific determinism which apparently undermine confidence in such action. The latter avoid explanations of human behaviour in terms of the conscious decisions of persons and threaten the very notion of 'a person', that is, a valuing, cognitively aware, responsible agent. (Evans, 1977: 14-15.)

Evans points out that various accounts of the human mind absorb human beings into the physical universe and try to understand human operations as machine-like. In their turn, computer scientists have increasingly claimed 'human' qualities for their machines, claiming that they can think, learn, and be purposeful. It is obvious that many disturbing theoretical and practical questions are raised by this mechanistic view of the person, but how, asks Evans, can these be addressed unless on the basis of values freely chosen after conscious, rational deliberation? (Evans, 1977: 21-33.)

A significant strand within sociology, like strands within physiology and psychology, has also looked for positivist scientific explanation of human behaviour apart from the conscious intentions of the people concerned. Social institutions are explained in terms of their functional value in maintaining a society, regardless of participants' understanding of them. Institutions are said to have 'latent' as well as 'manifest' functions. The concept of 'ideology' is used for the conscious motives and beliefs which serve to justify or legitimate institutions which have a functional value not obvious to the participants. If, however, Evans asks, all values are relative products of social conditioning, how can any society ever be improved, by sociologists, or anyone else? (Evans, 1977: 59-67.)

These various attempts to give a full and sufficient scientific explanation of human behaviour along naturalistic, mechanistic lines, are misconceived. Showing what causes a person's values or beliefs does not invalidate them. (Mayo, 1986: 79.) That can only be done in the context of justification through argument, through seeing the point of things and making a decision about them. A person's brain, body, and social relationships provide necessary conditions for action but any sufficient explanation for human action must take into account the reasons for the action. These reasons may be called 'causes' for the action, but they provide a purposive, rule-following model of explanation, quite different from scientific, causal explanation. Scientists may argue that all such reasoning is merely rationalization, the real causes being the natural underlying ones, but this is obviously not the normal situation. People do operate in terms of genuine reasons and not just phoney ones. In any case, just because a human action is causally determined does not mean that it is unavoidable. Indeed, knowing a cause of something is often a necessary condition of being able to avoid it. (Benn and Peters, 1959: 199-210.)

The idea of a single scientific method consisting of objective observation, impersonal causal explanation, and logic and mathematics, has had a powerful influence in the western world and remarkable achievements. (Evans, 1977:

15-19.) Increasingly, however, its limits, especially applied to the human sciences, are being emphasized (Evans, 1977: 101-16). The truth acquired in this fashion in those areas is limited because of human beings' essentially cognitive, creative, valuing nature. In fact, amongst the social scientists, some have always argued that unless they take a viewpoint close to the acting subject being studied they will not correctly observe or understand human actions. (Evans, 1977: 128.) Their 'scientific' method must be adapted to the subject. Within psychology, Maslow has identified a 'third-force' of humanist psychologies alternative to both orthodox Freudian and behaviouristic psychologies. These all have an emphasis on the person as a unified self or agent, the significance of choice in human life and the crucial role of values in both science and life. (Evans, 1977: 128-9.) Finally, in recent years some philosophers of the natural sciences have challenged the notion of science as value-free and emphasized the extent to which observations are influenced by the theories of the observers (Evans, 1977: 132).

It seems that in the modern, specialized, scientific world, 'the person' can get lost. Yet societies, nations, economies, social structures of various sorts do not exist without people living in and through them, giving point or meaning to them, creating them, demolishing them. In the fascination with things, systems and control, it is easy to lose sight of individual named people and their lives. Even when people are talked about they tend to be characterized on single dimensions such as their age, or their gender, or their level of intelligence, or their family status, or their work status, or their nationality, or their social class. Yet humans are obviously many-dimensional, and even when they are described on all such dimensions, a full and sufficient account of a person has not been given. That person is a cognitive, choosing, living creature, interpreting and interacting with his or her environment. He or she is not fully determined biologically or sociologically. If they were, notions of 'freewill', 'choice', 'responsibility' and 'rationality' would make no sense. A person's choices may be cruelly circumscribed, their level of responsibility low, their will timid, and their rationality limited, but the person cannot survive with any sense of identity, let alone flourish, without some performance on these counts, and all concepts of 'human well-being' are tied up with these peculiarly human notions. (Lawrence, 1984.)

A Model of the Dimensions of Ethical Conduct and its Assessment

Having traced what seems to be involved in planning to achieve human ends, or acting rationally, and the development of the idea that human well-being or the worth and dignity of every human person should be of paramount importance in human affairs, we can now construct a model of ethical conduct and its assessment incorporating both of these essential features. It is evident that both are essential because ethical praise or blame is brought to bear, not just on ends being sought but on the effectiveness and efficiency in their attainment.

The model concentrates on human well-being but can be extended to cover the well-being of all sentient creatures. In time, it can be anticipated that this will happen. Although vulnerable to accusations of 'speciesism' the more limited human well-being focus is difficult enough to encompass for most people at this stage of their moral thinking, and also the inclusion of all sentient animals may well have been counterproductive for it would complicate the explication even further.

A significant feature of the model is the assessment function which may run parallel with the steps of rational action, assessing the performance of them and which, in turn, raises issues of ethical justification. Another significant feature is that the model can apply both to individuals and collectivities. The same or different individuals, or the same or different collectivities can be involved at the various stages of rational action, and in the assessment function of such action. This is possible because the logic of rational action and the logic of assessment are similar whether pursued by individuals or by collectivities. When many different people are involved the process and assessment of it are obviously much more complex and hazardous, but it is the means-ends logic of rational action which continues to give them coherence and provides essential cognitive reference points for the participants.

Figure 2.1: The Dimensions of Ethical Conduct and its Assessment

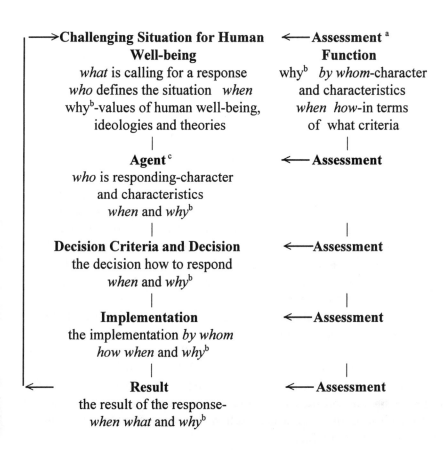

⟶**Challenging Situation for Human** ⟵**Assessment**[a]
  Well-being **Function**
what is calling for a response why[b] *by whom*-character
who defines the situation *when* and characteristics
why[b]-values of human well-being, *when how*-in terms
ideologies and theories of what criteria

| |

Agent[c] ⟵**Assessment**
who is responding-character
and characteristics
when and *why*[b]

| |

Decision Criteria and Decision ⟵**Assessment**
the decision how to respond
when and *why*[b]

| |

Implementation ⟵**Assessment**
the implementation *by whom*
how when and *why*[b]

| |

⟵ **Result** ⟵**Assessment**
the result of the response-
when what and *why*[b]

[a] May be performed by an individual or a collectivity.
[b] In each case the *why* covers values and ideologies, and also theories and assumptions about the way the world works. It is when the values are seen to be seriously related to the well-being of humans (and, for some, of other sentient beings as well) that the conduct is seen as of ethical significance, and is likely to come under ethical assessment.
[c] The agent may be an individual or a collectivity of people.

In the real world, people in their various sets of activities are engaged at different stages of this model. Since the various stages are logically interdependent, justification of any one set of activities will depend upon knowing where they lie in the rational action sequence and how they relate to logically prior considerations, and to later phases. The less clear-headed people are about these matters, the less likely they are to achieve the desired ends, and the more vulnerable they are to reflective criticism, either by their own conscience, or by an external assessor.

What makes this a model of ethical conduct rather than just of rational action, is the primacy given to human well-being. 'Human well-being' is a general concept covering as many human beings as are seen to be involved in any particular situation of planned action. When talking about the depletion of the earth's natural resources or the threat of nuclear war, for example, it extends to the whole of humanity present and future. On the other hand, it may relate primarily to the well-being of just one person, for example, some-one with a terminal illness and no known friends or relatives. With 'human well-being' as the prime value, the claims and interests of all the interested parties in a situation need to be identified and weighed otherwise further ethical challenge remains open.

The model points only to general criteria for the ethical evaluation of human conduct. Its application requires a theory, or at least assumptions, about what constitutes human well-being, and theories or assumptions how, in various circumstances, this can be achieved. In any particular instance of conduct in the real world, the greater the degree of agreement about what constitutes human well-being, and the greater the amount of knowledge of how to achieve it, the greater the likelihood of agreement about the moral significance of that conduct.

All actual human conduct is a person or persons acting in the situations of the real world. A particular type of human conduct may be treated as a particular instance of conduct, in isolation from the person/s whose conduct it is and the situation in which it occurred. Yet understanding the moral significance of an instance of the conduct must take into account the situation in which it actually occurred and the capacities of the person/s responsible for the action. As Hare pointed out (see p. 16), it is both possible and essential to develop standardized guides for ethical conduct, but the person or persons in real life must still decide when and how these are applicable.

The Components of the Model

There are five interlocking and interdependent phases in ethical conduct. First, there is a challenging situation which is seen by someone or by a group of people at some point in time to be of ethical or moral significance both because it substantially relates to human well-being and it is considered that something constructive can be done about it. Second, is the existence of an agent, either individual or collective, who assumes responsibility to respond to the situation. Third, is the process of policy decision of the agent deciding how to respond to the situation. Fourth, is the implementation of the agent's decision, by the agent or by others. Finally, is the assessment of the result of the response to, or intervention in, the original situation. At each stage, ethical issues are involved, because the decisions along the way are of crucial importance to an outcome which can be ethically justified, and also because more than just technical questions are raised by what is seen to be appropriate at each step in the process.

If human well-being is the paramount moral value, any human conduct which impacts seriously on human well-being is likely to come under moral scrutiny. This is why the model includes the parallel assessment function. At any stage, or all stages, rational action which claims to be ethically justified can reasonably be separately assessed - especially if the claimants to ethical justification are powerful and biased in their attitudes, or if there are public complaints of their behaviour, or if something has gone seriously awry, or action has been taken in conditions where adequate reflection was impossible, or the actor is relatively inexperienced. There are crucial ethical issues about who should undertake this separate assessment function, and how it should relate to the human conduct being assessed.

1. *An Ethically Challenging Situation*[4]

Human conduct is typically assessed as morally good or bad in the context of an ethically challenging real world situation. Two features define such a situation - it substantially relates to human well-being, and something constructive in terms of human well-being can be done about it. Traditionally,

---

[4] Fotion, 1968, argues that moral situations provide the broadest frame of reference for addressing moral questions, and this is preferable to the common concentration mainly on particular moral agents. Fotion's book also identifies a judge (or critic) role in moral situations, separate from an agent's.

scientific situations have been seen as only intellectually challenging, but as already indicated the situations in the social sciences cannot be ethically neutral, and also increasingly the methods and results of all the sciences are coming under moral scrutiny.

For a situation to be seen as substantially related to human well-being, this requires both knowledge or assumptions about the way the world works in the situation and some decision on what are the human values of well-being involved. We have seen already that despite cultural diversity, there is a considerable number of values common to human beings, particularly those living together in the same society, in terms of which judgments of comparative well-being can be made. Such values include security, income and wealth, health, housing, education, employment, recreation, civil and political rights, mobility, family well-being, friendship, love, and autonomy. Situations with implications for human well-being are those in which such human values are seen to be involved.

When there is some agreement on the factual and normative assessment of the situation, there is some possible basis to proceed further in response to it - either because human values are being threatened or denied in the situation, or because they could possibly be developed or enhanced. A fatalistic, or just realistic, judgment may be made, however, that nothing can be done that is likely to improve the situation, in which case it may continue to be of concern, but it is not a moral challenge, since 'ought' implies 'can'. For example, the situation may be viewed as too unstable, or relevant resources are not available, or the necessary technology does not exist, or the result of deliberate intervention is too uncertain or is likely to be too small for the effort required, or the unexpected consequences are feared, and so on. How sound are these arguments in a particular case is, of course, open to assessment. The more the original situation is seen as seriously involving human well-being, the greater the moral inducement to intervene constructively if at all possible.

It is obvious that in the process of defining the situation to be addressed at least some assumptions about the possibility of successful intervention are likely to be operating. Often, indeed, the original situation is defined with specific interventions in mind, by people with particular expertise, with the means determining the ends being sought rather than the other way round.

Perhaps the most crucial task confronting human beings is to define and select amongst the multitude of possible 'situations' which impact on human well-being, those that are morally most significant. Both individually and collectively, we organize and experience the world in terms of various situations in which we find, or place ourselves. How we characterize these, how many of them we can cope with at any one time, how they relate to each other, and who defines them as ethically important are continuing issues in the real world. Much of the political process can be seen as involving these issues. The government, political parties, pressure groups, people claiming various expertise, and publicists of different kinds are constantly engaged in defining and drawing attention to situations which they see as requiring action. The media is also heavily involved, but its choices of situations on which to focus often have little to do with a direct concern for human well-being and effective action.

In later stages of the action sequence, the initial situation may be redefined - as more becomes known about it, or people change their minds about it in terms of their priorities, or people engaged later in the process have different views from the original definers. Logically, however, there must continue to be an ethically challenging situation providing the justification basis for the rational action.

At the societal level the attempt to develop social indicators (Shonfield and Shaw, 1972) may be seen as a way of monitoring the processes of the society in terms of certain significant value indices, for example, infant mortality rates, and is suggestive of what situations deserve collective ethical attention. At the individual level, a person has the continuing ethical challenge of living their own life and deciding how they might contribute to human well-being more generally. Each person's moral life can be analyzed and assessed in terms of which, whose, and how many ethically challenging situations they are engaged in. Rational ethical action in relation to one's own life continually involves moving through the five action steps of the model - deciding on the situations which are most significant in relation to one's own well-being, accepting responsibility for action to this end, deciding what to do, carrying it out, and assessing the result. In relation to others' well-being, a person's involvement may, however, concentrate on only one of the five action steps. They may, for example, concentrate primarily on drawing public attention to one or more ethically challenging situations, but leave the rest of the phases of rational action to others.

It needs to be remembered that the ethically challenging situation may involve the well-being of any number of people, just as the assumed capacity to be able to do something about it may involve any number.

2. *The Responding Agent*

Once a situation is accepted as an ethical challenge, that is, one which substantially relates to human well-being and one which calls for an ethical response, who does respond and who morally ought to respond, and when and why do they respond? Ideally, the responding agent is the person or persons who are most likely to be effective and efficient in relation to the human well-being at stake in the situation. ('Agent' here is *not* being used in the particular sense of acting on behalf of someone else. It refers to anyone capable of responsible action, that is, action for which they can be held accountable.)

The people whose well-being is at stake are obvious candidates for being the responding agents whenever this is at all possible. They are likely to have a greater degree of both initial and continuing motivation to do something about the situation, they will have views on what constitutes their well-being which cannot reasonably be ignored whoever is the responding agent, and they are likely to be much better informed about various aspects of their well-being than anyone outside their situation. In addition to these pragmatic reasons for people to take responsibility for doing something about the situations which affect their lives, there is the value placed on self-determination or responsibility for self in its own right. At least some recognition of this is given in the various schemes for 'democratic participation' and 'consumer involvement'. However, such schemes typically arise in situations where already there are responding collective agents, agencies or organizations, that have taken, or have accepted prime responsibility for organized action in response to certain continuing situations of human needs and wants.

If an ethically challenging situation is a recurring one, a society is likely to have established particular roles and agencies, or organizations, to deal with it on an ongoing basis. People in those roles and agencies with those responsibilities are expected to bring special competence and experience to the task. The greater the human well-being at stake in the situations being addressed, the greater the likelihood that this will be the case. A multitude of occupations and agencies now claim special expertise in the handling of situations relevant to human well-being. People in modern society meet their needs and wants increasingly through the agency of others, and especially of formally organized others. This, however, greatly complicates their existence, because the interests and services of the agencies may not coincide with those of their clients.

In any ethically challenging situation, then, getting the attention and interest of those best able to respond is a crucial step. But deciding on who these are involves considerable knowledge and judgment. Each occupation and agency is necessarily specialized in particular ways and has its own history and interests, which must be taken into account when deciding on the appropriateness of its involvement as a responding agent to the situation. The challenging situation may well require response from more than one agency, which then raises the question of how responses are to be coordinated in terms of the human well-being at stake.

Again, as with the definition of the situation stage, this responding agent stage requires keeping in mind the various stages entailed in successful rational ethical action. For example, involving a responding agent without the capacity to ensure implementation of policy, either directly or even indirectly, indicates a lack of seriousness in addressing the original situation. Many policy recommending exercises commissioned by governments can, in fact, be seen in this light.

If ethically inappropriate people or agencies become associated with a particular challenging situation, it can become very difficult to get rid of them, especially if they have considerable economic or political power. They may claim to be addressing the original challenging situation, but, in fact, be more focused on other purposes - their social status, economic profit, using and improving their technology, retaining control over the situation, and so on. The more vulnerable the population whose well-being is at stake in the original situation - for example, where the population is very young, or very old, or very sick, or is intellectually handicapped, or is disorganized and inarticulate, or is socially and culturally distant from potential 'helpers' - the more safeguards need to be built into who appropriately is the responding agent or agency.

The moral virtues, or moral character, of the responding agent and of those responsible for a responding agency are particularly relevant in such situations. The responding agents may be clearly unsuitable - untrustworthy, unreliable, insensitive, lacking in relevant skills, timid, selfish, culpably ignorant, or incapable of focusing on the ethical challenges of the original situation. They may, however, have a mixture of both positive and negative attributes which makes judgments of their suitability more complicated.

3. *Decision Criteria and Decision*

An ethical agent, individual or collective, who is responding to an ethically challenging situation has to decide what kind of action will be most likely to be effective and efficient to the human well-being at stake. This requires deciding on specific feasible objectives to be achieved in the situation and on what kind of action should be taken to achieve them.

These crucial policy decisions are necessary for the guidance of a subsequent program of action, or implementation, and obviously need to be made with this in mind. At the same time, their relationship to the challenging situation needs to be clear. For example, the responding agent may in fact only be responding to particular aspects of the original situation, or may be reinterpreting the original situation in ways conducive to the agent's particular concerns, or the original situation may have actually changed before the responding agent could become active. Some agencies and some individuals continue with policies which long since have lost their connection with their originating situations. They may be fulfilling other purposes, but their original rational ethical justification has become lost or displaced.

A responding agent normally brings to any ethically challenging situation a range of existing commitments which they expect or are expected to honour. In a crisis situation which seriously involves human well-being, these may be temporarily put aside, but this may entail considerable human cost which no rational ethical response can discount or continue to ignore. Any responding agent that does not adhere to general ethical principles like truth-telling, keeping promises, and not harming people, which are so basic to continuing human well-being, is very vulnerable to ethical challenge, whatever the circumstances.

Organizations or agencies always have formal constitutions which state their formal objectives. Ideally their actual objectives should be regularly related to these and if they become too discrepant, action is necessary to close the gap by changing one or both sets of objectives. Without clear, widely-accepted and widely-known operational objectives, an organization cannot operate effectively and efficiently, cannot be held accountable, and cannot coordinate its work with other agencies. But in turn, the operational objectives only make ethical sense in the context of ethically challenging situations. If an agency is shifting in its concerns and commitments, this needs to be a conscious, public process, so that none of the interests of crucially affected people are ignored.

If the responding agent is an individual person, that person needs to be clear in what capacity they are responding - in some particular role which has certain commitments and expectations, or as a fellow citizen, or as a concerned fellow human being, and so on.

If human well-being is accepted as the basic moral value both for identifying situations which call for human action, and for determining the purpose and result of such action, this obviously leaves great scope for interpretation and argument around both factual and value questions. Yet the scope is not limitless, especially within the confines of living together in the circumstances of the same society. The responding agent's decision criteria must be related to human well-being and will necessarily be making assumptions about what is valuable or beneficial to human beings and what is harmful, and how the world works and is likely to work in the specific situation being responded to, in relation to these matters. At the decision criteria and policy decision stage, the responding agent will need to pin down much more carefully whose well-being is at stake in the challenging situation and in what respects and what is intended to be done about it. A wide variety of consultation and data collection techniques may be employed in the assessment of situations before relevant courses of action are determined. If the interests of any person seriously affected by the situation and the proposed course of action are neglected the decision is vulnerable to moral challenge. 'Interests' is a vague general term but people in real life when reasonably informed about their situation have a measure of agreement when things are going badly and things are going well, when their 'interests' are being harmed or enhanced, and when they are being treated unfairly in comparison with others in the same society in similar situations.

Attempts have been made to reduce the various decision criteria relating to interests into a single common measure, such as units of happiness, or satisfaction, or money, so that alternative courses of action can be compared more objectively. But happiness or satisfaction do not exist separate from the activities in which people are involved. The activities can be ranked in terms of their relative value to a person, but are not reasonably given quantitative measures. Money measures can be used for things which have an exchange market or economic value, but that does not necessarily reflect their value to the persons concerned with them, and many things of great human value are beyond money measures.

Policy decision is essentially a matter not just of calculation, but of judgment, balancing short-term and long-term considerations, the claims of different people, competing and complementary values, costs and benefits both economic and other, and degrees of probability. Especially when the decision clearly impacts on people's well-being, it is expected to be reasoned, and at least in an open democratic society, there is ongoing critical discussion as to what constitutes ethically justified reasons. Clearly some reasons are not acceptable, for example, those that are blatantly prejudiced, those that are partial, those that are only prudent for the agent, those that are ill-informed, and those that only reflect an emotional response.

4. *Implementation*

At the level of individual rational action, a person may have accepted that she or he should be a responding agent to some ethically significantly situation and may have made the necessary policy decision about the form of action needed, but then does not proceed further. This is often characterized as 'weakness of moral will'. The person knows what they ought morally to do, but they do not do it. Of course, there may be other good reasons why the person does not follow through with implementation, such as changes in the original challenging situation, or in the person's priorities, or in the capacities or resources of the person, and so on.

The same explanations can also be given for an organization not following through to implementation, except perhaps for lack of will-power, for a number of people are usually involved in an organization's sequence of rational action. In the organization, however, when those implementing the policies and programs are different from the policy-makers, what actually occurs may be very different from what was intended by the policy-makers, which can be a major obstacle to effective and efficient rational ethical action at the collective level. Only sophisticated organizational design, skilful leadership, staff training, and staff involvement in policy discussions are likely to avoid this occurring to any great extent. If the organization does not have the staffing capacity or inclination to implement the organization's policies in relation to the original ethically challenging situation, it is clearly not an appropriate responding agent.

5. *Result*

The whole point of the process of rational ethical action is to achieve a successful result in terms of the human well-being involved in the situation. Both short-term and longer-term results need to be observed and assessed. They may be better than anticipated, or worse than anticipated. There may have been unexpected consequences, both good and bad. It may be very difficult in complicated situations to know how much difference a particular course of action has made to that situation. Unless the prior stages are carefully monitored, especially in an agency's program, it will not be possible to know with confidence what course of action is having what kind of result. In the process of taking action, other goals may have displaced the original ones, and this obviously needs to be known at the result stage.

Once results have been actually experienced and understood, people can decide whether to continue with similar patterns of action, or to modify them, or to discontinue them. They complete the cycle of ethical learning involved in meeting ethically challenging situations. Some people and some organizations never fully complete the ethical action cycle, or do so very infrequently or spasmodically. They continue to behave in particular ways without checking to find out if these are effective and efficient. This obviously will have opportunity costs, that is, they will not know whether other uses of their resources and talents might be preferable. More seriously, they may unwittingly be doing more harm than good.

In handling situations which seriously affect human well-being, both good intentions and desirable results are needed. Good intentions not pursued to the logical and ethical conclusion of taking action and assessing its result are very much open to ethical challenge. They give 'good intentions' a bad name, when clearly all ethically justified conduct needs to retain 'good intentions' as an essential component. To describe a person or agency just as 'well-meaning' often carries the implication that they are also ineffectual.

The Assessment Function[5]

As already foreshadowed, because the process of rational ethical conduct necessarily involves the well-being of people, and sometimes quite vitally, any stage of the process or the whole process can come under separate ethical scrutiny and assessment, either formally or informally. This assessment function may be performed later by those involved in the original conduct, or by others. The others may be formally appointed to perform the task, with particular terms of reference - for example, a supervisor, or an inspector, or a peer review panel, or a committee of inquiry, or a committee of review. Or the others may be people specially concerned about the situation being

---

[5] See footnote 4, p. 43.

addressed, or concerned about alleged abuses, or generally interested in the activities under scrutiny.

Many situations and responding conduct call for independent ethical assessment, but this involves decisions by someone on which of these ought to be pursued, who should pursue them, when they should be undertaken, how the assessors should proceed, what criteria they should employ in their assessment and what should be done with the results of the assessment. It is obvious that the assessment function itself needs to be critiqued using the model of rational ethical action. Not least of the problems of an independent outside assessor is the difficulty of obtaining accurate information, especially when it is long after the event and no accurate records were kept at the time, and when the people whose conduct is being assessed choose not to cooperate fully or are no longer available.

The discussion in the earlier part of this chapter has indicated why it is reasonable in our sort of world to evaluate human conduct in terms of rational action and human well-being, and these two notions have formed the basis of the model that has been constructed. We can now examine the place of professional occupations in modern society and then evaluate their conduct in the light of the various dimensions of ethical choice indicated by the model.

3 What is Professional Conduct?

Description and Prescription of Professional Conduct

Having suggested a reasonable basis for the ethical evaluation of any human conduct, the rest of this book will focus on professional conduct and its evaluation. This is a particular form of human conduct which is claimed to be of especial significance for human well-being in modern society. Like any other form of human conduct, professional conduct can be both described and prescribed. Each of these tasks has its distinctive purpose, but the two are obviously related.

The purpose of description is to gain information, knowledge, and understanding about the reality of professional conduct - in the past, in the present, or in the future. If there is agreement on what the concept refers to, descriptive propositions about professional conduct can be supported in accordance with available evidence. But values and purposes are built into the describer's decisions on what to describe, how to describe it, and what constitutes evidence; and they are an integral part of professional conduct itself - what is being described.

Prescriptions about what professional conduct ought to be are logically distinct from descriptions, because they require a decision and commitment to achieve particular values and purposes. But unless prescriptions are based on reality and are informed by what is empirically feasible, they lose their prescriptive point.

This chapter examines how professions and professional conduct have been analyzed and described - by the professionals themselves and by outside scholars. It will be evident how description and prescription have been historically intertwined. Leaders of both older occupations and new aspiring ones have used the generally positive concept of 'profession' to try to secure or maintain high social standing and other relatively high rewards for their occupations and have not always been careful to distinguish between prescription and description. In this political process, what ought to be the case, or what one would like to be the case, can easily be confused with what one claims to be the case - especially when only fellow 'experts' can check the technical aspects of the claims. In later chapters when ethical assessment of professional conduct is discussed using its contribution to human well-being as the prime value, it will be obvious that such an ethical assessment depends upon a thorough ongoing understanding of where the conduct is located in a society's social processes and social structures - in its political, economic, and social arrangements. These are basically matters for empirical inquiry, and only such inquiry can reveal the effects of professional conduct on human beings.

The Division of Labour and Specialization of Human Tasks

Like all living creatures, humans expend effort to take from their environment what they need to survive. The human species is distinctive in that its efforts do not reflect any clearly definable set of instincts, but rather social choices which can vary widely in their form and reflect values which give point and meaning to human existence. (Watson, 1987: 82.)

The essentially social nature of our living has already been observed in the discussion of the pervasiveness of ethics in our lives. For any human society to persist a range of tasks has to be performed, such as getting sufficient food and water, providing shelter from the elements, protecting and educating the young, defending the society from outside attack, coping with illness and disease, settling internal disputes. Each member of the society cannot perform all these functions, so some degree of specialization of role or function is always present in every human society, but obviously not all members benefit to the same extent from this arrangement, and some types of society should not persist if the division of labour is unfair or hurtful to many or even some of its members.

In the early small hunter-gatherer societies the amount of specialization of tasks was limited. It was largely based on the obviously biological differences of age and sex, but such was the variation between societies in the expected age and sex roles that they were clearly more than just biologically determined, and this has continued to be the case in all later forms of human society. (Rueschemeyer, 1986: 2.)

Increasing complexity and division of labour has been evident as the main types of human society have evolved - hunter-gatherer, agrarian, industrial, and post-industrial. Social evolution towards ever-greater complexity was a central concept promulgated by founding fathers of modern sociology, but Rueschemeyer has warned against linear theories of ever-greater specialization, and has observed that 'the role of power has been greatly neglected throughout the long history of thought about division of labour' (Rueschemeyer, 1986: 1-3). His book demonstrates how power has been used to block and shape specialization of function. Like others, however, he does draw attention to the enormous increase in the division of labour with industrialization, especially in the production of goods and services. This was made possible by the growth in the size of populations, the use of high-energy technology, the vast expansion of scientific and technical knowledge, the pursuit of economic profits, the large-scale organization of production, and a vast increase in markets of consumers.

Beginning in Britain in the eighteenth century, then extending to other European countries, and countries of European origin in the nineteenth and early twentieth centuries, and becoming the world-wide ideology of 'economic development' by the mid-twentieth century, these various interrelated developments have been described by phrases such as 'the industrial revolution', 'the capitalist revolution', 'the great transformation', or just 'modernization'. However described, there can be no doubt about the revolutionary changes in traditional roles and relations in industrializing societies.

It is scarcely surprising that sociology, a subject which focuses upon the organization of society and social roles and relations, should have first appeared in European industrializing societies undergoing substantial structural changes. Social theorists like Adam Smith, Marx, Durkheim, and Weber, were trying to make sense of a new, emerging type of society and contrasting it with earlier and other forms of social order. (Watson, 1987: 2-3.) In one of the most influential accounts, Tonnies contrasted the large-scale, individualized, rapidly changing, urban scientific and rational modern society, with the small-scale, intimate, stable, rural, religious and traditional community which it was displacing. Work relations became specific, contractual and impersonal, and work was sharply separated from home and family. (Watson, 1987: 71.) The basis of work specialization shifted away from social statuses such as sex, birth or kin, and ethnicity, towards more universal criteria related to the ability to perform particular jobs. (Wilensky and Lebeaux, 1965: 63-6.)

The idea of post-industrial society has been largely associated with the work of Daniel Bell, especially his *The Coming of Post-Industrial Society* in 1973. For him it is a society where the emphasis is on services rather than goods, and on white-collar workers, many of them professional, managerial, or technical employees. It is a highly educated society where theoretical knowledge is the central resource. The division of labour is increasingly related to professionalization and the social division of knowledge. The post-industrial society ethic is said to be one of social responsibility and professional commitment. (Kumar, 1985: 633-4.) The term, however, can be misleading, because large-scale industrial production persists, and much of the white-collar and professional work continues to be in the service of existing products and processes. Industrialism is extended, not replaced by a new social order. Specialization continues but in work organized around occupations based on knowledge claims. Information technology is now assisting in providing a rapidly expanding, but changing knowledge basis for this division of labour, while at the same time it is giving much more general access to knowledge which previously has been seen as the preserve of specialized occupations. How this will impact on the occupational division of labour is uncertain.

Interdependence - Non-market and Market Transactions

Since people cannot survive, let alone flourish, by producing all they need or want through their own unaided efforts, they are dependent upon goods and services produced by others. The goods and services may be provided to a person because of his or her standing as a family member, a friend, a neighbour, or a member of various associations or 'communities' including his or her nation. Such transactions are part of ongoing relationships, which have continuing rights and obligations on both sides. They contrast with contractual market transactions where the medium of exchange of money enables buyers and sellers to disregard broader ties and obligations and limit their relationship to the economic exchange. It is through all these various social arrangements that people attain and experience their well-being, and informed social policy debate argues the pros and cons of the market and non-market mechanisms.

Monetary market exchange was a crucial feature in the revolutionary transformation into specialized modern social forms. It made it possible for producers to concentrate on particular products which could be exchanged for money by those who wanted the products in question, and they in turn could use the money in exchange for goods and services which they wanted. The 'invisible hand' of the market seemingly related supply and demand through the price mechanism. Money, then, served as a single measure of the exchange, or economic value, of very different goods, services and activities, and further, it served as a highly generalized way of storing economic assets. (Rueschemeyer, 1986: 4.) An individual's particular access to goods and services depended, however, upon whether they existed in the market in appropriate form, how much competition existed for them, how much priority the person was willing and able to give to them, and how much economic power, i.e. money, they had to purchase their ends.

The Labour Market

In the modern economic system a large proportion of the population is dependent for their livelihood upon selling their labour to an employer. In this way they achieve power on the economic market - considerable power if they receive high monetary returns for their work, very low power if they receive a low wage. In addition to money, an employee may receive other payment in the form of goods and services, and these so-called 'fringe benefits' have become a significant feature in the pay packages of high-level employees. (Titmuss, 1963: 34-55.)

A person may find employment with a private corporation whose prime purpose is economic profit, or with a private non-profit organization pursuing some public purpose, or with a government body with particular public functions. Alternatively a person can 'make their living' by working independently, providing goods and services directly to consumers and receiving from them a financial return. As we will see, this possibility has been significant in the history of certain high-status occupations in Britain and the United States.

The economic systems of western industrialized societies have provided changing employment opportunities. Very broadly, the 'mix' of primary products from the land, manufacturing products, and services, has shifted dramatically towards the latter two, with services becoming increasingly prominent. The numbers of independent operators have reduced in all fields, even in the high-status professional fields where private individual practice was the dominant model. They have found it increasingly difficult to compete with the larger organized units. The scale of the employers' operations, both government and private enterprise, has vastly increased, which has demanded the services of a managerial class and an extensive range of new expertise.

Government has become a major employer in the western so-called capitalist societies, regulating and stimulating economic activities, and providing a wide array of social programs. Depending on the interpretation, these are seen either as functional requisites for the perpetuation of the capitalistic economic system, or they are seen to represent significant political achievement for a socialist philosophy, meeting needs as a matter of communal responsibility outside the economic market system. In the former 'socialist' societies with their state-run 'command' economies, there was no place for the private-enterprise capitalist, although market mechanisms were beginning to be viewed more favorably in these societies before their recent dramatic economic and political collapse (Mishra, 1981).

Interdependence of Employer and Employee

In one sense, the employer and the employee depend on each other in that neither can apparently fulfil their purposes without the other. The terms under which they are working together can, however, vary enormously depending on factors such as - the strength of demand for the products they are producing, the cost of other factors of production besides labour, the degree and nature of expertise on the part of the employer and of the employee, the nature and extent of job satisfaction which employees are seeking, the availability to the employer of an alternative labour supply or of replacement by machines, the availability to the employee of alternative employment, government regulations, and so on.

The Right to Work

As has been mentioned (p. 33), the United Nations Covenant on Economic, Social and Cultural Rights includes the right to work and to fair wages. The governments of western industrialized countries after the depression of the 1930s included the maintenance of conditions of full employment as a major political, economic and social objective, an integral part of their national social security systems, and Keynesian economics seemed to provide an adequate means to achieve this, at least until the stagflation of the 1970s. What is crucial to recognize is that for most people in a modern, industrialized society, paid work provided by an employer is one's chief source of income, a key determinant of one's social standing, and a major commitment of time and effort. The part it plays in one's well-being in this sort of society is very large, as is shown by the devastating effects on people and their families of long-term unemployment.

Is Work Specialization Productive?

In classical economic argument, there is a clear connection between specialization in the division of labour and efficiency, but Rueschemeyer has shown how questionable this can be (Rueschemeyer, 1986: 17-19). Only under certain conditions and in relation to specific purposes is a given feature of division of labour likely to yield efficiency advantages. What is important is the overall productivity advantage. Virtually all aspects of the division of labour have side-effects. (Rueschemeyer, 1986: 20-1.)

Delimiting tasks narrowly and clearly facilitates tying rewards to performance, and more rational hiring and work assignment. Separating simple from complex tasks permits economies of training and recruitment. Dividing instrumental tasks makes concentration on a few activities possible, which is an especial advantage in the more demanding kinds of work. Specialization reduces the time used for switching from one activity to another. Rationalization of instrumental activities encourages the use of technical innovation. And once a pattern of division of labour is fully established, work roles and organizational units can, within limits, be arranged and rearranged as required by changing circumstances, new technology, and new goals. However, the separation of instrumental tasks for the rational pursuit of chosen ends in a work organization from other abiding human concerns can never be complete. People are pre-occupied with their family and other concerns which give meaning to their lives, and they need to feel part of their work group and to get along with each other. Also, the division of dominant from subordinate roles in work organization is not a division of labour among autonomous parties, but is primarily in the interest of authorities. (Rueschemeyer, 1986: 10.)

Functional explanations of the division of labour in a society make it appear that there are efficiency advantages for the whole society. Yet clearly when people have different needs, wants and values, what is 'functional' for some is not for others. Whose preferences and interests are dominant in the dividing of labour is a question which cannot be avoided. The presence of power, that is the ability to have one's own wishes to predominate over others, is important in the explanation of the form and extent of division of labour. (Rueschemeyer, 1986: 45.)

Economists argue that the economic market coordinates, aggregates and integrates individual patterns of evaluation in market prices, and this does not require shared values nor the exercise of power. Rueschemeyer points out, however, that many activities - in the home and in the government - are not marketed. In addition, market arrangements in the real world never approach the conditions of perfect competition which exist only in the economists' imagination. The state's laws are not neutral in their effects on the interests of different economic actors; access to markets is often as limited by custom and law as by capital and skill requirements; income is so unevenly distributed that the needs and wants of the poor do not affect the market choices as much as even superficial whims of the wealthy; and what is made available by the state outside the market and what is left to the market is very much a matter of politics, and the role of the state in the political economy. The market is, in fact, the means through which power is acquired and imposed. (Rueschemeyer, 1986: 45-6.) 'Political economy', the older term for 'economics', makes this clear.

In this assessment of work specialization by Rueschemeyer, it is evident that at least implicitly he is assessing such activity in terms of its effectiveness and efficiency in achieving human well-being. His insistence on analyzing the division of labour in terms of whose interests are being furthered is indicative of some of the more recent writing in the social sciences. Social arrangements like the division of work do not just occur as a result of impersonal, objective processes. They are at least partly the result of conscious human striving and of political processes through which human beings develop, maintain, and extend their interests - both in cooperation and in competition with each other. Accurate description requires taking this into account, and it also indicates the extent to which division of work is a legitimate subject for ethical evaluation.

The Scope and Nature of Professional Work

So far this chapter has briefly outlined the place of work in human society, and especially in the more recent industrialized societies. With this in mind, we are now in a position to examine directly professional work which is the particular form of work of prime concern in this book.

In the present overall work scene, the numbers of professionals are substantial. They can, however, be exaggerated, and the notion of present-day professionals being typically 'independent' practitioners is grossly inaccurate. Even on a loose definition of 'professional', professionals still constitute only a relatively small proportion of the contemporary work-force. In 1986, they constituted 14.8 per cent (8.8m.) of the work-force in the United States, 15.7 per cent (1.9m.) in Canada, and 15.9 per cent (4.1m.) in the United Kingdom. In each of these societies, only about 8 per cent of the professionals are employers or working on their own account; all the rest are classified as employees. (1986 Year Book of Labour Statistics.)

Is 'Professional Work' a Meaningful Descriptive Category?

Like any other human activity, all actual professional work is specific in time, in place, and in persons involved. How much, and which aspects of it are subsequently described and analyzed will depend upon the nature of the surviving record of the work; and the number, interests, purposes, and resources of the writers. Rather different accounts may be given by the various participants in the work, both of their own participation and of the participation of others, and by outside observers, both at the time of the activity and later. But what makes these accounts of 'professional' work in the first place? Is this a meaningful classification of work - within societies, between societies, and over time?

In one sense of the word, all work done for a living is done 'professionally', or for payment. This contrasts with activity done on a voluntary basis or as an amateur, that is, without monetary reward. As early as the sixteenth century, the term 'profession' could be used in the English language to refer generally to a person's occupation. For example, in the opening scene of Shakespeare's *Julius Caesar*, a carpenter and a cobbler are asked to state their 'profession'. In the French language 'professional' continues to be synonymous with 'occupational', and the word 'profession' was used interchangeably with 'occupation' in Eastern European socialist societies (Jackson, ed., 1970: 8). In addition, some more recent scholars have argued that because the term 'profession' is an essentially disputed term, with variable meaning - amongst social scientists, and amongst other community groups, the various occupations said or claiming to be 'professions' should be studied primarily as occupations, and not as 'professions'.

Huntington, for instance, following Freidson and Johnson, does not see 'professions' as categorically different from occupations *per se*. She suggests that the image of taking, seizing or holding territory, conveyed by the word 'occupation', is, in fact, especially apt for those occupations with an ideological commitment to professionalism, for this is a particular form of occupational organization that attempts to achieve control over the occupation's activities. Yet the image conveyed by the word 'profession' is not of actively claiming a function, but rather of professing or declaring, or being called to a function or position. (Huntington, 1981: 3-4.)

Structural and cultural components of an occupation are seen by Huntington as 'potential resources to be used in claiming and defending occupational territory' (Huntington, 1981: 32). Structural elements include the occupation's age, the size and characteristics of its members (age, sex, marital status, class of origin, and educational attainment), their work settings, their level and type of income, and their clientele (Huntington, 1981: 7-48). Cultural elements include the occupation's mission, aims and tasks; its focus and orientation; its knowledge; its technology and technique; its language and terminology; its ideology or dominant value orientations; its identity or image of itself; the status and prestige of the occupation; and the ways it relates to patients or clients, and to other occupations (Huntington, 1981: 49-154).

Turner and Hodge also propose a framework for the analysis of occupations, rather than of professional occupations alone (Turner and Hodge, in Jackson, ed., 1970: 33), but they acknowledge that what constitutes an occupation is, in turn, contentious. In modern society occupational labels proliferate, and even so, often still contain a division of labour within them (Turner and Hodge, in Jackson, ed., 1970: 33-34). An occupation can be seen to exist whenever similar activities are being carried out within a general scheme of division of labour. The persons involved may not be aware of the similarities and may not be in any social relationship with each other. Occupational organization does, however, require the development and maintenance of social networks and patterns of social relationships between people engaged in similar activities. This may occur both through non-formal association with each other, or through more formal association. It is through such organization that members of the occupation identify and pursue their collective occupational interests, to the extent that this can be achieved, and may also pursue sectional and non-occupational interests. Turner and Hodge observe that the processes of occupational organization are poorly understood. (Turner and Hodge, in Jackson, ed., 1970: 35.)

Shared occupational interests can take a wide variety of forms, each providing a possible basis for occupational association - common theory, similar techniques, working on the same materials, using the same equipment, similarity of work situation, shared claims to the right to perform particular work, and a shared location. Further, any person may be a member of several occupational groups, networks and associations. (Turner and Hodge, in Jackson, ed., 1970: 36.) Turner and Hodge suggest that occupational organization can be achieved by the development and transmission of substantive theory and of practical techniques; by the provision of materials and equipment, by the regulation of working conditions and market conditions; by the identification of practitioners and recognition of qualifications for practice; and by the promotion of standards of practice, internal relations between members, and public recognition. (Turner and Hodge, in Jackson, ed., 1970: 37.)

Like Huntington, and other more recent writers, Turner and Hodge place special emphasis on the basic resources involved in an occupation. Their 'resource approach' to studying occupations requires examining the potential and actual resources of the occupation and the processes of resource creation, management and control. (Turner and Hodge, in Jackson, ed., 1970: 25-6, 49-50.) In contrast with the rather static approaches which just identify the major dimensions of an occupation, a resource approach is essentially dynamic and goal-oriented. It is apparent that the nature and existence of an occupation in any society depend on the extent to which societal resources are engaged in the activities connected with it.

At the beginning of the twentieth century, Durkheim saw occupational groups as providing a solution to the *anomie* arising from the forced division of labour in the economic life of industrial society. He argued that an occupational activity could be 'efficaciously regulated only by a group intimate enough with it to know its functioning, feel all its needs, and able to follow all their variations'. (Durkheim, 1902, 1947: 5.) 'What we especially see in the occupational group is a moral power capable of containing individual egos, of maintaining a spirited sentiment of common solidarity in the consciousness of all the workers, of preventing the law of the strongest from being brutally applied to industrial and commercial relations.' (Durkheim, 1902, 1947: 10.) He drew parallels of what he had in mind with the medieval guilds and the Roman Collegia. Collective activity was always too complex to be able to be expressed through the single and unique organ of the state, and moreover the state was too remote from individuals. Secondary groups, such as occupational groups, were needed between individuals and the state, otherwise society disintegrated. (Durkheim, 1902, 1947: 28.)

Durkheim saw the development of occupational groups as inevitable:

> When a certain number of individuals in the midst of a political society are found to have ideas, interests, sentiments, and occupations not shared by the rest of the population, it is inevitable that they will be attracted toward each other under the influence of these likenesses. They will seek each other out, enter into relations, associate, and thus, little by little, a restricted group, having its special characteristics will be formed in the midst of the general society. But once the group is formed, a moral life appears naturally carrying the mark of the particular conditions in which it has developed. For it is impossible for men to live together, associating in industry, without acquiring a sentiment of the whole formed by their union, without attaching themselves to that whole, preoccupying themselves with its interests, and taking account of it in their conduct... When

individuals who are found to have common interests associate, it is not only to defend these interests, it is to associate, that is, not to feel lost among adversaries, to have the pleasure of communing, to make one out of many, which is to say, finally to lead the same moral life together. (Durkheim, 1902, 1947: 14-15.)

The Study of Professions as a Distinctive Occupational Group

General Observations

Additional to the general use of the word 'profession' for 'occupation', the English language also has a usage which refers to a particular group of occupations, originally the 'learned' occupations of medicine, law, and the clergy associated with the medieval universities of Europe. Today in all industrial nations, the concept of profession can be used for a broad group of relatively prestigious but quite diverse occupations, identified more by the higher educational status of their members than by their specific occupational skills.

There is, however, another usage that uses 'professionalism' as a way of organizing an occupation, which produces distinctive and highly significant occupational identities for the members of the occupation. (Freidson, in Dingwall and Lewis, eds, 1983: 23; Freidson, 1986: 21-6.) The title of the present book is using the concept of 'professional conduct' in this more restricted sense. The purpose is not to discuss the ethical evaluation of all occupational conduct, that is, conduct involved in making a living. Nor is the focus on the occupational conduct of people with higher education. Rather we are concentrating on the occupational conduct of people who make a living as members of occupations which are said to be 'professions' in this more special and restricted sense. But what are the distinguishing characteristics of such occupations which can give 'professional conduct' this more specific meaning?

Our current understanding of 'professional conduct', in Anglo-American societies and in other societies they have strongly influenced, comes from an historical process of writing about 'the professions' in such societies. General reviews have noted significant shifts that have occurred in this writing.

(Freidson, in Dingwall and Lewis, eds, 1983: 19-22; Freidson, 1986: 27-30; Rueschemeyer, in Dingwall and Lewis, eds, 1983: 38-40.)[1]

Until the 1940s, the most important writing was largely British. An optimistic and positive view of the professions tended to be taken, seeing them as a constructive way of controlling and organizing work in the public interest. Then for some thirty years after the World War II, study of the professions was dominated by American scholars, mainly sociologists trying to develop general analytic concepts applicable to more than one period or nation. Yet paradoxically, there was a virtual absence of intercultural and international comparison. Both the scholars and professions themselves were grounded in a middle-class culture developed since the nineteenth century. The institutional context of American society was taken largely for granted. Like their British predecessors, the main emphasis of the American scholars was on 'the special character of knowledge and skill of the professions and on their special ethical or altruistic orientation towards their clients' - even though deficiencies in the actual performance of professions were recognized and criticized.

The 1960s began to see in both the United States and Britain, significant changes in emphasis and attitude in the writing about professions. Their failings rather than their virtues were emphasized and their political, economic and status positions received particular attention. According to Rueschemeyer, the shift came from several sources - a hostile attitude towards status privilege; scepticism about the idea of progress based on expanding knowledge and applied technology; a diminished awe towards occupations distinguished by their higher knowledge; and attempts of new occupational groups to acquire professional status in a situation of vastly increased competition. In this more recent period, various writers emphasized as critical distinguishing features of professions their unusually effective monopolistic institutions and their high status, rather than their knowledge, skill and ethical orientations which are now treated more as ideological claims to gain or preserve status and privilege.

More recent historical work is said to have 'both reflected and reinforced' the changed view. Gerald Geison has claimed that much has been gained from 'the shift of perspective and widening concerns', even though the tone of some of the resulting literature has sometimes been 'strident and conspiratorial'. Detailed historical work has shown that neither the benign 'functional' model

---

[1] The following two paragraphs are drawn from these sources.

of professions, nor the alternative 'capitalist' model can account for the richly diverse forms and distributions of professional groups. (Geison, ed, 1983: 5-7.)[2] Robert Dingwall has observed a broad consensus amongst recent scholars on the need for comparative empirical study, which places professional work in a much wider historical and contemporary perspective, but with the continuing importance of the social division of knowledge being reaffirmed (Dingwall, in Dingwall and Lewis, eds, 1983: 11-12).

In 1987, Wilfrid Prest still argued that the history of the professions in England was a relatively new and unexplored field (Prest, 1987: 1). He pointed, however, to the quickening of scholarly interest amongst historians over the past decade or so - arising from intellectual curiosity, dissatisfaction with the available literature, a wish to place the history of particular disciplines in their social context, concern with the social dimensions of educational change, and some awareness of the relatively recent professionalization of their own occupation of historians. The aim had been to write the history of professions as social history at least, if not total history. This had required paying as much attention to lower status and less prominent or successful practitioners as to leading lights, who may well be untypical. It had required investigating and relating to each other both the social identity of the occupation and the nature of its work. It had further required understanding professions as cultural or intellectual artefacts. (Prest, 1987: 6-7.) (These various dimensions are essential not only for adequate social history, but also for assessing the ethical significance of professions.)

Prest claimed that work on these lines had effectively demolished the myth that the industrial revolution was the single crucial turning point in the history of the professions in England. It was now clear, he said, that both the numbers and socio-economic impact of professional occupations in England before the mid-18th century had been drastically underestimated. This had been largely due to the continuing acceptance until recently of *The Professions* by Carr-Saunders and Wilson. These authors, in an admittedly very sketchy account of the professions, had stressed their limited and socially dependent character before the industrial revolution. They were seen as largely serving and being recruited from the gentry and nobility, and therefore lacking distinctive occupational identity or set of values. This contrasted with

---

[2] This book was a result of a special historical project on the professions at Princeton University.

their proliferation and development in the 'modern' or 'post-industrial' period. (Prest, 1987: 1-5, 7-8.)

Prest acknowledged, however, that although it was now apparent the membership and clienteles of early modern professions were by no means as socially restricted as had been previously supposed, there were still important differences between the early professions and their modern counterparts. Before the 19th century, most of the professional occupations lacked any kind of formal structure - no standardized training or formal qualifications and no occupational organization. Further, professional commitments were often part-time and typically they were life-long and not restricted by retirement policies. Also it now seems that those who used the services of the early professionals often took a more active and demanding role than would be normal today. (Prest, 1987: 14-17.)

As a 'working convention' for historians, Prest suggested that the one and only characteristic common to all professional persons, past and present, was their ranking within a broad middle class, situated above the workers but below the elite whose livelihood was in no way dependent upon their personal exertions. This shifted attention away from sociological ideal-type models of what a profession should be to the complex realities of what professions actually were, and are. (Prest, 1987: 17.)

More Detailed Examination of the Scholarly Writing

Some further examination of twentieth century Anglo-American writing on the professions will help to fill out the general observations that have been made. This will enable us to consider more fully the various dimensions of 'professional conduct' as we might reasonably understand the concept, and will provide some necessary background when the ethics of professional conduct is being considered in Part 2 of the book.

A Seminal Pioneering Study

In 1933, Carr-Saunders and Wilson produced their monumental pioneering work *The Professions* (Carr-Saunders and Wilson, 1933). Remarkably this was being described in 1972 as a seminal work in the sociology of the professions still unsurpassed (Johnson, 1972: 93), and in 1987 as 'still the standard general history of the professions in England' (Prest, ed., 1987), although, as already mentioned, the work of historians was then calling for revised understanding of professions before the industrial revolution. Carr-Saunders and Wilson contrasted the scholarly attention given to trade unions with the almost complete neglect of professional associations, and yet, they asserted, within the ranks of the professions were to be found most of those upon whose special skill the functioning of modern society depended (Carr-Saunders and Wilson, 1933: iii).

Numerous practical problems relating to the organization of the professions and the availability of their services had forced the public to take an increased interest in professionalism - problems like a public medical service, legal aid, the place of professional education in universities, and the 'closure' of professions by state registration. In addition, political theorists were particularly interested in the position of associations within the state, and few associations were more important or powerful than those formed by professionals. (Carr-Saunders and Wilson, 1933: 1.)

The authors argued that without information about the professions, no informed guidance could be given on the practical issues, nor could there be any hope of settling the widely divergent views about the value of professionalism held even amongst people of similar political affiliations. To one writer, professions were 'objects of deep suspicion', and to another, 'conspiracies against the public', while for another, the professionalization of business was 'one of the most promising methods of social reform'. [The writers were not named, but they are likely to have been Laski, Shaw, and Tawney. Laski had warned of the 'limitations of the expert' in a 1931 Fabian Tract and wrote on 'the decline of the professions' in a 1935 article. He wanted state control and elimination of private practice (Laski, 1931; 1935, 656-7). Shaw's much-quoted line 'All professions are conspiracies against the laity', had appeared in his play 'The Doctor's Dilemma', first published in 1906. In 1921, Tawney had argued that the extension of professionalism throughout the society would make its organization 'functional' to community needs, and would combat rampant 'individual self-interest' in the 'acquisitive society'. He saw the increase in the number of salaried managers in business, performing specialized functions, as already an indication of such a movement. The following year, however, American sociologist MacIver had observed that while business managers might have specialized expertise and standards of ethics, they usually did not have associations that transcended their business enterprise to enforce these standards. (Tawney, 1961, 1921; MacIver, 1922, in Vollmer and Mills, eds, 1966: 50-5.)]

Carr-Saunders and Wilson observed that generalizations on the subject of professions could have 'little behind them' until they were informed by many investigations, 'approaching the subject from different angles'. Opinions could be no more than 'expressions of like or dislike of certain aspects of professionalism which, from lack of investigation, may not have been thoroughly understood'. The authors were concerned with 'professionalism in the society of today and tomorrow'. They included some account of the origin and development of existing professions, because past facts were, to some extent at least, relevant, and the historical work had not yet been done. It was acknowledged that study by outsiders was difficult, because every profession lived in a world of its own. (Carr-Saunders and Wilson, 1933: 1-2, iii.)

What later became known as 'the definitional problem' (Freidson, 1986: 31), was already very apparent. Carr-Saunders and Wilson acknowledged that there was no more agreement about the boundaries of professionalism than there was about its value. Their pragmatic procedure was to review those vocations which by 'common consent' were called professions, together with others which claimed that title or whose organization or other characteristics resembled in some degree those of the acknowledged professions. They saw the term profession as standing for a complex of characteristics. The acknowledged professions exhibited all or most of these. They stood at the centre, and around them were grouped vocations exhibiting some but not all of these features. (Carr-Saunders and Wilson, 1933: 3-4, 284.) The ancient professions of law and medicine were seen as the 'typical' professions, and the first major section of the study was devoted to an historical and contemporary survey of these. Then followed much briefer accounts of an array of other occupations.[3] For different, and rather weak reasons, the church and the army were excluded from the study (Carr-Saunders and Wilson, 1933: 3).

The authors concluded that it was the existence of specialized intellectual techniques, acquired as the result of prolonged training, which gave rise to professionalism and accounted for its peculiar features - the rendering of a specialized service to the community for a fixed remuneration (fee or salary), the concern, sometimes shared with the state, for the competence and honour of practitioners as a whole, and the building of associations to achieve these ends. Yet they acknowledged that whatever the nature of a vocation's

---

[3] Dentists; nurses; midwives; veterinary surgeons; pharmacists; opticians; masseurs and biophysical assistants; the merchant navy; mine managers; engineers; chemists; physicists; architects; surveyors, land and estate agents, and auctioneers; accountants; actuaries; secretaries; public administration; teachers; journalists; authors and artists; brokers; and banking and insurance.

technique, it was closer to the professional 'centre' if its practice aroused a sense of responsibility. (Carr-Saunders, 1933: 285-7.)

Additional to their account of the separate occupations, Carr-Saunders and Wilson provided a brief general account of the professions since the early Middle Ages (Carr-Saunders and Wilson, 1933: 289-97). The industrial revolution was seen as opening the floodgates with new vocations proliferating alongside the ancient professions. The practical application of scientific knowledge, the momentum of scientific research, the large-scale industrial organization, the new uses for landed property, the large-scale social organization, the increase in government services, organization and legislation - all stimulated the emergence of professions based either on science or on knowledge of human institutions.

In the general history of professionalism in England, the authors traced the development of professional training and the testing of professional competence. Special attention was given to the new system that developed from the beginning of the nineteenth century, when the responsibility for training passed from professional organizations to institutional education, the universities recaptured part of the field, and 'most important of all', the modern examination was invented. (Carr-Saunders and Wilson, 1933: 310.) Under the former apprenticeship system, the apprentices picked up whatever theoretical knowledge they could in the course of their instruction. Under the new system, practical and theoretical knowledge were separated, although sometimes practical training was given in, or under the supervision of the institutions providing the theoretical training. (Carr-Saunders and Wilson, 1933: 316-17.)

Carr-Saunders and Wilson noted that if universities began to examine, the associations were usually willing enough to recognize a university degree as admitting to membership. In many cases associations had requested universities to set up courses, and in some cases had founded teaching posts and scholarships. However, certain professions, such as accountants and actuaries, remained largely outside the university. (Carr-Saunders and Wilson, 1933: 318.)

In a concluding section, the authors speculated on the future of professionalism. They anticipated that the extension of professionalism 'upwards and outwards' would be fairly rapid, while its extension 'downwards' to those engaged in manual labour or in routine intellectual occupations would be gradual. A system of specialized careers open to all on a basis of trained and tested talent would tend to reduce social injustice, make for social stability, lead to greater social efficiency, and reinforce professional pride in the proper conduct of business. The greatest danger would be the reappearance in a new form of a segmentary social organization, with people locked into their specialized vocations. (Carr-Saunders and Wilson, 1933: 493-4.)

The authors argued that professionalism could only exist when practitioners were free to associate for common ends. Of the many centres of association none was more compelling that a person's vocation. The scientific professions were seen as being progressive in the sense of being borne along by the progress of the knowledge on which they were based, and they in turn tended to influence the professions whose technique was institutional and which could stagnate. Professional associations were seen as stabilizing elements in society, inheriting, preserving, and handing on a tradition. (Carr-Saunders and Wilson, 1933: 495-7.)

Whitehead's criticism of the narrowness of professionals was accepted as generally true. He had said: 'Each profession makes progress, but it is progress in its own groove... The remainder of life is treated superficially'. Carr-Saunders and Wilson asserted that professionals did not grasp the essential features of the social and economic structure and the place of professions in it. When they did take an interest, they often failed to display 'the same standards of exactitude and judgement' as they demanded in their immediate spheres. Yet in a democratic society, they had a large part to play 'to bring knowledge to the service of power', both through their professional associations and as individual citizens. In addition, it was important that organizations should be regarded as instruments to be created and remodelled where necessary by those who rendered specialized services. If people found in vocational associations 'their permanent anchorage and shelter', they could shape organizations into instruments for the fulfilment of their purposes. (Carr-Saunders and Wilson, 1933: 495-503.)

This pioneering work raised a number of interrelated and overlapping issues for the study of professions - the need to define what constitutes a profession; the nature and form of the prolonged education and training which typifies professions; the essential role of professional associations; the need for external or public recognition; the communal aspects of each profession, and importance to its members; the impact of professions on society; and the adequacy of information and knowledge about the professions, both contemporary and historical, and individual and collective. We will look at each of these in turn, in the light of some of the main contributions to scholarship on the professions.

What Constitutes a Profession?

What are the distinguishing characteristics of occupations called professions in Anglo-American societies? There is a problem of definition confronting any writing on these occupations, and the way it is dealt with has both theoretical and practical implications. We have already noted (p. 69) the pragmatic approach adopted by Carr-Saunders and Wilson, but their exclusion of two major employed traditional occupations, the church and the army, could well have helped to skew general analysis away from employed occupations. Since the idea of a profession has been associated with notions of status, autonomy, and functional privilege for an occupation's members, obtaining recognition as a profession has important practical implications for its members, and also for its clients, its employers, its occupational competitors, and the state.

One of the first to try to identify the characteristic features of a profession was Abraham Flexner (Flexner, 1915: 576-90), an American educationalist with German experience, and a key figure in the reform of American medical education (Starr, 1982; Larson, 1977: 37, 162-4). In 1915, he stated that to make a profession 'in the genuine sense', certain current 'objective standards', 'criteria', or 'earmarks', needed to be established - although these would change from time to time.

Flexner identified six professional criteria. The activity was essentially intellectual in character. It was derived from learning. It had a definite practical purpose in a definite field. It had a technique or skills which the professional practitioner had to master to attain professional objectives, and these were able to be communicated through an orderly educational process. A profession formed a democratic brotherhood, whose activity completely engaged its members; qualifications for membership were determined by the nature of the professional responsibility alone, and were not conditioned on some qualification not essentially related to the activities involved. Although still self-interested, the professional organization was increasingly expected to advance the common social interest. (Flexner, 1915: 578-81.)

The American sociologist Theodore Caplow asserted in 1954 that professionalization involved quite definite and sequential steps. (Caplow, 1954, in Vollmer and Mills, eds, 1966: 20-1). Similarly, some ten years later Wilensky described a 'natural history' of professionalization. (Wilensky, 1964: 142--6). Subsequently, however, this sequence was criticized as being 'historically specific and culture-bound' (Johnson, 1972: 28-9), and such attempts to set down a sequence of steps were said to be 'neither empirically correct nor theoretically convincing' (Goode, in Etzioni, ed, 1969: 274). In his 1964 study of the role of qualifying associations in the development of professional occupations in Britain, Millerson observed that many of the authors of definitions were pleading a special cause, having their occupations in mind. (Millerson, 1964.)

In 1957, Ernest Greenwood gave an influential summary account of the five 'distinguishing attributes' of a profession agreed upon in the sociological literature - a basis of systematic theory, authority recognized by the clientele, community sanction and approval, a code of ethics regulating relations with clients and colleagues, and a professional culture sustained by formal associations. Each attribute was a matter of degree and was not the exclusive monopoly of the professions. Greenwood argued, however, if one were to single out the attribute that most effectively differentiated the professions from other occupations, it was the existence of a professional culture. Greenwood emphasized that what he had produced was an internally coherent ideal type, much sharper and clearer than the actuality observed in the occupational scene. It structured reality to bring order out of apparent disorder, thereby illuminating the goal for which professionalizing occupations were striving. (Greenwood, 1957: 44-55.)

William Goode asserted in 1960 that any traits used in the definition of the term 'profession' must be conceived as variables, forming a continuum along which a given occupation may move. Instead of the dichotomy of 'professional-non professional', he used the variable of 'professionalism', and asked how far an occupation had moved in the direction of increased or decreased professionalism. He noted that definitions of a profession varied but did not contradict one another. Two traits were, however, sociologically central because they were the main determinants of the others - a prolonged specialized training in a body of abstract knowledge, and a collectivity or service orientation. (Goode, 1961, in Vollmer and Mills, eds, 1966: 35-6.)

In their well-organized book of readings under the title of *Professionalization*, Vollmer and Mills avoided using the term 'profession' except as an 'ideal type' of occupational organization, which did not exist in reality but would if any occupational group became completely professionalized. 'Professionalization' referred to the dynamic process whereby many occupations changed in the direction of a 'profession'. 'Professionalism' was seen as an ideology found in many and diverse occupational groups aspiring to professional status. It was associated with the values of expertise, autonomy, commitment, and responsibility. (Vollmer and Mills, eds, 1966: vii-viii.)

A 1969 book edited by Amitai Etzioni focused on a group of new professions - teachers, nurses, and social workers - whose claim to the status of doctors and lawyers was 'neither fully established nor fully deserved'. Their training was shorter, their status was less legitimated, their right to privileged communication was less established, there was less of a specialized body of knowledge, and they had less autonomy from supervision or societal control than 'the' professions. These were described as semi-professions. Almost all were employed by organizations and the large majority was female. It was asserted that the norms and values of professions, organizations, and female employment were not compatible. Studies in this book dealt exclusively with the tension in these occupations between administrative, hierarchical authority and professional, individualized, essentially knowledge-based authority. (Etzioni, ed., 1969: v-xvii.) One of the studies argued that bureaucratic control in organizations was strengthened when a female workforce predominated (Simpson and Simpson, in Etzioni, ed., 1969: 196-265). Goode concluded in his contribution that many aspiring occupations and semi-professions would never reach the levels of knowledge and dedication to service necessary for a profession (Goode, in Etzioni, ed., 1969: 266-7).

Like earlier authors, Wilbert Moore proposed in his 1970 book a number of criteria of professionalism (Moore, 1970: 5-16), which, he argued, provided common questions, even if the answers differed from occupation to occupation. The range of skills and positions in a nominally uniform occupation presented a problem; the status of an occupation could not necessarily be properly judged by its ideal-typical representatives. (Moore, 1970: 17-18.)

Elliott constructed a professional ideal type, whose features linked together in a self-supporting whole. Recognized professions usually demonstrated these features most strongly. He distinguished four important components in the professional role - the performance of the professional services themselves; the development of the knowledge on which such services were based; the communication of this knowledge to professional successors and/or wider publics; and the administration of an employment setting within which such performances could be carried on. These were given different emphasis in different practice settings, at different levels in the same profession, and at different stages of the same career. (Elliott, 1972: 101.) In contrast to professional work, non-professional work called for technical craft or skill, and was routine and programmed; its ends were decided by society or other institution; the worker's identity came from outside work which was a means to non-work ends; there was occupational or class advancement, not individual career achievement; and education for the work was limited and the work role was specific. (Elliott, 1972: 96-7.)

Johnson observed, in 1972, greater public scepticism of professional claims than was evident in much of the sociological literature. Elements of professionalism selected by professionals and accepted by sociologists, appeared to be what ought to be, not necessarily what actually existed. In addition, the elements chosen tended to reflect Anglo-American culture at a particular time in historical development of a very few professional bodies. Few scholars had attempted to establish the space and time dimensions and limitations of the concepts which they used. (Johnson, 1972: 24-7.)

According to Robert Dingwall in 1976, the central problem of the various attempts to define 'profession' was their assumption that it had a fixed meaning. All that could be done was to elaborate what it appeared to mean to use the term and to list the occasions on which various elaborations were used. Dingwall examined the use of the term 'profession' by health visitors in Britain in relation to their own or others' behaviour in elaborating 'professional' and 'non-professional' conduct, and its usage to establish the activities of health visitors as a 'profession' rather than an 'occupation'. It was suggested that occupations sought to establish themselves as 'professions' through certain kinds of appeals. (Dingwall, 1976: 331-5, 347.)

The empirical study of health visitors revealed that competent performance as a professional appeared to involve giving attention to a number of elements. These elements provided relevant orientation points for the management of situations encountered. Together they indicated some more or less organized interpretive scheme held by members of the health visiting community. The scheme had six main components. The field health visitor was a professional because: she was a certain sort of person; she had autonomy in her work and knew what was best for her clients; she was a member of an occupation which selected its recruits, had formal qualifications, was self-governing, had its own body of knowledge, had a history, and had research done on it; she had responsibility for supervising others' work; she was equal to all other professionals, but had a discrete area of work; and she acted towards others on the assumption that they shared this definition of her social location. (Dingwall, 1976: 336-7.)

Freidson observed, however, in 1983, that if 'profession' was to be described as a 'folk' concept rather than a scientific one, phenomenological research would need to study not only how everyday members accomplish profession through their activities, but also how sociologists accomplish profession as a concept, and how official agencies accomplish profession as an administrative category - and how these interact. Freidson did not think the problem of definition could be solved by struggling to formulate a single definition which it is hoped will win the day. (Freidson, in Dingwall and Lewis, eds, 1983: 28-30, 35.) Freidson's 1986 book focused on the official conceptions of professions in the United States and the formal institutions that sustained them (Freidson, 1986: 32, 35-6).

In his award-winning *The System of the Professions*, 'an essay on the division of expert labour',[4] Abbott said it was unclear whether we should identify professions by group claims or by the functional realities. The importance of professional social structure lay in its effect on professions' abilities to maintain themselves in a competing system. Once a group entered into competition what mattered was what it actually was. (Abbott, 1988: 81-2.) [According to Abbott, a profession's social organization consisted of professional groups of diverse forms; professional controls (schools, examinations, licences, ethics code, and informal controls); and worksites of great variety (some controlled by the profession, others controlled by groups outside the profession). The strength with which individuals were tied to this organized structure varied. Also individual professionals could develop enduring identification with specialty work. (Abbott, 1988: 79-81.)]

Earlier, in another substantial contribution to the study of professions, Larson had argued that the ideal-typical constructions did not tell us what a profession was, but only what it pretended to be. The cognitive and normative elements of a profession were used as arguments in a process that involved both struggle and persuasion, as particular groups attempted to negotiate the boundaries of an area in the social division of labour and establish control over it. Persuasion tended to be directed to the outside - to the relevant elites, the potential public or publics, and the political authorities. Conflict and struggle marked the process of internal unification of a profession. As professions gained autonomy, they could develop with increasing independence from the ideology of the dominant social elites. The production of knowledge played a strategic role in the dynamics of these special occupations. Privileges could always be lost, however. (Larson, 1977: xii.)

In summary, then, 'profession' is not an abstract scientific sociological concept, although it could possibly become one if agreement could be reached about core determining characteristics which are generic across occupations

---

[4] It won the Distinguished Contribution to Scholarship Award of the American Sociological Association in 1991.

and cultures, and which would separate professional from non-professional occupations. In the meantime, the term is still meaningfully used in Anglo-American societies for occupations that are organized in particular ways that give them considerable autonomy and power, and whose conduct is of special concern because of its impact on the rest of society. But as scholarship on the professions has, by now, made clear, different uses of the term can lead to confusion, especially when they are not distinguished. As a descriptive concept, it may be used for impressions and speculation, or for generalizations soundly based on empirical study. As a prescriptive concept, it may be used aspirationally - what an occupation aspires to be. Or it may be used normatively - what an occupation ought to be if it is to conform to a particular model of occupation, or what an occupation ought to be morally.

The Nature and Form of Professional Education

The writing on the professions has consistently emphasized their claims to specialized knowledge and intellectual skills gained from a formal educational process. In 1915, Flexner said that the adjective 'learned' really added nothing to the noun profession. The steady stream of facts and ideas from the laboratory and the seminar kept the professions from degenerating into mere routine. On the basis of agreement about the profession's specific objectives and the requisite skills to attain them, a profession had arrived at an understanding as to the general and specific training needed for admission into the professional school, and as to the content and length of the professional course. (Flexner, 1915: 579-80.)

As already mentioned (pp. 69-70), specialized intellectual techniques acquired as a result of prolonged training in educational institutions, were seen by Carr-Saunders and Wilson, as central to professionalism, and one of the issues they highlighted was the place of professional education in universities.

Soon after World War II, in their polemic to sustain what they saw as 'the professional heritage', Lewis and Maude discussed a variety of educational issues under the title of 'Educating the Expert'. These included: the need for breadth and depth in the education of specialists; the need for a technologist to understand and apply several sciences; the respective roles of the universities, universities of technology, technical colleges, and professional institutes; the need for education in administration both within professional work and a separate function; the need to understand the social impact of the expert's activities; the need for longer and better training countered by pressures to increase the numbers qualified and to curb rising costs; the shortage of well qualified teachers; and the creation of new classes of technical assistants, who aspired to higher status, but on an even more narrow and inadequate basis than the technologists. (Lewis and Maude, 1953: 151-71.) The authors were stimulated by economic and social change in Britain, including the post-war growth of a welfare state. Their educational issues have continued to resonate.

In 1960, Everett Hughes noted that North American writing on the professions reflected the concern for individual and group social advancement, and increasingly the place of minorities and of women. A great number of people were attempting to improve their lot by gaining the education and other qualifications for entry to professions, yet there was no assurance any occupation would retain its position for the length of a professional career, or that what was learnt would not become obsolete. (Hughes, 1960, in Vollmer and Mills, eds, 1966: 65-6.) Hughes observed that in all of the older professions, the distinction between careers of practice and careers of research, education, and administration, was becoming marked, and was also emerging in the new professions where prestige was more clearly going to those removed from practice (Hughes, 1960, in Vollmer and Mills, eds, 1966: 67).

In 1961, Bucher and Strauss observed that the interests of segments within a profession might run along different lines, and were frequently in conflict. Segments and emerging specialties competed in gaining access to institutions, in recruitment, in curriculum space, and in relations with the outside. (Bucher and Strauss, 1961, in Vollmer and Mills, eds, 1966: 191.)

The modern professional system was seen by Talcott Parsons, in 1968, to have two main branches, the academic, with its two primary functions of research and teaching, and the applied (Parsons, in Sills, ed, 1968: 537). Parsons reviewed the historic position of the western university, and then the new university system especially as it developed in the United States where professional training was brought overwhelmingly within the university system (Parsons, in Sills, ed., 1968: 539-44).

In 1970, Wilbert Moore saw professional socialization as involving complex issues about educational levels and requirements, including the relation of education to practice and the forming of professional identity. It also required keeping up with new knowledge and new techniques, and building a career which ideally showed progress and self-imposed responsible behaviour. (Moore, 1970: 79, 81.)

Elliott observed that the study of professional education and training had received the most attention, in contrast to the study of professional practice (Elliott, 1972: 76). With the appearance of the academic-subject specialist oriented towards a career in the subject and expecting to move from institution to institution, occupational professionalism among university teachers made it difficult to achieve the university ideal of a liberal education (Elliott, 1972: 52). Speaking in 1867, J.S. Mill had asserted that there was 'tolerable agreement' that the university was:

> not a place of professional education. Universities are not intended to teach knowledge required to fit men for some special mode of gaining their livelihood. Their object is not to make skilful lawyers, or physicians, or engineers, but capable and cultivated human beings. (Elliott, 1972: 51.)

Elliott noted that educational organizations, in fact, varied in their goals. Some, like the military academy, were 'doctrinal communities', where the goal was the acquiring of patterns of behaviour acceptable to people in the future status position. Others, like the technical colleges, provided role socialization in terms of the skills involved. The two types tended to come together, although there was still considerable variation between different occupations. (Elliott, 1972: 78-80.) The concept of socialization usually was used with an emphasis on the individual being shaped to fit the social situation. But, said Elliott, this put too much emphasis on shaping and fitting, it implied a very passive view of humans in society, it concentrated on similar values and behaviour patterns rather than on the clash of opposites, and it assumed a tendency toward harmony and equilibrium rather than an ability to live with tension and conflict. (Elliott, 1972: 90-2.) Elliott suggested that the idea of socialization should be related to the individual learning to use elements in the social situation. This implied purpose. It saw a human as a social actor with goals and an orientation towards the future and an ability to act in relation to both positive and negative influences in the environment. To know how people would react to situations it was necessary to know who they thought they were, where they had come from and where they were going. (Elliott, 1972: 93.)

According to Larson, professionalization was the process by which producers of special services sought to constitute and control a market for their expertise. Because of the element of marketable expertise, it was also a collective assertion of special social status and a collective process of upward social mobility. Legitimacy was founded on the achievement of socially recognized expertise, or more simply, on a system of education and credentialing. The focus on the constitution of professional markets led to comparing different professions in terms of the 'marketability' of their specific cognitive resources. (Larson, 1977: xvi-xvii.)

In *Professional Powers,* published in 1986, Freidson undertook a detailed analytic description of the institutions of professionalism in the United States, in order to clarify the actual relations between knowledge and power (Freidson, 1986). Explicitly connected with the idea of profession was training in higher education for knowledge-based pursuits and for university teaching itself. It implied a method of gaining a living while serving as an agent of formal knowledge, and that bodies of formal knowledge, or disciplines, were differentiated into specialized occupations. (Freidson, 1986: 15, 20.)

The credential system of the professions established positions which provided a living for ordinary qualified practitioners and for those members of the profession who occupied administrative, teaching and research positions. Freidson pointed out that credentialism could take many forms and could not be dealt with sensibly in global terms. Credentials could be binding, advisory, or ignored. Formal credentialing in the United States consisted of two distinct methods which were intermeshed. In occupational credentialing, licences, degrees, diplomas and certificates were issued to individual members of occupations performing particular kinds of work. In institutional credentialing, charters, operating licences, articles of incorporation, and accreditation, were issued to institutions that organized particular kinds of services to the public, including the training or education of prospective members of an occupation. Freidson demonstrated that in the United States private sources of credentialing were much more important than public sources. (Freidson, 1986: 63-4.)

Freidson asserted that at the foundation of the credentialing system, both generating it and being generated by it, were institutions of higher education. The formalization of professional education in the early part of this century was an attempt to meet the need for some degree of predictability and uniformity in the market for professionals and not merely based on a desire to raise the profession's prestige and restrict the supply of practitioners. Freidson demonstrated how important accreditation was for the survival of both general and professional institutions of higher education in the United States and how intermeshed it was with the state systems of occupational licensing and institutional chartering and licensing and with the distribution of federal funds. (Freidson, 1986: 73, 77.)

Freidson acknowledged that the formal credential system merely established the possibility of gaining a living for an individual professional. Choice by clients and employers of particular professionals depended, in addition to the formal credentials, on a variety of informal credential criteria - personal testimonials, the prestige of institutions attended by the professional, and discriminatory criteria like gender, race, religion, ethnicity and class. (Freidson, 1986: 88.)

After discussing the various changes in the social structure of jurisdiction, Abbott examined three great cultural changes that had also remade the work of professions - changes in the amount and complexity of professional knowledge, the new legitimacy claimed for this knowledge, and the rise of universities. These were three facets of the rise of rationality. (Abbott, 1988: 177-211.) He noted that contrary forces pushed abstraction in professional knowledge towards an equilibrium between extreme abstraction and extreme concreteness. Amalgamation and division helped professions to maintain an optimum level of abstraction. (Abbott, 1988: 104-5.)

The Role of Professional Associations

Professional associations in Britain numbered only 27 in 1880; by 1970, the total was 167. These, according to Perkin, along with the employers' associations and trade unions were the harbingers of the new society based on human capital created by education and enhanced by strategies of closure which excluded the unqualified. Modern society, in Britain, as elsewhere in the developed world, was made up of career hierarchies of specialized occupations, selected by merit and based on trained expertise. (Perkin, 1989: 1-2, 18-20.)

In his 1928 Herbert Spencer Lecture, Carr-Saunders claimed that in the early days of every profession there were strong motives for practitioners to form professional associations, and there was a tendency towards the dominance of a single professional association in each profession. Three main reasons were given for professional associations - the recognition of all practitioners with at least minimum qualifications and their inclusion in the association, the definition and maintenance of rules of professional conduct, and the raising of the status and remuneration of the group. (Carr-Saunders, 1928, in Vollmer and Mills, eds, 1966: 3-9.)

In their 1933 book, Carr-Saunders and Wilson insisted that a profession could only be said to exist when there were bonds between the practitioners through formal association (Carr-Saunders and Wilson, 1933: 298). In the new wave of association that gathered momentum in the nineteenth century, members were conscious of being in occupations not 'fit for gentlemen', and their declared objects almost always included the raising of status. The associations which arose out of study societies in the earlier part of the century first added functions relating to the competence and honour of their members, and later included protection of material interests and concern with matters of public policy relating to their special knowledge and experience. Later-formed associations usually included these four aims at the outset, and generally also included study activities. (Carr-Saunders and Wilson, 1933: 301-3.)

In response to pressure from the various professions, legislation reserved all or some professional functions to practitioners of proved competence on an official list or register of practitioners. According to Carr-Saunders and Wilson, the state's intervention in setting up a register had profound effects upon professional associations, since they could no longer take effective action in relation to admission to and expulsion from the profession. Members of the profession continued to exert influence, however, through their membership of the regulating body, and the professional associations still retained their protective and public activity functions. (Carr-Saunders Wilson, 1933: 305-7.)

Bucher and Strauss observed in 1961 that professional associations were not everybody's association but represented one segment or a particular alliance of segments. Codes of ethics, licensure, and the major professional associations were not necessarily evidence of internal homogeneity and consensus but rather of the power of certain groups or segments. Those who controlled the professional associations also controlled the organs of public relations. The outsider was not necessarily aware of the inner circle or the peer struggles behind the united front. (Bucher and Strauss, 1961, in Vollmer and Mills, eds, 1966: 190-3.)

Moore noted, in 1970, that professional socialization received various reinforcements - from the occupational norms internalized by the professional, from peer expectations, from the continuing need to market services, from the standards and sanctions of the occupational association, from possible damage suits instituted by an aggrieved employer or client, from the removal of a licence, and even from a possible charge of criminal misconduct. The probability was high that socialization worked. (Moore, 1970: 8.) In 1972, Elliott observed that in both American and English professions disciplinary enforcement of professional behaviour was weak. Three main types of offence were disciplined - poor service to clients, breaches of social norms which might involve conduct with clients, and attempts at competition or trade practices barred by the profession. (Elliott, 1972: 123.)

Freidson observed that the powers that individual practitioners wielded were highly variable and in most cases were considerably less than those ascribed to their professions. Neither they nor their colleagues in administration and in teaching and research created and sustained the credential system that established staffing standards for employers and standards for the content of professional education. Who then established what was acceptable professional work, and who negotiated with the state to secure official adoption of these standards? (Freidson, 1986: 185-6.) Professional associations characteristically attempted to work through legislation and other formal agreements concerned with occupational and institutional credentialing. Those entitled to act on the profession's behalf were in positions of potential power in the world outside the profession. Their influence over the activities of their members varied. By and large, professional associations tended more to provide services to members than to exercise control over their ethical or technical work behaviour. (Freidson, 1986: 186-7.)

In Washington, professional credentials were virtually required for certain high-level political appointments in the executive arm of government itself, depending on the political strength of the particular profession involved. Below these positions, civil service regulations influenced by the lobbying of professional associations, resulted in the employment of particular professionals such as engineers, natural scientists, and especially lawyers. Virtually all federal judges, a majority of presidents and legislators, many civil servants, and a large proportion of the staff serving Congress members had legal credentials. Most major professions controlled at least one specialized professional agency in government, but professionals in government were likely to have a rather different perspective on policy issues than did professional associations. (Freidson, 1986: 193-6.)

Freidson pointed out serious limits to the capacity of professional associations (and of their officers) to speak monolithically and forcefully, because of differences among members. Individual distinguished professionals could in fact have greater influence than formal representatives of a professional association. These could be public celebrities, or influential insiders serving major advisory panels, or influencing public policy through their testimony and organization of special interest groups. Officers of professional associations were not consistently distinguished as individuals.

(Freidson, 1986: 197-9.) In addition to their other activities, the professions were deeply involved in establishing official standards for goods and services. It was in standard-setting committees that the professions in general and professional associations in particular could have the most unequivocal influence. (Freidson, 1986: 200-9.)

External or Public Recognition

Goode argued, in 1969, that each person and each group of persons made demands on the money, power, and prestige markets of society. A united occupational group could gain what an individual could not. Occupations that sought recognition as professions engaged in transactions within all three markets, but with varying success. To be accepted as a profession, an occupation required special transactions in mainly the prestige markets. Clever transactions that yielded power and money were not sufficient to achieve acceptance as a profession. (Goode, in Etzioni, ed., 1969: 267-9.) In the short run, there was only so much money, power, or prestige to be shared. In the longer run, however, professionalization could yield greater production for the society as well as economic advantages and improved prestige for the occupations involved. Power was seen as largely derived from status and income. Goode observed that almost no occupation had risen from a low rank to the top. Upward mobility was more limited for occupations, than for individuals. Competition was strongest among similar or overlapping occupations. (Goode, in Etzioni, ed., 1969: 270-2, 310.)

There were a number of consequences if occupations could fall or rise. The outcomes of the exchanges between occupation and the society altered the terms of individual bargaining. An occupation had to expend some of its collective resources even to maintain its position. Because the individual shared in the rise of the occupation, some people had to decide how much of their personal resources to invest in the corporate enterprise. The total effort to maintain or improve occupational position was a large part of the total allocation of energies and resources in the society. Finally, Goode noted that the efforts of all occupations, but especially the semi-professions and professions, was a source of social change. (Goode, in Etzioni, ed., 1969: 273-4.)

The task of the four traditional person professions, law, medicine, the ministry, and university teaching, required trust in the handling of intimate personal knowledge (Goode, in Etzioni, ed., 1969: 266-7). Goode spoke of a 'corporate bargain', in which the profession was given a mandate to obtain potentially dangerous information about its clients because in fact there was no option; the client otherwise could not be adequately helped. In exchange, the profession itself proclaimed its intention of preventing its members from exploiting its clients. Such a corporate bargain could not be made or carried out unless the profession was cohesive enough to be able to impose controls over its members. (Goode, in Etzioni, ed., 1969: 299.) Goode argued that because client-professional relations in the person professions were more likely to become emotional than in others, and their clients felt more vulnerable, these professions were more likely to be socially salient. They were universally known, unlike technical-scientific specialties they figured in novels, stereotypes were created about them and they were more definitely recognized as distinct occupations. (Goode, in Etzioni, ed., 1969: 299.)

As already mentioned, Turner and Hodge suggested a 'resource approach' to studying occupations. They discussed four interrelated areas: the degree of substantive theory and technique, of monopoly, of external or public recognition, and of organization. External recognition involved several possible publics: the 'clients' - individuals, groups, or large-scale organizations; co-workers outside the occupational group; other occupational associations, complementary or competitive; employing units and employers' associations; government bodies involved in the regulation of occupational activities; educational and training institutions; and other individuals, groups, and organizations - the general public - with sectional interests and differential knowledge. (Turner and Hodge, in Jackson, ed., 1970: 26-38.)

According to Abbott, jurisdictional claims occurred in three arenas - the legal system which could confer formal control of work, the arena of public opinion, and the workplace. The existing and changing balance of power between the three required empirical inquiry. Jurisdictional claims entailed only secondarily an obligation to in fact accomplish the work claimed. General social obligations were more formal among Continental professions than among Anglo-American ones, because of the relative power of the Continental governments to enforce this. (Abbott, 1988: 59-60, 68.)

Claiming public jurisdiction of tasks was a pervasive activity - in newspapers, magazines, handbooks, television programs, and vocational guidance manuals. Public images of professions were fairly stable and sometimes out-of-date. Differences of public jurisdiction were differences between archetypes. It was also assumed tasks were objectively defined. At stake was the right to define certain problems culturally and to dominate the social structure dedicated to solving them. (Abbott, 1988: 60-2.)

Jurisdictional claims made in the legal system might include a monopoly of certain activities, of certain kinds of payments by third parties, control of certain settings of work, and control of certain kinds of language to describe tasks and concepts. Contests for legal jurisdiction occurred in the legislature, the courts, and the administrative or planning structure of government. Abbott noted that legal jurisdictions for professions were even more durable than were public jurisdictions. (Abbott, 1988: 62-3.)

In the workplace arena, jurisdiction was a simple claim to control certain kinds of work. The typical professional worksite was an organization, although some professionals worked in solo or group practices in open markets. In open markets, jurisdictional boundaries between competing professions were established by referral networks. Within an organization, the standard interprofessional division of labour was replaced by the intraorganizational one, which often located professionals with many extraprofessional tasks and ceded many professional ones. In most professional work settings, actual divisions of labour were established through negotiation and custom. They were relatively short-term and vulnerable to organizational perturbations. Boundaries between professional jurisdictions tended to disappear in worksites, particularly in overworked worksites. In most professional worksites, the mix of workers was so broad that assimilation was considerable. This organizational reality had to be countered by active jurisdictional maintenance. (Abbott, 1988: 64-6.)

Abbott distinguished six possible settlements of jurisdictional disputes, and discussed each in turn. (Abbott, 1988: 69-79.) Every profession, he asserted, aimed for a heartland of work over which it had complete, legally established control, but there were only so many full jurisdictions to go around. Hence the existence of more limited settlements. The dominant arena of interprofessional competition had changed over time. Administrative and legislative authority had emerged as a central professional audience in both Britain and the United States in the last fifty years. The legal arena had long dominated in countries like France and Germany. (Abbott, 1988: 157-64.) Professional publics were both judges of general claims made in professional media statements and consumers of professional services. Clients had become less atomized. Organizations had become clients - of lawyers, accountants, architects, librarians, social workers - and individual clients had created cartels to negotiate with organized professions. An active role for the public audience was new. (Abbott, 1988: 166.)

Professional Community and Culture

The idea of professionals being part of a professional community and culture which is of great significance to them has received considerable attention. Carr-Saunders and Wilson wrote:

> Every profession lives in a world of its own. The language which is spoken by the inhabitants, the landmarks so familiar to them, their customs and conventions can only be thoroughly learned by those who reside there. (Carr-Saunders and Wilson, 1933: Preface.)

As already noted, Greenwood argued if one were to single out the attribute that most effectively differentiated the profession from other occupations, it was the existence of a professional culture. One of the central concepts of this culture was the concept of 'career', which involved complete absorption in and devotion to one's work, with the work being an end in itself and not primarily for monetary gain. Work was an all-pervading influence in the lives of professionals. (Greenwood, 1957: 52-3.)

This was 'the professional heritage' which Lewis and Maude had seen as under threat by developments in post-war Britain. For them, this heritage was a valued culture which involved complicated or subtle techniques whose development and application required peculiar incentives and particular conditions of life, and an irreplaceable tradition of 'self-examining integrity and self-forgetful service'. They acknowledged, however, the heritage could be held of no account because it had been too exclusive, too sheltered, and a 'pious fraud' when there was evidence that the professional tradition was neither universally followed nor always conducive to progress. (Lewis and Maude, 1953.)

Writing at the same time as Greenwood, William Goode also emphasized the 'community' aspects of professional groups. He saw them as colleagues bound by a long-term identity, status, language and group sanctions, with shared values and agreed role definitions, and reproducing themselves socially through selection and training processes. (Goode, 1957: 194-200.)

The 'process' model proposed by Bucher and Strauss in 1961 viewed a profession as 'a loose amalgamation of segments which are in movement.' As already noted, their focus was on conflicting interests and on change. Identification with segments limited and directed colleagueship and directed alliances with neighboring occupations. A unity of interest among professionals had been too readily assumed by sociologists. The interests of segments might run along different lines, and were frequently in direct conflict. This was the first significant challenge to the prevailing structural-functional approach to professions which saw them as relatively homogeneous stable communities serving agreed community functions. (Bucher and Strauss, 1961, in Vollmer and Mills, eds, 1966: 186-95.)

Elliott observed that professionalism was largely a cultural phenomenon which rested on a series of contradictions and paradoxes. These included individualism and collective defence of common interests, traditional status and occupational achievement, non-vocational education and vocational training, an alternative to capitalist economic theory yet dependent on its fruits, an elitist basis for a service claimed to be universally applicable, and creativity and individual judgment and routinization from professional norms and standards. (Elliott, 1972: 144.) The more professions achieved the status of a community within a community, the more they were likely to have a divisive as well as a cohesive influence. (Elliott, 1972: 12.)

Bledstein's 1976 book aimed to rectify the neglect of the culture of professionalism in American history. (Bledstein, 1976.) He argued that by this cultural process the middle class in America had matured and defined itself in the nineteenth century. Most Americans now took for granted that all intelligent modern persons organized their behaviour according to it. (Bledstein, 1976: ix.) The American university had generally come into existence to serve and promote professional authority in society. The professional person was seen as possessing esoteric knowledge about the universe which if withheld from society could cause positive harm. Science as a source for professional authority 'transcended the favoritism of politics, the corruption of personality, and exclusiveness of partisanship'. While professional ambition had liberated the creativity of self, regard for professional expertise had, however, undermined self-confidence and discouraged independent evaluation. (Bledstein, 1976: x, 90, xi.)

The mid-Victorians cultivated a new vertical vision of individual fulfillment through the pursuit of the professional career (Bledstein, 1976: 105-7). Career meant scheduled mobility, the coherence of an intellectually defined and goal-oriented life, commitment to a continuous performance in the service of universal ends (Bledstein, 1976: 112, 159-202.) Character was the internal symbol of continuity. Within the context of democratic opportunity, the culture of professionalism structured American life vertically, 'so that every person should know and accept their rightful place in society'. (Bledstein, 1976: 112, 129-58.) Bledstein observed that higher education in America was a social necessity and a source of public acceptance. It had been forced to be far more flexible and diversified than European systems. (Bledstein, 1976: 125-7, 287-331.)

According to Freidson, in 1986, the occupational community of professions was often divided internally by specialty and variable career success, but what enabled them to maintain their position was the dimension of authority over the content and organization of professional work. Their own teacher-researchers produced and legitimized new knowledge, and controlled the recruitment, training and certification of their members. Their administrators controlled working conditions, supervising, directing and evaluating the work of practitioners as well as shaping organizational policy. Their elites worked with their associations to shape social policy. Located in different positions in the system, practitioners, administrators, teacher-researchers, and professional elites had different duties, interests, perspectives, and powers. (Freidson, 1986: 211-14.)

The Impact of Professions and Their Future

Robert MacIver observed in 1922 that it was especially typical of professional groups to develop standards about their behaviour with clients and other outsiders, as well as standards within. The attempt of professional groups 'to coordinate their responsibilities, relating at once the individual to the group and the group to the wider community' was 'an important advance'. But the economic, technical and cultural elements in 'the general professional interest' could sometimes pull in opposite directions. These provided 'a rich mine of ethical problems, still for the most part unworked'. The relation of the profession as a whole to the community was the least effectively developed aspect of professional ethics. 'Specific group biases' limited the social effectiveness of professional groups. Group ethics would not by themselves suffice for the guidance of the group unless they were 'always related to the ethical standards of the whole community'. (MacIver, 1922, in Vollmer and Mills, eds, 1966: 50-5.)

In the view of Caplow in 1954, it was difficult to exaggerate the importance of the general phenomenon of professionalization for the structure of the economy (Caplow, 1954, in Vollmer and Mills, eds, 1966: 20-1), while for Talcott Parsons in 1968, the professional complex had become 'the most important single component in the structure of modern society', representing new leadership based on 'moral and intellectual authority rather than on political power and economic success' (Parsons, in Sills, ed., 1968: 545).

We have already referred to Goode's 1969 observations on the impact of professionalization on the money, power, and prestige markets of society - that it was a source of social change, and that in the longer run professionalization could yield greater production for the society as well as economic advantages and improved prestige for the occupations involved, although there were offsetting costs.

Lieberman warned against 'the tyranny of the experts' in a 1970 book subtitled 'How Professionals are Closing the Open Society'. Although it was acknowledged that the professions had been effective in improving the general tone of professional conduct, they were seen as dividing the world into spheres of influence and keeping the public out on the grounds that they lacked insight into the professional mysteries. The public was losing power to shape its destiny. Lieberman claimed that 'inherent tendencies' in all professions constituted a pervasive social problem. Private associations of specialists, like lawyers, doctors, and funeral directors, already wielded vast power. (Lieberman, 1970: 2-5.) The consumer in the modern economy was spread across an infinite variety of goods and services, facing producers increasingly organized in large units. The professional movement could be viewed as an attempt by many groups to endow themselves with power as producers that they did not have as consumers. (Lieberman, 1970: 139-40.) The economic power of the professional class had serious inflationary consequences. The Catholic belief of a just price, which had provided the context for the monopolistic medieval guilds, no longer held. (Lieberman, 1970: 155.)

The rise of professionalism was also seen as a threat to democracy, because of its beliefs that citizens, like consumers, were incompetent to make important decisions affecting their lives. It entailed the management of public affairs by groups not representative of the public. (Lieberman, 1970: 7-8.)

In the course of propounding a theory of the professional class, Lieberman insisted that at least three separate motivations went into the mix which activated the professional: the service goal, the profit goal, and the desire for autonomy. It was useless to hunt for 'primary' motivation among them. (Lieberman, 1970: 66-7.)

Lieberman noted the failure of education to help the public understand issues relating to the professions. He challenged the traditional distinction in American education between 'liberal arts' and 'professional' subjects. The professions in fact constituted a great part of social, political, economic and institutional history. There was a need to teach the public how to evaluate the deeds and statements of professionals. The entire educational system was effective in blocking the development of generalists. The media had no theory of the professions and did not report their activities systematically. They failed to demand generalists capable of reporting specialist doings to the public. (Lieberman: 1970, 262, 264.)

Bledstein commented at the end of his 1976 book that Americans had never been so aware of 'the arrogance, shallowness, and potential abuses of the vertical vision by venal individuals who (justified) their special treatment and (betrayed) society's trust by invoking professional privilege, confidence, and secrecy'. He asked, how could professional behaviour be made accountable to the public without curtailing the independence upon which creative skills and the imaginative use of knowledge depended? (Bledstein, 1976: 334.)

In introducing the book on *Disabling Professions* edited by Illich in 1977, the publishers said that traditional and newer professions had been acknowledged as being selflessly devoted to the good of society. Now, however, the question had to be asked whether the professions in fact provided their services so altruistically, and whether people were really enriched and not just subordinated by their activities. (Illich, ed., 1977: 9.) Illich was a trenchant critic of the teaching and medical professions, and of professionalism in general. He claimed the twentieth century would be known as 'The Age of the Disabling Professions', a time when people had 'problems', 'experts' had 'solutions' and scientists measured imponderables such as 'abilities' and 'needs'. The illusions on which the age was based were increasingly visible to common sense. Professionals told you what you needed and claimed the power to prescribe. The professional corporation carried out for itself a social mission. In any area where a human need could be imagined professions, dominant, authoritative, monopolistic, legalized - and, at the same time, debilitating and effectively disabling the individual - had become exclusive experts of the public good. The public acceptance of domineering professions was essentially a political event. Public affairs were passing into the hands of a self-accrediting elite. (Illich, 1977, 17: 19-20.)

As needs were broken down into ever smaller component parts, each managed by the appropriate specialist, the consumer experienced difficulty integrating the separate offerings of his or her various tutors into a meaningful whole that could be desired with commitment and possessed with pleasure. To be ignorant or unconvinced of one's own needs had become the unforgivable anti-social act. (Illich, 1977: 23-4.)

In a discussion on professionalized service and disabling help, McKnight observed the growing proportion of services in the gross national product of every modernized society. This stage of economic development had unlimited potential; there was no end to the needs for which services could be manufactured. The creation and allocation of services were the central political issues in modernized economies. (McKnight, in Illich, ed., 1977: 70-1.) In the modernized service society professions said to the citizen: we are the solution to your problem; we know what problem you have; you can't understand the problem or the solution; and only we can decide whether the solution has dealt with your problem. The disabling effects were intrinsic to professional service. Benefits had to be weighed against them in a political process which would restore the political definition of citizenship. (McKnight, in Illich, ed., 1977: 89, 91.)

A very different view of the professions had been taken by a British book written by Paul Halmos, published in 1970. In *The Personal Service Society*, he criticized the generally pessimistic sociological accounts of the professions, accusing them of negative bias. In contrast, he explored the ways in which at least the personal service professions contributed to social betterment by providing intellectual and cultural leadership. (Halmos, 1970: 4-7.) The medium of achievement in an increasingly professionalized society was increasingly the 'services rendered' and decreasingly the 'goods provided'. The manpower required to render personal services in health, welfare, and education need have no bounds. In a personal service society which was developing, the terms and direction of achievement would have changed. A service-orientation could not develop without sensitivity, imagination, and sympathy. (Halmos, 1970: 9-10.) Professional workers realized their personalities, at least partly, through realizing certain professional goals which were other than the enhancement of their status or income. The contribution made by professionalization to cultural change had been grossly underestimated. Halmos refused to allow a cynical account of professional motivation and aspiration to claim the monopoly of objectivity. (Halmos, 1970: 193, 195.)

Elliott observed that studies of occupational prestige in Britain and the United States had consistently shown that the older professions were still accorded the highest status. Professional income was also higher than average. There was, however, a sharp difference between the incomes of those in the older self-employed or 'higher' professions, and those in the newer or 'lower' professions, who were generally salaried employees. (Elliott, 1972: 58.) The professions were not easy to place in the general class and status structure. Although professionals might share common experiences, their emphasis on separation, autonomy and the individual career, could well have divisive consequences for any general professional class. (Elliott, 1972: 61, 143.) Professional selection and recruitment was, however, heavily skewed towards the high-class and status groups, the main exceptions being the technological professions and those associated with education itself. (Elliott, 1972: 71.)

The state and profit-making organizations were the professions' main competitors in their attempts to define their own ends and means. Both used criteria for allocating resources and evaluating future courses of action which were fundamentally different from professionalism. Economic authority rested on judgments of profitability, political authority on what was practical and desirable, given the wishes and interests expressed through the political system. Professional authority appeared more absolute; based on the claims to unique responsibility for some aspect of the public good and knowledge of how it should be achieved. There was, however, the problem of control of any system of paternal elitism. Further, conflicting aims of different fields had to be resolved, and scarce resources allocated between fields. An even more fundamental difficulty was that the absolute claims within a field reflected the particular socio-economic situation of a profession and its practitioners rather than the potential of available knowledge. (Elliott, 1972: 147-8.)

The main strength of the professions was, according to Elliott, their ability to exploit their particular expertise to counter the control of other groups and the claims of rival ideologies. Their place in society was not secure. In some ways the growth in the number of professions and professionals had undermined rather than strengthened the claim of the professional group as a whole to its position in society. (Elliott, 1972: 151.)

Freidson, in 1973, saw the growth of the professions in the twentieth century as a rebirth of the occupational principle for organizing and controlling work. This contrasted with the administrative principle which had effected a revolution in the organization and control of work during the industrial revolution, when management instructed the worker about what should be done and how it should be done. (Freidson, in Freidson, ed, 1973a: 19-20.) In this century, the authority of management over the organization of work had been modified by government regulation, and by the rise of industrial trade unionism. The latter was an instance of the occupational principle, but largely tried to influence terms and conditions of work rather than its content. Management remained fairly free to continue to fragment, mechanize and rationalize tasks. (Freidson, in Freidson, ed, 1973: 21.)

Professionalization of occupations constituted another source of control over work, which removed or withheld from management the authority 'to create and direct the substance, performance and even the goals of the work itself. When such work goes on in an organization, management can control only the available resources, not most of what the workers do or how they do it. In a professionalized service organization, the strategic task of an organization is formulated, controlled, and evaluated primarily by the workers. (Freidson, in Freidson, ed., 1973: 22-4.)

Freidson pointed out that administrative authority was not the only possible coordinating mechanism. On the basis of claimed and recognized expertise the work of many other occupations can be coordinated around a professionalized service, with the professionals coordinating the division of labour in the organization. (Freidson, in Freidson, ed., 1973: 25-6.)

Futurologists were agreed on an increasing dependence on specialized knowledge, but little attention had been given to how this would come about. Freidson observed that those engaged in the process of creating, communicating and applying knowledge were identified and identified themselves with recognizable, increasingly organized occupational groups. It was the concept of occupation, and particularly profession, which provided the sociological link between knowledge as such and its organized role in present-day society. (Freidson, in Freidson, ed., 1973: 28.)

Freidson observed that both the occupational and administrative principles seemed to be strengthening in post-industrial society. Bureaucratization by both private and public management, seemed never stronger, and professionalization could be considered a major social movement of the twentieth century. Would the professionals lose control over their work and become mere 'technical workers', a special category of skilled labour in the organizational charts of management? Could management extend the rationalization of work from manufacturing to services, breaking down the work of professionals into a series of discrete, simple operations? This could support the exercise of managerial authority, if it produced the same product as was previously produced by the professional worker. (Freidson, in Freidson, ed., 1973: 35.)

The authority of expertise or skill, however, provided a challenging alternative to the authority of office, and was a principle inherent in a truly 'knowledgeable' society. Freidson commented that if esoteric knowledge and skill were really necessary to perform most of the work of the future, the occupational principle would take precedence over the administrative principle, whether or not professionals were employees. Control over the content of work was not necessarily weakened by being an employee. Also occupational organization and action by professional workers would provide a counterforce to the extension of the administrative principle to the control of professional work. It was possible that with the continued growth of the occupational principle, the post-industrial society would be the professional society. (Freidson, in Freidson, ed., 1973: 36-7.)

A 1983 essay by Rueschemeyer focused on the social control of expertise (Rueschemeyer, in Dingwall and Lewis, eds, 1983). The issue arose because the recipients of professional services were not themselves adequately knowledgeable to solve the problem or to assess the service received. He pointed out that it was only in the Anglo-American 'functional' literature that it was seen as 'functional' for the experts themselves to have control of the use of their expertise. Yet there was no causal necessity for this arrangement of professional self-control. Expert services could be controlled by at least two other institutional arrangements - control by consumers, and control by third parties, especially the modern state. The different types of control were, in fact, generally found in mixed form. There was too a further possibility, and that was where there was no effective social control of expert services. This was especially likely to occur where service recipients were economically, socially and politically weak. Rueschemeyer observed that economic and more recent sociological analysis saw the machinery of professional organization primarily as a tool for acquiring and maintaining a privileged autonomous position, and only secondarily, if at all, as an instrument of professional self-control. (Rueschemeyer, in Dingwall and Lewis, eds, 1983, 41-8.)

Did the professions constitute a 'new class'? One theory of a new professional-managerial class saw it as neither working nor capitalist class (B. and J. Ehrenreich, in Walker, ed., 1979). Freidson pointed out, however, that since specialization was divisive, the occupations were not unified by their class position. Nor did they act as a class; they were far too heterogeneous, both between each other and internally. (Freidson, 1986: 42, 45-6, 59-60.) Abbott noted that enthusiasm for professionalism could be seen as a new class consciousness, but professionals did not generally support a fellow profession's attempts to gain legal protection, and there was no general, class opposition to the authority of corporate employers (Abbott, 1988: 175).

Abbott acknowledged the existence of dominant power and conservatism in the professional system, but argued the issue was one of their degree. No profession delivering bad services could stand indefinitely against competent outsiders. Jurisdictions were renegotiated in workplaces over two- to three-year periods, in public over ten- to twenty-year periods, in law over twenty- to fifty-year periods. Professional power retarded these processes. It built up in incumbency; it could also arise from aspects of the professional task, such as lawyers' association with the courts; and it could also come from association with the state, or universities, or a particular social class, or the elite corporate sector. (Abbott, 1988: 135-9.)

Having provided an abstract model of the professional system, Abbott examined the real historical environment whose social and cultural changes had worked their way through the system of professions opening and closing jurisdictions. He concluded there was no uniform pattern of 'professionalization' or of 'deprofessionalization'. For individual professions, the jurisdictional results of general social change depended on their particular situations. (Abbott, 1988: 144-50.) The varied writings that asserted the professions were losing their privileged position had already been evaluated by Freidson. He found that theories of deprofessionalization and proletarianization lacked empirical support. The relative prestige of the various professions, and of the professions in relation to other American occupations had been quite stable; the 'knowledge gap' between professionals and their clients was not closing; professionals controlled what use was made of computers; and neither competing occupations nor consumer self-help movements had seriously threatened the licensed professions, while new areas of work were being invented. (Freidson, 1986: 109, 111-12.)

British social historian Harold Perkin, in 1989, asked what sort of society has brought us in the more economically advanced countries to the present brink of unprecedented power both for creation and destruction. The title of his book, *The Rise of Professional Society*, gives his answer. Whole armies of experts had contributed to this promising and perilous situation. Modern society in Britain, as elsewhere in the developed world, was made up of career hierarchies of specialized occupations, selected by merit and based on trained expertise. Where pre-industrial society was based on property in land and industrial society on managed capital, professional society was based on human capital created by education and enhanced by strategies of closure which excluded the unqualified. Landed and industrial wealth still exerted power but it was increasingly managed by corporate professionals. The professional hierarchies cut across the horizontal solidarities of class. (Perkin, 1989: 1-2.)

Professionalism, Perkin claimed, permeated society from top to bottom in two ways. More and more jobs became subject to specialized training and claimed expertise, with their occupants demanding the status of a profession and the rewards of a profession, such as a secure income, a rising salary scale, and fringe benefits. Also the society was permeated by the professional social ideal, which emphasized human capital, highly skilled and differentiated labour, and selection by merit defined as trained and certified expertise. (Perkin, 1989: 3-4.)

The professions lived by persuasion and propaganda, by claiming that their particular service was indispensable to the client or employer and to society and the state. Only in post-industrial society had the professions as a whole been able to establish human capital as the dominant form of wealth. Professional control of the market in a particular service created an artificial scarcity in the supply. Professional capital gave the professional security and confidence to press the professional ideal upon the other classes. This ideal implied the principle of a just reward not only for the particular profession but for every occupation necessary to society's well-being. (Perkin, 1989: 6-8.)

The professional society was structured around the principle of vertical career hierarchy, and social conflict (the struggle for income, power and status) took the form of a competition for resources between rival interest groups. Many competed for public resources. (Perkin, 1989: 9-10.) By far the most important division between the interest groups was between the public sector professions, funded directly or indirectly by the state, and the private sector professions, chiefly managers of private sector corporations. Another large and important group of professional occupations was employed by a wide range of not-for-profit institutions. They, in fact, tended to lean towards the public side of the divide. (Perkin, 1989: 11.) The modern bifurcation of the two rival groups of professions rested on the concrete foundations of incompatible interests. Both groups wished to capture control of government. The nineteenth-century rhetoric of class conflict was for both a weapon in their competition for income and status. (Perkin, 1989: 17.)

Perkin argued that the principle of the division of labour had, in 200 years, transformed Britain (and a large part of the world) from a predominantly agricultural system through an industrial mass-production economy to a post-industrial society increasingly based on services. Division of labour had two aspects, specialization and integration. Specialization led directly to professionalism. The increasing complexity of the modern world generated specialization and organized professions. But specialization also required integration by management which in turn became divided by specialized areas. (Perkin, 1989: 22-5.)

In the final chapter, Perkin described the backlash that had occurred against professional society during the adverse economic conditions in the 1970s and 1980s. Special interest groups of all kinds came under attack, but especially the organized professions. (Perkin, 1989: 472-83.) The backlash against individual professions particularly those employed by the state, and professionalism in general was inevitable, argued Perkin, because of the condescension of professionalism, the suspicion that professions were a conspiracy against the laity, and the rivalry and mutual disdain many professions felt for each other. The most obvious source of an effective body of hostile opinion was the revival of the free market ideology. Professional organization deliberately excluded unqualified competitors. But there was already 'a tide of popular displeasure at the pretensions, and privileges of individual professions'. (Perkin, 1989: 475.)

The Adequacy of Information and Knowledge About the Professions

To rectify the problem of unfounded generalizations about professions, scholars and others clearly need a great deal of data and cumulative scholarship about the occupations. Modern technology has revolutionized capacity for data collection, storage, and retrieval, but has not obviated judgments about its quality and the purposes to which it can be put. The research arm of a profession is particularly involved in these issues, but how much attention is paid to the availability and adequacy of data about the profession itself is worthy of systematic examination. In sociology, one can expect occupational sociologists to take a particular interest. Political scientists may be interested in data concerning the political power of these occupations, and economists with data about their use of resources and their restraints on competition. Professional associations may also be active in stimulating adequate data systems about their profession and its circumstances. Political concerns may, however, limit such an interest, particularly if the data is likely to reflect adversely on the profession.

A society could be well informed about its professions if an accurate up-to-date occupational profile were available, built on continuing, reliable, meaningful data. This could be constructed by official statistical bodies, and/or by reasonably objective researchers in professional schools and associations. The occupation's size, age, ethnicity, gender, socio-economic composition, educational attainments, income, political interests and influence, and economic resources, would be included; also its distribution in work settings and type of work, its geographic distribution, and the nature of its clientele. Data on the relevant professional associations would be covered, and the educational activity of the profession would also be an important section of the profile.

A contemporary profile, in conjunction with serious historical work on each profession, such as Paul Starr's *The Social Transformation of American Medicine*, and Richard Abel's *American Lawyers*, can obviously give substance to people's understanding of what reality is being referred to when a particular occupation is mentioned. Remarkably, as recently as 1961, Goode noted that he knew of no adequate history of any profession (Goode, in Vollmer and Mills: 37). Abbott's work on the professional system does, however, bring into question historical study that focuses just on the one occupation. His theory of professional development focused on groups with common work rather than organizational structures of professions. He argued that the development of the formal attributes of a profession was bound up with the pursuit of jurisdiction and the beating of rival professions. Each profession was bound to a set of tasks by ties of jurisdiction. The professions made up an interacting system within which professions competed. A profession's success reflected as much the situation of its competitors and the system structure as it did the profession's own efforts. Forces external to the system periodically created, abolished, or reshaped tasks within the system. (Abbott, 1988: 20, 30.)

Without people willing to pursue professional careers, the notion of profession would not exist. Additional to information and knowledge about professions as a whole, serious biographical writing is needed on the members of professional occupations and this should not just concentrate on desired role models, important though these may be in the professional socialization of subsequent generations.

Whatever the adequacy of knowledge and information about professions in contemporary Anglo-American society, they clearly have significant impact on the production, availability, and suitability of services and goods; on the use and distribution of scarce human, physical, and financial resources; on the production, organization, and utilization of knowledge; on the purposes and organization of human work; on education systems; and on the lives of their members and those of their families and friends. It is evident that the ethics of professional conduct is too important a topic to be left just to the professionals themselves.

4 Dimensions of Individual and Collective Professional Conduct

It is apparent from the last three chapters, that the idea of 'professional conduct', like the idea of 'ethics', is complex and controversial. Yet it cannot be ignored because of its continuing significance in at least Anglo-American societies, and indeed in any society concerned about the responsible use of specialized knowledge to make a living.

In such a society, 'professional conduct' typically, though not exclusively, refers to the conduct of a professional or a person in a professional role, or it refers to the conduct of a professional collectivity - consisting of members of the same profession, or of members of different professions. The idea of a profession in such a society is an organized occupation with characteristic social structures - educational institutions or schools concerned with the development and transmission of relevant values, knowledge, and skills; a professional association or associations with educational, industrial, and social policy functions; and work organization allowing sufficient autonomy for professional practice. The organized occupation strives for social recognition and respect - in the workplace, in the public arena, and in the legislative and government arena. An occupation organized on professional lines provides a way of organizing the personal work careers of its members.

Although a nation-state has been the usual frame of reference for describing a profession, in fact, a modern profession is increasingly an international phenomenon as well, with its international organizations and international meetings, the development of international missions, development and sharing of professional knowledge across national boundaries, and the opening up of career opportunities beyond a professional's own nation-state. Particularly in smaller and/or less economically developed countries, international professional influences can be powerful and problematic (Midgley, 1981).

A Descriptive Model of Professional Conduct

This chapter will propose a descriptive model of professional conduct which pays due regard to the various dimensions of professional conduct illustrated in writing on professions and professionals, and experienced by the author in his own work as an educator of professionals and as a user of a variety of professional services. Since the purpose of this book is to focus attention on the ethical evaluation of professional conduct, it is important to be as clear as one can on the dimensions of what it is that is being evaluated.

Whose Conduct?

The Professional Agent - Individual, Collective

Any instance of human conduct entails an agent and what that agent does, or how that agent acts. The agent may be an individual or a collectivity. An instance of professional conduct entails action by a professional agent. '*Whose* conduct is it?' is always a relevant question to ask when reference is made to an actual instance of professional conduct, and at the very least the answer must refer to the individual agent in some sense having membership of a particular profession, or the collective agent being in some sense connected with a profession or professions.

Membership of a Profession

Individual membership of a profession is a clear-cut concept when a person has the recognized educational qualification for professional practice, is working as a practitioner of that profession, is a member of the relevant professional association, and has a conscious commitment to the obligations of professional membership. The concept becomes blurred, however, when one or more of these conditions does or do not operate. For example:
- when a person has not undertaken the recognized educational qualification, but may have some adjacent qualification, or has an out-of-date qualification, or a qualification from another country;
- when a person is not working specifically as a practitioner of the profession for which they are educationally qualified, but is engaged in adjacent work for which their qualification is useful, or when a person is not currently working professionally;

- when a person has membership of more than one professional group from holding double qualifications, or being involved in the education or administration arms of a profession which also gives membership of the profession of university teachers, or the profession of management or public administration;

- when a person meets the other conditions of professional membership, but has not taken out membership of the relevant professional association for financial or other reasons; and

- when a person meets the other conditions of professional membership, but does not have a conscious commitment to meeting the obligations arising from professional membership.

To talk meaningfully about professional conduct relating to an individual agent, requires clarity on the extent to which these various conditions are present in the agent concerned. A particular instance of conduct may not be reasonably described as 'professional' conduct if the agent concerned does not have unambiguous membership of an occupation organized on professional lines.

Professional Collectivities

Where the agent is a professional collectivity rather than an individual, answering the question 'Whose conduct is it?' requires establishing the nature of the connection with a profession or professions. Again, a particular instance of collective conduct may not be reasonably described as 'professional' conduct if the collectivity concerned does not have an unambiguous connection with a profession or professions.

Professional collectivities are variously called professions, associations, institutes, schools, ad hoc or standing committees, working groups, teams, agencies, units, or departments. The clearest instances of professional collectivities are those composed of people with unambiguous membership of a single profession, or of the various professions involved if it is a multiprofessional collectivity. The more the collectivity contains people with ambiguous membership of a profession or of the professions involved, the less it is reasonable to describe the collectivity as a 'professional' collectivity.

The most general case of a collective professional agent is the profession as a whole, a concept which calls for answers to the same boundary questions which arise when individual membership is the focus - what are the educational, practice, association, and commitment conditions for membership of the profession referred to? Often, however, the collective agent is not the profession as a whole but a group or groups claiming to represent the profession, usually professional associations and their office-bearers. Collectivities within a professional association will include general governing groups, and standing and ad hoc groups focused on particular concerns such as educational standards and opportunities, employment conditions and opportunities, and action to improve the society's policies based on the profession's expertise. The actual relationship between those acting on behalf of a profession, and the total membership of that profession requires clarification to answer the question 'Whose conduct is it?' when the collective agent referred to is a profession as a whole.

Within a profession, collective professional agents can take many forms. The particular collectivity may be a specialty with its own professional association and educational institutions, which is typical of specialty development in the medical profession. Alternatively, the specialty may stay as a sub-group within the general professional structures.

Whatever the pattern of specialty development, a profession has three interdependent groups usually described as educators, administrators, and practitioners, each of which can give rise to distinctive professional collectivities within a profession. In fact, both the educators and the administrators are engaged in essential functions, and it seems conceptually odd not to see them also as practitioners, albeit practitioners of a particular kind.

A profession's educators may be organized in various collectivities - a general association of educators which covers all who perform educational functions; a general association of schools; a standing committee of heads of schools; a professional school with its governing structures, and various groups concerned with the basic professional curriculum, its postgraduate and other continuing education programs, and its research program.

A profession's administrators perform essential organizational functions - including coordination and resource allocation - in agencies which provide professional and sometimes other services, in the profession's educational institutions, and in its professional association/s. They may form professional collectivities, like an association of secondary school principals, if they are numerous enough and have sufficient interest to maintain an organized collective existence. They may, however, instead make common cause in collectivities consisting of administrators with various professional and other backgrounds. Such a collectivity may concentrate on public administration, or on business administration, or it may try to cover both.

However significant may be a profession's educators and administrators, the great bulk of its members are its 'practitioners'. These work together in a wide variety of collectivities in their employing agencies, and their professional association/s, and in some settings in collaboration with people from other professions.

It is evident that knowledge of professional conduct must include an understanding of the collective organization of professional life. It cannot concentrate solely on the individual professional agent.

Characteristics of the Individual Professional Agent

Once it is clear *who* is the individual or the collective agent when an instance of professional conduct is being referred to, a wide variety of other information about the agent may be relevant in describing and trying to understand the conduct of the agent.

An individual professional agent will always have a wide range of personal characteristics. How relevant these are in a particular instance of professional conduct requires empirical verification.

The professional will be a particular chronological age, which will be related to biological age, life and work experience, and career stage. Although the significance is changing, the professional's gender can have influenced career choice and career opportunities, and may influence concurrent commitments. The professional's ethnicity may be that of the dominant culture or of a cultural subgroup in the society where he or she is practising, and may be the same or differ from that of clients and professional peers. The professional will have a particular record of educational achievement, both in the initial professional qualification and in subsequent continuing education. The professional's work experience may be extensive in scope or depth, or both, or the professional may be a novice (every professional must be one at the beginning of a career, and in dealing with new situations throughout a career). The professional may be experienced in more than one profession.

How and where the professional is currently employed are likely to be highly relevant information in understanding an instance of professional conduct. The professional may work for private for-profit enterprise; for private non-profit enterprise; for government at national, state, or local level; be self-employed; or be employed with rights to 'private practice'. The work setting can be that of a single independent operator, a partnership of multiple colleagues of the same profession, a for-profit professional agency employing members of the one profession or a mixture of professions, a professional unit in a large bureaucracy, private or government, again either with a mixture of professionals or professionals of the same kind, and headed by an administrator with the same or different qualifications. And there is the further possibility that the instance of professional conduct is an instance of the professional working in a 'voluntary capacity'. However the professional is employed, the work setting of the professional will have a geographic location which will strongly influence what work is undertaken. The circumstances of professional work are different in large cities, in suburban centers, in provincial towns, and in rural environments.

The social status of individual professionals will vary according to the general social standing of their particular profession, and the status of their particular work within the profession. The status of a professional agent will influence what work can be undertaken and with what degree of perceived legitimacy.

The agent's character and temperament cannot reasonably be ignored in a description of an instance of professional conduct. What are the character traits and what is the temperamental disposition of the person whose conduct is being described are highly relevant questions in assessing that conduct. They emphasize the continuity and integrity of the person whose conduct it is. Every instance of professional conduct contributes to understanding by the professional and others, about the kind of person they are.

Any individual professional engaged in any instance of professional conduct has a range of concurrent commitments which may influence the particular conduct in question. The professional has other work commitments - to other clients, to professional and other work colleagues, to an employing agency, to the profession. In addition are commitments to family, to friendships, to other social groups, and to being a citizen in a democratic society. Behaving in an ethically justifiable fashion requires balancing the claims of all these commitments of a person who is a professional agent. Their professional agency in an instance of professional conduct cannot reasonably be isolated from the rest of their conduct if one is concerned with ethical justification of that conduct.

Characteristics of the Collective Professional Agent

It seems, then, that understanding any instance of professional conduct involving an individual professional can require a variety of information about whose conduct it is. The same can be argued about any instance of collective professional conduct. The collectivity consists of a number of professionals, of the same or different professions. It has particular age, gender, ethnic, and status characteristics. Its members have particular characters, temperaments, educational qualifications and work experience, as well as concurrent commitments. In addition, the collectivity as such may have concurrent commitments, and a typical decision structure and process. For example, the collectivity may be an ad hoc committee dealing with a particular instance of conduct; it may be a standing committee dealing with particular types of conduct; or it may be a general group like a professional association handling multiple functions in a limited time period, or continuously over a long period.

Whenever 'professional conduct' is under consideration, the 'who' dimension calls for the sort of careful clarification sketched in the above analysis. These main dimensions of individual and collective professional agents are indicated in the first section of the descriptive model of professional conduct at the end of the chapter.

What Conduct?

Descriptive Professional Conduct

To be meaningful, the concept of professional conduct needs to be not only actor-specific, but also conduct-specific. Conduct is not a very precise term, but generally it refers to actions taken by a person or a collectivity of persons, and actions imply purposive human behaviour. By definition, all professional agents, individual and collective, are engaged in actions as professionals. To gain and maintain their professional status, they must conform to acceptable standards of conduct.

Action and Inaction

This second part of the descriptive model of professional conduct provides categories of conduct in which professional agents may be expected to engage. Since each conduct category is agent-specific, it must be related to a professional agent described in the first part of the model. Although the concept of 'conduct' is sometimes used to refer to 'right' or 'good' behaviour, the usage here is descriptive, not prescriptive. The prescriptive discussion comes in the final section of the book, when professional conduct is discussed in the context of ethical evaluation.

Generally, 'conduct' refers to activity on the part of an agent, but there are instances where the 'conduct' in question is 'inactivity', for example, where an individual or collective professional agent is accused of misconduct because of an error of omission, or the agent is pursuing a policy of 'studied neglect'. An agent's 'activity' or 'conduct' can cover thinking, discussing and deciding, as well as taking physical action.

An instance of human conduct may be analyzed in terms of where and when it takes place, what does the agent do? what is intended by the agent? who and what are affected? In an instance of professional conduct these questions are asked and answered in the context of undertaking work organized on professional lines.

Where and When

Actual professional conduct occurs in a particular place and time. 'Professional work' tends to be concentrated in a professional's workplace, wherever that is located, and to take place during 'working hours'. Professionals' working hours may not, however, be rigidly adhered to and their work with and for clients may be done away from their office - in clients' homes, in clients' offices, in others' work settings, or in their own homes out of office hours. Professional collectivities can also be located geographically. Where things take place can, of course, influence what takes place. The time element in professional conduct is often critically important. Unless you know when conduct is taking place, you cannot know what has preceded it, what is concurrent with it, and what is likely to occur when, in the future.

Intentions, Methodology, Effects

What gives coherence to an instance of conduct is the purpose being pursued. It may be argued, with MacIntyre (see p.19), that any instance of human action, or conduct, is goal-directed. What is intended by a professional agent is, then, critical information in the classification of professional conduct. Without knowledge of what is intended by the professional agent, the conduct cannot reasonably be described, let alone evaluated ethically. But an adequate description of an instance of professional conduct requires reference not only to intentions or purposes, but to methodology - how the purposes are pursued - and also to results of action including unintended consequences. The question 'What has the professional done?' is always relevant to be asked at the conclusion of an instance of professional conduct.

So far it has been asserted that each instance of a professional agent will be engaged in conduct which has a location and time, will be motivated by particular intentions, has a methodology, and will have effects both intended and unintended. The intentions, the methodology, and the effects may relate to people, to other living creatures, and/or to the physical world.

People-Related Conduct

A professional agent's conduct in relation to people can include - a client or clients served by the professional; the self; an employer; professional peers in one's profession, in the same organization, in other organizations, working independently, or in a professional association; professionals in other professions, in the same organization, in other organizations, or working independently; and administrative, technical and other workers in the employing organization, and elsewhere.

Service to clients   Service to clients provides the very rationale for the existence of the professional occupation, with all its activities assumedly having an instrumental relationship to achieving client well-being. The concept of 'client', however, requires careful analysis, as does the idea of 'service'. A client is usually thought to be a person or a collectivity who employs the 'services' of a professional agent. A profession, a professional agency or organization, or an individual professional obviously cannot continue without clients, and clients presumably use a professional agent to pursue certain purposes which they otherwise could not pursue. Each is dependent on the other, but the terms of this dependence will vary greatly, according to the nature of the professional agent, the nature of the client, and their respective purposes in interaction with each other.

Characteristics of clients   Matching the variety amongst individual and collective agents, is a similar variety amongst individual and collective clients. The individual client will have personal characteristics which may or may not be relevant to the professional service they receive - age, gender, ethnicity, family, education, work experience, social status, income and wealth, character and temperament. A collective client may be a couple, a family, a group of people with similar concerns, an association, an employing organization. Again, they will have a wide variety of potentially relevant characteristics.

Purposes and outcomes Clients will enter their relationship with a professional service with certain concerns in mind. A client's continuing interaction with a professional service will be sustained by the purposive activity of both parties. Whether the 'service' is 'of service' to the clients depends on agreement on assessment criteria and on evidence of the effects of the actions of the professional agent. An instance of professional service may produce an outcome which is seen as beneficial to a client by the client, by the client and the professional agent, or by the professional but not the client.

Payment for individual professional service Except when working in a voluntary capacity, the individual professional agent will always receive a financial return for providing a service to a client. Although professionals may be so involved and interested in their work that they 'live to work', they, like most others, must 'work to live'. For some professionals, the financial incentive is predominant, with financial profitability being the main criterion of success. Other professionals expect a reasonable level of financial return related to criteria such as the social usefulness of their work, their levels of education and training, their experience, and the degree of difficulty and level of responsibility of their work.

Arrangements for paying individual professionals take many forms. The professional may be paid for each instance of service, with the level of payment being set - in advance, or after the event - by the professional, the professional and the client, a professional association, or the government, or some combination of these. The payment is often based on time spent, and/or the procedures involved. It may be conditional on a successful outcome. It may be based on a percentage of the overall financial cost of a project; or a percentage of a payment made to a successful client arising from the professional's service. Instead of payment for each instance of service or each project, a professional may be paid a retainer to provide ongoing services to a client whenever they are needed. Either full or subsidy payments on behalf of clients for professional services may be made by the government, insurance companies, or employers. Such arrangements are common for medical services.

The actual financial return to a professional for work done is the net return, after his or her costs are deducted, including overheads. How much the individual professional bears the costs of providing a service will, however, vary greatly. The costs will include the cost of the professional's initial and continuing education, and may include the costs of accommodation, of support staff, and of technical equipment. These costs may be borne by a professional's family, by an employing agency, or by the government.

Employment conditions A professional directly employed by an organization or agency typically receives an annual salary, paid in equal amounts on a monthly or two-weekly basis, irrespective of the actual work done. The professional may also receive other rewards - 'fringe benefits' of various kinds such as superannuation or pension contributions, holiday and sick leave, a car, housing and education subsidies. The level and type of remuneration are set down at the outset in a contract of employment between the agency and the professional, which typically includes a 'duty statement' covering the work the professional is expected to perform, the duration of the appointment, and a statement of the working condition - salary, fringe benefits, support staff, review, resignation, and dismissal procedures, and so on. Such 'contracts' can vary greatly in their level of specificity. The working conditions may be standardized for particular categories of professional staff, and be strongly influenced by action external to the agency, such as actions by industrial tribunals, professional associations, and governments. Some individual professionals can, however, negotiate an individually tailored employment contract.

Work done by professional staff in an organization is paid for by the organization. An organization in turn must gain financial resources to be able to do this. Depending on the nature of the organization, its money will come from government taxes, sale of goods and/or services, benefactions, and donations. Any of these sources may earmark the expenditure of the funds. An organization may gain funds to employ professionals on a particular project. Clients of professionals working for organizations may pay no fees to the organization for the service, some fees, or full economic fees. For example, for a period, university students in Australia paid no tuition fees; now students from overseas must pay full economic fees, and the rest pay reduced fees which may be deferred until after graduation.

It is evident that the availability of financial resources and conditions connected with their availability will often have a critical influence on the amount and nature of professional conduct. Except in voluntary work, professionals cannot work without payment, but it is clear that payment can take many forms, including payment by third parties.

Payment for collective professional service The work of a professional collectivity is actually paid for by an employing agency when the collectivity consists of employed professionals operating in agency 'work' time, with the money coming from the various sources of agency funding which pays agency salaries. If the collectivity operates outside agency 'work' time, the professional members may be donating their services free. A professional association and its various professional collectivities usually depend heavily on the voluntary services of its office-bearers and participating members, and the paid services of a secretariat financed from membership fees. How much and what kind of work can be done by a professional collectivity depend on the availability of finances to pay for the work, and/or the willingness of member-professionals to work voluntarily, or without payment.

The self The self is implicated in all instances of professional conduct through the notion of agency. The agent is always a particular person or a particular collectivity, and as such is considered responsible for action taken - what was intended, what was done, what was the result, what were the opportunity costs. A professional agent's reputation in their own eyes, and in the eyes of others, depends on answering these kinds of questions.

To gain and maintain recognition as a responsible professional agent, an individual must make a considerable initial and continuing personal commitment of time, money, and effort, to learn and understand the requisite knowledge and skills of the profession concerned, and values which justify their use. Professional education and training means *self*-development in order to perform the work of the profession. Some forms of professional work, for example, psychiatry, clinical psychology, and social work, require more than the appropriate use of relevant knowledge and skills in the service of specified values. These require heightened levels of *self*-awareness on the part of the professional agent to avoid the personal needs of the professional interfering with service to clients. If a professional's educational preparation is too narrowly drawn, and/or the professional's work is very limited in scope, the 'development' of the professional's self may be highly specialized and restricted.

A professional, like every other human being, has an ongoing responsibility for self. Because professional work can be so personally demanding and occupy so much of a person's adult life, relationship to self is a significant dimension of professional conduct. The relationship clearly can have positive and/or negative effects, and cannot be ignored in any ethical justification of that conduct. The effects of professional conduct on the well-being of the professional agent is a matter of description after empirical investigation. The agent's intentions may give little attention to self, or pay regard to self primarily as an instrument in the well-being of clients and/or others, or may be pre-occupied with considerations of self to the detriment of clients and others involved in the agent's conduct. The intentions of agents in their conduct do need to be distinguished from the effects in an accurate description of the conduct

Collective identity Notions of 'self' tend to be associated with individual professional agents. However, a professional collectivity also has an ongoing identity which has claims to consideration in professional conduct. The conduct can be focused on developing the capacity of the collectivity, on developing and maintaining its reputation, on ensuring its survival, and so on. Without some attention to the collective 'self' - often provided by senior administrators and management boards in large collectivities, and chairpersons and team leaders in small ones - a collectivity cannot provide service to others. It is all too easy, however, for collectivities to become 'ends in themselves' rather than means to the achievement of professional purposes. The modern insistence on operationalized mission statements and specified goals and objectives are conscious attempts to counter this.

Employer-related conduct When a professional agent is employed by others to provide a professional service to clients, a significant dimension in the agent's conduct is the nature of the relationship with the employer. As already seen, the employer usually pays the professional a salary to undertake specified work, but the degree of specificity can vary greatly and professional staff can in fact enjoy considerable autonomy. An employment contract is usually with an organization; not with its senior executives or its governing body. In fact, however, the latter act on behalf of the organization in personnel matters. If they have the same professional qualifications and background as the professional staff whom they engage on behalf of the organization, there is likely to be greater understanding of technical matters and greater agreement on values and objectives, than when the senior executives or board members are 'laypersons' as far as the professional staff are concerned.

Even when a professional is employed in a single-profession professional agency, like a law firm, that is, one where the governing group, the administrator, and the main professional staff all have the same professional background, the professional's autonomy will be limited by agency policies and priorities. The employing agency can, of course, be seen as enabling the professional to undertake work which the professional otherwise could not do and so has a very great influence on professional conduct. For example, an employed professional has a guaranteed income, accommodation, clients, collaborative professional staff, support staff, and equipment, none of which is immediately available to a sole practitioner. In addition, the employed professional can usually be expected to have at least some influence over the organization's policies which determine the availability of these resources.

Fellow workers - categories and characteristics A significant feature of a professional's conduct is his or her conduct in relation to various categories of fellow workers. Relationships may be cooperative, competitive, or indifferent; and will vary according to whether the fellow worker is a member of the same profession, is of a different profession, is a technical worker, is neither technical nor professional, or is working in the same organization, in another organization, or independently. In addition, other characteristics of the fellow worker may influence the conduct.

Same profession - professional colleagues, 'peers': If professionals of the same profession are indifferent to each other, the identity and persistence of the profession are in jeopardy. To be recognized as belonging to a professional occupation, a significant proportion of the members of that occupation must engage in cooperative activity with each other to establish and maintain professional education and a professional association to deal with common concerns, including standards of values, knowledge, and skills. Within the occupation, members will compete with each other for positions, influence, and resources.

The educational arm: The educational arm of a profession consists of educational professionals, the full-time teachers and researchers in professional schools, those performing professional educational functions in agencies, and in associations, and practitioners who are involved in educational programs. In all cases, the direct clients or students are future practitioners of the profession in question, so the overall purpose is provided by that profession. People engaged in educational provision are increasingly educational professionals, with typical qualifications and career paths. How practitioners and educationalists relate to each other in a profession is of critical importance to both enterprises and the profession in general. Every professional practitioner is, at least partly, the product of a professional education process, and professional education makes no sense unless related in some way to professional practice.

Professional peers - peer review: A person begins to learn how to relate to professional 'peers' in the educational processes of a professional school. Fellow students and teachers are future professional colleagues. People in the same profession are commonly described as colleagues because it is assumed they have chosen to share together common purposes, knowledge, and skills. The idea of 'peer' review for assessing a professional's work is widely asserted and accepted. How much a professional is involved in actual peer review will, however, vary greatly depending on the work setting.

Peers in the same organization; in other organizations: A professional's relations with fellow professionals in the same agency are often of great significance in the conduct of the professional. They may be mutually supportive and cooperative, or competitive and antagonistic. Working with fellow professionals from other agencies can be easier than where agency employees do not share the same professional background. But just as professional agents can vary on a wide range of characteristics, so too can fellow professionals as people who will affect the conduct of a professional agent.

While each professional is expected to adhere to reasonable standards of professional practice, referral of clients by fellow professionals will reflect assumptions of particular competence. Receiving and providing referrals is a significant aspect of intra-professional conduct.

Peers in association: When professionals join in the work of their professional association, they may be aiming to further the general aims of their profession, or be pushing particular specialist interests, or be focusing on selfish achievement. Those professionals who do not participate in the collective associational life of the profession, may be members of smaller professional collectivities. Professional reputations can be built on more than one basis, and can vary according to the audience - clients, fellow specialists, fellow professional members, other professions, the general public.

Competitive jurisdictions and settlements As emphasized by Abbott, each profession has to win and maintain jurisdiction over its work in competition with other occupations. There are three arenas in which this competition takes place - the workplace, the public arena, and the legislative arena. Various 'settlements' are reached as a result of this competition with a particular occupation having full, partial, or shared jurisdiction. Clearly the conduct of the profession involved is shaped by the particular settlement outcome. It will affect whether these professionals are working in collaboration with workers from other professional and/or technical occupations and the nature of their relationships.

Collaboration between occupations A multi-professional collectivity, by definition, has members of more than one profession working together, apparently for the purposes of the collectivity. It is, of course, both possible and desirable for workers from different organizations and different professions to collaborate when there are shared purposes - around individual cases, policy issues, or community concerns.

Relating to managers As already indicated, a person in a managerial or administrative role can only achieve credibility in a professional collectivity if he or she is respected by the professionals involved, and this usually means not only sharing the values and purposes of the professionals but also their substantive knowledge. To achieve this, management education has become an important specialization within many established professions. An alternative model is for management to develop as a profession in its own right, with its practitioners claiming jurisdiction across all areas of management irrespective of the purposes and substantive knowledge involved. At the very least, general management education and professional organization tend to subdivide between business and public administration. Given the coordination and resource allocation significance of the management role, these different patterns of management education will clearly affect how individual professional agents will relate to the managers of the organizations within which they work.

It is apparent, then, that further important dimensions of a professional agent's conduct relate to fellow workers and their respective purposes, backgrounds, and roles.

Other People Affected

As a fellow citizen and/or fellow human being, a professional agent cannot ignore the moral claims of other people affected by professional conduct. These provide inevitable moral constraints.

Conduct Related to Other Living Creatures and the Physical World

The discussion to this point has concentrated upon people-related aspects of professional conduct. This will include 'environmental' concerns which impact on the current and future well-being of human-beings. But the intentions, methods and effects of professional conduct may also be seen to impact on other living creatures and the earth's physical environment which are concerns in their own right and not only in relation to humans.

The second section of the following figure sketches the main dimensions of conduct which might be carried out by the professional agents sketched in the first section of the figure. Together the two sections constitute a model for the analysis of professional conduct.

Figure 4.1: The Dimensions of Individual and Collective Professional
Conduct

A. **Whose Conduct?**
The Individual Professional Agent
membership status in a profession
educational qualification, practising, association membership,
professional commitment
personal characteristics
age, career stage, gender, ethnicity, education, work
experience, how employed, where employed, social status
(of the profession, of work within the profession),
character and temperament, concurrent work commitments
(to other clients, to work colleagues, to employing agency,
to the profession), concurrent other commitments (to family, to
friendships, to other social groups, to citizenship)
Collective Professional Agents:
Single Profession
profession as a whole
educational profile, practice profile, association
membership, professional commitment
professional association
general governing groups, standing and ad hoc groups
(educational standards and opportunities, employment
conditions and opportunities, social policy action, specialty
practice groups)
professional specialty association
governing and other collectivities
the profession's educators
a general association of educators, a general association of
schools, a professional school (governing structures, groups
for continuing education - postgraduate degrees and other
programs, groups for research programs)
the profession's administrators
in the provision of services, in its educational institutions, in its
professional association/s
the profession's 'practitioners'
agencies, units, departments (ad hoc committees, standing
committees, working groups, teams)

Multiple Professions
collectivities of a mixture of professions
in agency settings, in educational settings, in research settings

Characteristics of a Collective Professional Agent
number and type of professionals, characteristics of the membership, concurrent commitments of the collectivity, structure and process of the collectivity

B. What Conduct?

Descriptive Professional Conduct
action and deliberate inaction
where - workplace, elsewhere
when - working hours, chronology
agent's intentions, methodology, intended and unintended effects

People-Related Conduct
clients
service to individual clients
client characteristics - age, gender, ethnicity, family, education, work experience, social status, income and wealth, character and temperament
service to collective clients - couple, family, group with similar concerns, association, employing organization
purposes and outcome
payment for individual professional service
criteria for payment, determination of payment levels, bearing the financial costs (client, professional, employing agency, government), fringe benefits, contracts of employment (working conditions)
payment for collective professional service
by an employing agency (sources of agency funds - taxes, sales, benefactions, donations, fees), voluntary unpaid work
self
responsibility, reputation, commitment, education, self-awareness, effects on self, intentions re self
collective identity
survival, development, reputation, purpose

employer-related conduct

   contract-specificity, organization's representatives -
   qualifications, restrictions on autonomy, expansion of
   capacity

fellow-workers - categories and characteristics

   cooperation, competition, indifference

   same profession - colleagues, peers

      educational arm (educational professionals, others, relation
      to practitioners), professional peers peer review, same
      organization, other organizations, referral patterns,
      peers in professional association

   other occupations

      competition for jurisdiction - in the workplace, in the public
      arena, in legislative arena   jurisdictional settlements

   collaboration between occupations

   managers

      credibility with professionals, specially educated part of
      profession, profession in their own right (business
      administration, public administration)

other people affected

**Conduct Related to Other Living Creatures and the Physical
World**

   'environmental' concerns

      people-related, in their own right

PART 2: THE ETHICAL JUSTIFICATION OF
PROFESSIONAL CONDUCT

Given that professional conduct is a particularly significant form of human conduct in modern society, what is its ethical justification? The rest of this book engages in a discussion of the kinds of arguments that professions and professionals need to mount and to refute when justifying their conduct in present-day circumstances. The framework for this discussion is provided by the model of ethical conduct built on the notion of rational action for human well-being - with its five interdependent stages and parallel assessment function. To do justice to the topic the discussion must give adequate consideration to concurrent and sequential dimensions of both human well-being and ethical action, and also to both individual and collective dimensions of professional agency.

5 Individual Ethical Agendas and Professionals

As stated earlier (p. 44), perhaps the most crucial task confronting human beings is to define and select from amongst the multitude of possible situations they might respond to those that are morally most significant. If in the justification of human conduct, the value of human well-being is to be genuinely paramount, those situations that are most significant for human well-being and about which something constructive can be done first need to be identified. It will be recalled that the selection and definition of an ethically challenging situation is the first logical stage in ethical action (pp. 43-5). This and the next two chapters discuss what would be on the human agenda if human well-being were the prime ethical value and what role professions and professionals might play in shaping such an agenda.

Professions and professionals obviously are concerned about their own well-being, but they could not in fact make a living unless their specialized knowledge and skills are seen as 'useful' by other human beings. Further, they at least claim to be acting 'in the public interest', however that is interpreted, and many of them use 'service' language. Also they value their autonomy and are likely to be heavily engaged in selecting and defining situations for action which reflect their particular knowledge and values, and their action potential. It is already evident from the writing on the professions that people in professional work roles often play a highly significant part in determining what gets on the human agenda. In brief, then, what are the agenda implications if human well-being is accepted as the prime ethical value, and how do professionals help or hinder the drawing up of this ethical agenda?

Humans interact in a multiplicity of ways, but they associate for a purpose. A feature of modern society is the extent to which humans coordinate their actions in associations deliberately constructed and reconstructed to seek specific goals (Etzioni, 1964: 1-4). By combining ideas, talent and resources, organized collectivities can accomplish what individuals in isolation cannot. In 1986, Charles Perrow claimed it was generally accepted that 'all important social processes either have their origin in formal organizations or are strongly mediated by them'. Within two decades it would be accepted that 'the study of organizations must be at the core of all social science'. (Perrow, 1986: vii.) Already the study of organizations has emerged as a major topic for social scientists, and their work has become a central feature in management education, and in the education of professionals who necessarily work in various organizational contexts.

Among human associations, the state is unique, because it has a comprehensive legal jurisdiction over the people and organizations in its geographic area, and can enforce its will by the use of armed force. No other association has the same degree of power or comprehensiveness of scope, and more often than not its geographic boundaries determine what is called a society, whatever may be the ethnic and other divisions amongst the people living within its boundaries. For its laws to be valid, however, it must operate in accordance with the constitution, and it can only achieve moral legitimacy if its law-making and administration can be justified in moral terms. A democratic government is expected to serve the interests of all the people, and not just those who happen to vote for the political party which won the last election, or those who will keep it in power, or those who make the most noise, or those who articulate their interests best, or those who use the media effectively. The role of professionals in ethical agenda-setting for a democratic government will be the focus of the next chapter.

No matter how concerned governments may be about human well-being, they cannot be its sole agent, for no one monolithic organization can possibly cater for the range and diversity of needs and interests in the population of a modern society. Many other collectivities are also involved - families, for-profit or commercial organizations, and voluntary or non-profit organizations. The role of professionals in ethical agenda-setting for these different types of collectivities will be discussed, in turn, in Chapter 7. The final section of that chapter, and of these three chapters dealing with professionals' involvement in ethical agenda-setting, will be a discussion of ethical agenda-setting for the collectivities of each profession, and in particular, its professional associations and educational bodies. As is evident from the earlier chapters on the idea of professional conduct, if the idea of professionalism is to have any significance, moral or otherwise, it must be associated with an identifiable professional identity, and this can only come when people can and do freely associate around their occupational role.

Freedom of association is a central tenet of a liberal democratic society. It enables people to associate together in a multitude of collectivities, additional to the state, in the pursuit of human ends as rich and varied as the human imagination. Trying to determine what ought to be the relationship between the state and the numerous freely formed and freely maintained associations within its boundaries is a continuous moral challenge (see Benn and Peters, 1959: 235-332).

The present chapter considers professionals' involvement in ethical agendas for individuals. Human well-being does not exist separate from each person living their particular life; other people and collectivities can help or hinder the process, but cannot live a person's life for them. It is understandable in a large complex society to concentrate on ethically justified agendas for collectivities, but a prime concern for human well-being must never lose sight of each person's own responsibility for ethical agenda-setting, not only in relation to their own lives but in relation to other human beings as well.

People with different political philosophies emphasize one or other of the three agenda-setting arenas - 'liberals' emphasize freedom of the individual, social democrats the government, and liberal democrats private collective enterprise, but none denies the existence and validity of the other two. The preamble of the United Nations Universal Declaration of Human Rights insists that 'every individual and every organ of society' shall strive to secure recognition and observance of the rights and freedoms prescribed in the Declaration (United Nations, 1948). Although the United Nations is essentially an inter-governmental body, it is clearly not just talking about a government's responsibility.

We are, then, focusing on the contribution of professionals in identifying and determining ethically challenging situations for each of the main agenda-setting arenas in modern society - individuals, the government, families, commercial organizations, and not-for-profit organizations. The story is complex, but so is modern living - especially if human well-being is accepted as the prime value.

The 'Agenda' Concept

We are all familiar with the idea of having an agenda in the context of a committee meeting. It consists of a list of items or situations which a committee member brings to the attention of the committee for consideration and suitable action. It is a way of organizing the time and attention of the committee. The chairperson is expected to ensure that the item is relevant to the purposes of the committee, that the discussion is relevant to the item, and that the item receives adequate consideration before any decision is taken. At any one meeting, only a limited number of items can be considered. Items necessarily compete for the time and attention of members. Unless someone places an item on the agenda, the situation it relates to will not be addressed by the committee. It is obvious that effective attention to human well-being depends on getting the most relevant situations which impact upon human well-being on the action agenda.

Individual Ethical Agendas and Professionals

Perhaps the most obvious situation that has implications for human well-being is that each person has a life to live, and while others can greatly affect the circumstances of that life the ultimate responsibility rests with the person whose life it is. A commitment to human well-being as the prime ethical value entails a special commitment to one's own well-being because that is the human being you have a continuing responsibility for throughout the years of your life, and are in a unique, but not exclusive, position to do something about. A commitment to human well-being also entails doing what you can to improve the lot of the human species. This usually means being able to take at least some constructive action in relation to those close to you in time, culture and social circumstance. The personal attributes, and the time and social location of any one person will place constraints on what can realistically be placed on that individual's ethical agenda.

As a person moves through the different age stages, and their circumstances change, so too will the items on their agenda. For instance, different items will come into prominence, as a person moves from primary, to secondary and to other modes of education, as they gain employment and change jobs, as they start voting, as they make a home of their own, with or without other people, as they enter into relationships of various kinds, including a marital or other intimate long-term relationship, as they procreate and bring up children, as they join associations of one kind or another, as they shift location, as their children leave home, as they retire from work, as they decide how to spend the rest of their days. People may deal with these sorts of situations in a very pragmatic fashion not giving careful thought to the claims and interests of all the people involved. Even when an individual is more ethically careful and systematic at one of life's review points, rarely will the main items on the person's life agenda be formally recorded. A few who keep diaries or take seriously the making of new year resolutions may commit their revised individual agenda to paper, but this is rare. When professionals are involved, they will generally keep records for their own use, but these will concentrate on the professional intervention, not on the life agenda of clients, although this may receive passing reference.

An individual's agenda becomes and remains ethically justified to the extent that it is focused on human well-being. Such a focus would seem to require that the individual develop his or her capacities to the full and to use these capacities to pursue values which enhance human living, both for themselves and for others. There seems to be no room on an ethical individual agenda for an exclusive focus on the well-being of self or of selected others, and harm to self and/or others has no place unless counter-balanced by human benefits.

Professionals, like everyone else, are individuals with life agendas. For them, their work is typically an important item on their individual agendas, but how ethically justified is it? Certainly the essential intellectual component combined with the degree of autonomy associated with professional work can give it inherent interest to its practitioners, it can provide clear and well-rewarded career paths, it can provide a sense of community and shared purpose amongst its practitioners, and its human service component can give it ethical purpose. However, as some of the more recent writing on the professions has suggested (see Chapter 3), this is often more of an ideal type of professional conduct rather than a universal reality.

Many circumstances can place in jeopardy professional work being included on an individual's ethical agenda. The professional may not be able to keep abreast of relevant professional developments; the professional may not be confident about the profession's technology; the professional may be unjustifiably paternalistic; the professional may have no say on how knowledge will be used by powerful clients; the professional may only serve already privileged groups; the professional may be inundated by clients; the professional's health and family life may be undermined by the pressures of work; the professional may be more interested in making money than providing a professional service where it is most needed; the professional may disagree with the agendas and main policies of the professional association/s and/or the professional schools, but be powerless to change them; the professional may prefer to work in another profession but cannot afford to change; and so on. In the present generation, there is no longer an easy acceptance that a commitment to professionalism is beneficial to both the community and the professionals themselves.

Professionals who disregard other interests and responsibilities, on account of their work, may be able to give ethical justification for their individual agenda if the outcome is a notable contribution to human well-being. There can, however, be a price to pay in the narrowness of their interests and understanding outside their particular field of expertise, and the neglect of those close to them, including themselves. All professionals are lay people when receiving the services of other professions. Professionals can become acutely aware of the limitations of the various forms of professionalism when they, or the members of their family, are receiving a professional 'service' in relation to some aspect of their life, but they may be poorly equipped to deal with them because of the dominance of their own professional work in their life and thinking.

Only empirical study would indicate the extent to which professionals influence other people's individual agendas and whether this is in the ethically justified direction of enhancing human well-being. Professionals working in a society's educational system, particularly in its primary and secondary schools, impart values and provide role models as well as knowledge, which will affect what pupils value and their ideas about their futures. In recent years explicit moral education has become a conscious aim, but there is still considerable concern that it can become indoctrination, rather than helping young people to cope in a reasoned way with the inevitable value choices which every human being must make.

Schools sponsored by organized religion, and run and taught by education professionals, have the daunting task of preparing their pupils not only for this life, but for 'life in the world to come'. However successful they may be in their first objective - and many are amongst the best in Australia at least in terms of academic results - religious faith may, in fact, be no stronger amongst those who attended church schools than amongst those who attended purely secular schools.

Religious doctrine may assert that there is 'life after death', but if the concept is taken literally it is an obvious contradiction. Death means the cessation of life. What form any continuing existence of a person can take after their body, including their brain, has ceased to function is difficult for most modern minds to comprehend. The person's ideas and historical actions may continue to influence people. Loved ones are often described as 'living on in our hearts and minds'. But this way of talking cannot obscure the reality of their actual biological death or that they no longer are a source of moral consideration in the actions of the currently living.

Ideas that a human should live this life in preparation for a life or lives to come have been associated with various religious doctrines, and they make obvious complications for having any clarity in a concept like human well-being, because it is not at all clear what the entity is that persists beyond biological death and how notions of well-being can therefore be associated with it. It is literally a mystery, something beyond human reason. It is expected to be accepted as a matter of faith on the basis of divine revelation in historically located religious texts, and subsequent writing if this is seen as suitably inspired. Religious doctrines may make claims covering personal salvation, in this world and/or the next, or in later lives. They may cover a 'chosen people', or all people. They may concentrate on relations with a single god or many gods, or on relations between people, or between people and the rest of creation. Ideas of human well-being are greatly involved in such doctrines, especially since the very concept of religion has binding and grounding implications for the humans involved.

Although the modern world is increasingly secular, religious doctrine continues to be propagated, especially by professional clergy of one kind or another. Some faiths are more actively proselytizing than others, but all believe they in some sense know a transcendental reality which humans ignore at their peril. Fundamentalist faiths leave no room for doubt or choice, and are immune to intellectual challenge from outside or within. Other faiths are more open to challenge and change. Historically, religious doctrine has been used to justify human conduct that has apparently had disastrous effects on human well-being - religious wars fought with particular ferocity, denial of scientifically-established knowledge, differential advantage to believers over non-believers, discrimination against specific categories of people such as women, homosexuals, lower castes, and those possessed by the devil. There are, of course, counter examples, where religious doctrine is cited as the basis for real achievement of human welfare, and especially of 'spiritual' welfare. Indeed, some argue that a genuine commitment to ethics can only come from religious faith, and if faith is eroded so too must be ethical behaviour. On this view, standards of ethical behaviour are determined by God, not by human argument and decision. The obvious problem with this, however, is how do we establish that a particular standard is God-given. Religious traditions often conflict, and there is the further issue of something being ethically right because of the persuasiveness of the supporting arguments, not the authority of the source of the arguments - even when that source is seen to be divine. A prime ethical commitment to human well-being tends to be dismissed as mere humanism, but logically is not a concern for the salvation of every individual a form of humanism?

The role of religious professionals in the modern world in trying to define each individual's agenda is obviously highly contentious, and an ongoing source of basic moral disagreement. Religious traditions have, perhaps inevitably, relied on professionals, people who have spent their working lives in the vocation of their particular religious ministry. These people, in interaction with each other and their congregations, and in competition with professionals of different religious persuasion, sustain and shape their particular tradition. The concept of a Christian church is intended to cover all believers, but it is significant that the term is often used to refer just to the professionals in it. The religious professionals, however, ignore the laity at their peril, especially as the laity become better educated and questioning about religious traditions.

It is apparent that in Anglo-American modern society, there is not a single religious ministry. Each religious tradition has its own characteristic organization with a professional ministry usually being an integral part. How much the professionals control the organized structure will vary, according to the part played by the laity. The religious professionals typically are trained in the theological training institutions of that religious tradition, and subsequently pursue a professional career within that tradition. If they are not more broadly educated, for example by a university liberal education, they are unlikely to achieve wide-spread credibility. Some religious professionals do undertake additional general education, and/or education in another specialized professional field such as social work, teaching or psychological counselling. This can give them and their religious tradition continuing credibility in the eyes of the public, but can raise questions of ambiguity of role when a person seems to be straddling two or more professions.

This brief discussion of the role of religious professionals in influencing the human agenda arose from a consideration of the idea of life after death. It seems from what has been said that religious faith can greatly affect what gets on the agenda at least of the faithful. Any serious consideration of ethical conduct in the contemporary world cannot ignore religious faith because of its effects on the lives of the religious adherents but also because their behaviour affects the lives of others.

As has been indicated, educational and religious professionals may be especially influential in individual agenda-setting. This is because of their strategic initial position in the socialization process, and because both claim a concern for the general well-being of their students and congregations, and not just concern with particular bits of learning, or particular aspects of a person's life. Educationalists talk about 'educating the whole person', and clergymen talk of their total concern for each person's 'mind, body and soul'. How much these declared concerns assist in the production of coherent individual ethical agendas will vary greatly, as will the agendas themselves.

In many instances, the declared concerns can be no more than empty rhetoric, because the professional concerned in reality does not have the same continuity of responsibility, or breadth of concern as the individual whose life it is, or significant others like parents and friends. The balance of influences over individual agenda-setting will change as the person moves through the life cycle. Each influence needs to be assessed in terms of the extent of its effects on an individual's agenda, and how those effects relate to human well-being.

Additional to teachers and clergy, other professionals also proclaim a concern for 'the total person', and therefore cannot avoid issues relating to individual agenda-setting. Amongst the so-called 'helping professions', social work's commitment to social well-being (see p. 147), and its traditional emphasis on 'client-determination' can lead to more ethically-justified individual agendas. However, the profession's weaknesses and limitations (see pp. 145-7) have restricted its ethical influence on individual agenda-setting.

It is evident that the various parts of the medical profession vary greatly in the extent to which they influence individual agenda-setting. In societies like Britain and Australia, where government national health systems make medical services generally available, almost all members of the society provide doctors with fairly regular access to aspects of their personal lives. They seek the help of doctors when they are worried by symptoms which may signify disease or illness, and accept a doctor's functional need to inquire into a patient's habits, lifestyle and values, to the extent that these are seen as relevant to the doctor's diagnosis, treatment and prognosis. The main focus is, however, on an episode of illness and restoration of health, and as will be discussed (see p. 153), maintenance of an individual's health is only one item on any individual's ethical agenda. An ethically sensitive doctor will not only help an individual to regain his or her health as effectively and efficiently as possible, but will do this with due regard to the individual's life agenda as determined by that individual. Doctors can help people to understand the health implications of various activities to the extent that doctors know them, but their medical knowledge does not entitle them to prescribe what should be the life agendas of particular individuals. Compared with their specialist medical colleagues, general practitioners may have a broader scope and greater continuity of medical concern, but in the modern world they in fact know relatively little about many of the dimensions of human well-being in a modern society, and so are not well-placed to help individuals develop ethical agendas. If they attempt to do so, they can be accused of going well beyond their professional mandate based on specialized knowledge, and also of using their social prestige and influence to impose their values on others who are often vulnerable because of illness.

Given the continuing bias of modern medicine in favor of individuals with acute illness (see pp. 156-7), and the brevity and superficiality of most medical consultations, it would be hard to argue that medical professionals play a significant role in persuading individuals to include even health maintenance and disease prevention on their ethical agendas, despite the inclusion of public health and community medicine in their training. A 1980s Australian study of 'alternative' health practitioners found that they spent more time with their patients, were more prepared to listen, and showed more interest in the person's broad life situation, rather than purely physical problems. Users were impressed with the focus on prevention and the apparent treatment of cause rather than symptoms. (See Palmer and Short, 1989: pp. 156-7.)

When professionals of various kinds express concern for 'the whole person' there seems to be some recognition that each person's individual agenda has many items and they all contribute to the person's sense of identity, integrity and purpose. Psychological counselling provided by psychologists, psychiatrists, or social workers, may concentrate on certain troublesome aspects of a person's emotional and mental life. Dealing with these may enable people to engage more confidently in individual agenda-setting, but this will only be an ethical agenda if they give primacy to the value of human well-being.

In a modern society, professionals of all kinds tend to be influential in individual agenda-setting, because typically they claim special knowledge about what can and cannot be achieved in important functional areas. Indeed, professionals make their living from persuading people in the population that the concerns which they address are significant for some aspect of human well-being and that they are specially educated and trained to deal with it. Individual agendas can become cluttered with concerns stimulated by the different professional groups. The concerns may be ad hoc, spasmodic, or continuous, and may be central or peripheral to human well-being. The more educated a society becomes, the more individual agendas will be influenced by professionals, both because professionals make people aware of 'problems' and because people become aware that they can achieve some control over their destinies, even if this often means seeking well-informed professional help.

Only empirical study, together with agreement on what constitutes human well-being, will reveal the extent to which any one person's agenda is influenced by professionals and whether this is in ethically desirable directions. Professional influence is likely to be morally negative on an individual's agenda-setting: when a professional places undue emphasis on the attainment of values important to the professional but not so much to the client, when the professional undermines the person's sense of autonomy, when the cost of the professional's services absorbs a great deal of the person's financial resources, when the professional pays no regard to the moral claims of non-clients, when a person's life is greatly disrupted by the professional's technology, and when the side effects are serious and disregarded by the professional. Conversely, professional influence on individual agenda-setting is likely to be morally positive: when the professional ensures that the client's values are respected in the help provided, when the professional respects the autonomy of the client but at the same time is enabling him or her to make more effective and efficient choices, when the professional provides a service that is within financial reach of those who can benefit from the service, when the professional insists that a client pay due regard to the rights of others, and when the professional informs the client about the likely effects of the professional technology on the life of the client and associated others.

Compared to individuals in traditional societies, individuals in modern, democratic, industrial societies have been seen to be much freer to determine their own destinies, particularly if they take advantage of educational opportunities not previously available. However, the 'fear of freedom' can give rise to new dependencies, such as occur in fascist political regimes under dictatorships (Fromm, 1942), and the patterns of opportunity and individual initiative can still vary considerably along social class, gender, ethnic, and geographic lines.

There is no question of the heightened sense of individuality in modern society. Yet awareness of, and responsibility for, one's own life agenda can be difficult, if not unbearable, in modern circumstances - when the individual is faced with a hostile social environment, when significant others are indifferent to the individual, when the individual is merely a means to the ends of others, when personal and/or social resources are inadequate for the tasks to be done, when social roles are being undermined by rapid social change, and when it seems that an individual living in a mass society is helpless to change the collective anticipated future for human beings.

Unless a biological condition clearly makes it impossible for a person to be responsible for their behaviour, like it or not, each human individual is held responsible for their conduct. (The word 'conduct' is typically used to signify behaviour for which a person can be held responsible, or accountable.) Individuals may escape agenda-setting for their own life by ending it through suicide, a distressingly common option taken by young people in Australian society. Or they may merely adopt uncritically roles expected of them by their families, or the wider community, without being able to provide ethical justification for their validity, often feeling detached and emotionally and intellectually unengaged in how they are spending (or 'expending') their life. Or they may just drift throughout life, staying clear of any lasting commitments, living merely for the present and its bodily gratifications, and possibly devaluing attempts to draw up and pursue life agendas and strategies, seeing them as naive and misguided.

A society is in good ethical shape when its members have ethical individual agendas which genuinely give point and meaning to their actions and projects, and therefore their lives. From what has been said, such agendas cannot be the prime and direct responsibility of any outside authority - parental, educational, governmental, or professional - no matter how well-intended. Authorities of one kind or another, backed by power, status, and/or special knowledge, can greatly influence individual agendas, telling people what they can, must, or ought to do, but only decision and commitment on the part of the individual concerned, based on reasons relating to human well-being, will constitute an ethical individual agenda for that person. Again, it must be emphasized that, while an individual agenda must not ignore the individual's long-term responsibility for self, it will also reflect concern for the well-being of other human beings not just as means to the individual's own ends, but as ends in themselves.

6 An Ethical Agenda for Government: the Role of Professionals

A democratic system of government which is said to be 'of the people, by the people, and for the people' (President Lincoln's Gettysburg address, 1863), makes strong claims to moral legitimacy if human well-being is the prime moral value. People, not things or institutions, are its prime concern. 'For the people' means in the interests of everyone, and not just in the interests of people who are rich, powerful, or vocal. 'Of the people' means everyone comes within its jurisdiction; none can escape except by migrating to another government's jurisdiction or becoming stateless. 'By the people' means, in modern society, all (adult) people are expected to share responsibility for controlling their government by periodically electing representatives to govern on their behalf, and by engaging in critical discussion of government action.

The development and maintenance of democratic systems of government in nation-states has been a major historically recent achievement for those committed to human well-being as the prime ethical value. Making such a system work is perhaps the most obvious and important ethical challenge for each generation - because of the power and influence of modern government, and because of the effects on human well-being of alternative systems of government. And it does not stop there, since people and their states must also take responsibility internationally as well as nationally.

Reformers and sometimes revolutionaries in earlier generations have contributed to the development of a democratic system of government. In many countries, however, democratic government has still not been achieved. Even where it exists, it can be eroded when the interests of minorities are consistently ignored, vested interests become too powerful, citizens become apathetic, government functionaries lose their credibility, and so on. More dramatically, democratic government can also be threatened by army take-overs and external invasion.

This chapter concentrates on the part played by various professionals, and people in occupations with ambiguous professional standing, in agenda-setting by a democratic government. It is a topic central to both the ethical justification of professional conduct and of government itself.

Government's Concern for the General Welfare

National governments, at least in democratic societies, are supposed to be concerned with 'the general welfare' or the 'commonweal'. Each department of state justifies its activities as a contribution to 'the general welfare', because effective pursuit of its purposes is said to be vital to the well-being of its society. Often functional language is used to make the point. The purposes, or 'functions', are based on cultural values, that is, commonly held values which give point and purpose to the activities of people living together in the same society. These will include education, income security, health, housing, legal justice, productive employment, national and personal security, mobility, sport and recreation, trade, and good external relations.

Departmental Agendas

The agenda of each department is determined by both its ongoing statutory and customary obligations, and the political agenda of the currently elected government. Depending on the prevailing political philosophy, the particular cultural values at stake, and the local history, a government department may monopolize the function, or play a much smaller role amongst the various value-attainment mechanisms operating in that society.

In the Westminster parliamentary system, the department is headed by a minister who is a politician of the political party with a majority of seats in the parliament, and by a senior bureaucrat who is formally responsible to the politician for the work of the department. Increasingly the senior bureaucrat is also a political appointee. Also ministers now have their own personal staff. The British television series 'Yes Minister' portrays in amusing fashion various processes which might operate at the senior levels of a government department - empire-building, interdepartmental rivalry, ministerial manipulation by a department, personal political ambition, crisis management, electoral considerations, coping with pressure groups, handling the media, and so on.

The agenda of a government department is periodically reviewed at budget time, when the minister and/or administrative head changes, and when the government changes. Occasionally the focus of its work may change as a result of a general public service review, or an outside or inside specific review of some aspect of its work.

To what extent are professionals of one kind or another caught up in all these processes of government which influence what gets onto the agenda of government?

The justification of having an elected citizen, the minister, to head a government department, is so that the work of the department can be politically accountable to the parliament and the elected government. The departmental experts are supposedly 'on tap not on top'. The minister has the role of interpreting and defending departmental action in the parliament, in the party room, and in the public arena.

Any adult citizen can become a politician by winning an election to the legislative body of their state. Although it is not widely recognized as such, politics is an important modern professional occupation, with a potential breadth of concern about human well-being which is unmatched by any other occupation. Politicians, in the platforms and programs of their political parties, set out a broad agenda which they claim will benefit the people generally. When elected, they claim to represent the interests of all their constituency and not just of those who voted for them. Depending on the voting system, single issue candidates may be successful at an election, but an elected politician is expected to consider and vote on a broad spectrum of issues.

Politics as a Profession

Increasingly politics offers a life-long profession to elected members of the main political parties. Certainly they make a living as a politician, and many pursue typical career paths. They do not have to acquire formal educational credentials to become or remain politicians, but many now have tertiary educational qualifications - in law, and other professional fields, and many acquire considerable knowledge on the job about particular substantive issues, the political process, and the structure of society and government.

Politicians do not have a professional association as such, but they depend heavily on their membership of a political party, with its shared ideology and traditions and its particular organization, to draw up an electorally viable political agenda, to give them endorsement as a candidate for election, and to give them access to a role in government. In addition to the professional politicians each major party now relies heavily on party managers, who are professional in outlook. They do it for a living; they have relevant special knowledge; and they aim to help the party win and attain office assumedly because they believe this would be for 'the good of the country'. In drawing up their electoral platforms, political parties now call on advice from a variety of sympathetic professionals whose expertise collectively may cover most aspects of government. An incumbent political party is better placed to receive such advice from departmental professional sources, than an opposition party.

The Profession of Public Administration

Senior government bureaucrats often contrast their 'professionalism' with the 'amateurism' of politicians, including the political head of their particular department. In what sense are senior bureaucrats professionals? Do they see themselves as members of the profession of public administration, and/or members of different professions working in the public service, or not members of any particular profession? They may belong to a public administration association which discusses matters of common concern, they may read and contribute to a public administration journal, many may be described as 'career public servants', and their career is usually significantly shaped by their education and training. How their particular form of professionalism affects departmental and political agenda-setting can only be discovered by empirical study.

The Prevalence of Economic Rationalism

In the mid-1980s, Michael Pusey discovered patterns amongst the Australian government's senior public servants which had important implications for their agenda-setting roles. A disproportionate number came from privileged social backgrounds, and the more privileged the background, the more individualistic and 'anti-social' they tended to be. Fifty four per cent had qualifications in economics and business, and this directly influenced their views about the role of the state. The top public servants were, in fact, more conservative in their political views than they believed they were. (Pusey, 1991: 59, 74.)

In his survey, Pusey identified three main groups of government departments - the central (or coordinating) agencies, the market-oriented departments, and the program and service departments. The executive staff in the central agency group were the youngest, they were from the most privileged social backgrounds, and about 70 per cent had a business-oriented education in economics, accounting or business administration. By contrast, the executive staff in the program and service departments were the oldest group, and were twice as likely to have a university education in the social sciences, humanities or the law. The staff in the market-oriented departments had older staff than the central departments, but also had about 70 per cent with economic/business qualifications, and more with qualifications in the 'hard' (natural) sciences. Pusey found these various characteristics were reflected in strongly patterned differences in basic orientation to public policy. (Pusey, 1991: 76-8.)

The aggressive economic rationalism of the central agencies had 'no historical memory' and it was 'quickly burying the interventionist state of the market-oriented departments', in order to get the economy working on sound economic principles. The senior staff of the program and service departments tended to be demoralized and on the defensive, with the perceived legitimacy of their welfare state programs badly undermined. The central agency departments were perceived as 'setting the agenda and terms of argument'. What was prevailing was not practical rationality, but a very concentrated formal rationality which entailed 'a narrowly reductive view of the economy, politics and society'. (Pusey, 1991: 107-9.) The top public bureaucrats surveyed by Pusey saw economic problems as the main problems facing Australia. They held a 'systematic' economic framework, but not a coherent social or political one. According to Pusey, 'the economy' was certainly hardly ever seen as a subordinate part of Australian society conceived in some coherent way *as a society*. (Pusey, 1991: 43-4.)

Pusey noted that 'positivist' economics had become the most commonly shared educational experience of both ministers and top bureaucrats which gave them a similar understanding of their common mission as system managers and 'strategic missionaries' (Pusey, 1991: 189-90).

The most striking example of an economic rationalist trying to set the overall agenda for the Australian national government occurred in the early 1990s. A professional economist and former economics professor, John Hewson, as Leader of the Opposition lost the 'unloseable' national election of

1993, with a political program focused on tax reform. He subsequently conceded that he was not a professional politician and that his focus had been too narrow, not giving sufficient attention to social concerns.

Limitations of Economic Theory

How the assumptions, abstractions, model-building, and mathematical character of economic reasoning relate to human well-being is a complicated question, to be tackled at both theoretical and practical levels. Fruitful cross-disciplinary cooperation around theory is not at all common. Economists themselves are in a state of intellectual ferment concerning basic questions of macroeconomic management. (Bliss, 1987: 54-5.)

What seems to have given economists recent access to such a wide range of human enterprise is their concern for the value of 'efficiency', and their focus on exchange values measured in money terms. It seems reasonable to use resources in the most 'economical' fashion in achieving one's goals, especially when resources are in scarce supply or will become so in the future. Economists' models supposedly contribute to human well-being by helping individuals, organizations, and societies explore the implications of different simplified but still realistic assumptions (Bliss, 1987: 51), and this can help them think more clearly about their use of scarce resources. But deciding what and whose ends are to be pursued should be matters for social and political decision, and without detailed substantive knowledge necessary for effective action in the many specialized areas of human enterprise, economists cannot know what should be on the action agenda. 'Efficiency' is in fact a meaningless concept divorced from a notion of effectiveness, and effectiveness in turn only makes sense in terms of the values being pursued.

Buying and selling in a market is the typical focus for the economist. Economists have influenced thinking about the production and distribution of goods through market exchanges, and have emphasized the utility of markets in achieving human wants and desires. Much of the political pressure to 'privatize' government activities has, in fact, come from economists and those influenced by their thinking. The most frequent complaints against economists as general agenda setters is that they neglect equity issues, their production models and measures concentrate on money measures, they ignore the interests of others not directly involved in market transactions, and they do not make explicit the social and political values they are often actually prescribing. If government is genuinely concerned about human well-being, it seems odd that this particular discipline has achieved such a prominent place in recent government agenda setting, both at political and bureaucratic levels. The Australian story has its parallels in the Reagan government of the United States, and in the British Thatcher government, at least partly because economics is now an international discipline heavily influenced by American writing (Bliss, 1987: 55).

Economics a Profession?

It is not obvious that economics is a profession, and that economists are professionals. Certainly economics is a discipline in the sense that it is a distinctive branch of learning and dialogue recognized by institutions of education and research (Bailey, 1980: 24), and economists belong to their own learned associations. Generally, however, economists do not have well-developed arrangements for their own occupational control such as accreditation of courses and codes of ethics. There is the further issue that many who set the agenda of government may draw heavily on economists' thinking, without identifying themselves as economists. They may have some other occupational identification/s which may or may not be professional in character.

The Contribution of Sociologists

This discussion is at present focused on the involvement of professionals in government agenda-setting and whether this is beneficial for human well-being. Another significant modern discipline with ambiguous status as a profession is sociology. With their focus on social relationships and social arrangements within something called 'a society', it might be expected that sociologists would have an important contribution to make in helping government to set an agenda genuinely focused on human well-being. Modern sociology had two sources, the empirical study of social problems and theoretical understanding of replacement of small traditional community with impersonal modern society. (Kent, 1981; Shils, 1987: 227.) Sociologists have mainly sought to improve society by making known to the decision-makers existing social conditions as revealed by objective study. What social structures they study and how they study them are still influenced by their personal and group values. Perhaps no other subject is more likely to be riven with controversy because of the extent to which this is the case.

After a period of institutional growth in the 1960s and early 1970s, sociology appears to have lost ground in achieving perceived legitimacy. In 1980, a British writer, Joe Bailey, described the paradox of sociology being taught to increasing numbers of people, yet the discipline suffered internal schism and external hostility. Sociologists were not strongly organized on professional lines, but many professions such as social work and planning used the knowledge provided by sociologists and thus depended upon sociology's 'theoretical propriety'. Bailey argued that the pluralism of sociology should be guided by a return to a concern for intervention to reduce human misery, promote happiness and in some way deal with the problems of men and women. Too much of its institutional existence in universities appeared 'self-indulgent and inwardlooking'. (Bailey, 1980: 1-2, 32-3.)

In 1986, Peter Berger observed that contemporary sociology was dominated by 'two equally depressing factions, the narrow positivists grinding out masses of mostly trivial data and the ideologues propagating various more or less odious political agendas'. It could be argued that sociology had always been more of a perspective than a field. Sociological consciousness as originally understood had liberating qualities for all modern thought. [He could have cited Berger and Luckmann's *The Social Construction of Reality* (1966) as a case in point.] Berger admitted that he himself had become very much alienated from the ongoing life of sociology as an organized discipline, and he had worked mainly with people from other fields. (Berger, 1986: 234-5.)

The Influence of Lawyers

It is scarcely surprising that those who have specialized in the study of laws, legal procedures, and legal systems - lawyers - play a significant role in modern government. They monopolize the judiciary, and control the attorney-general's department; and play an increasingly important role in all departments of state. They are also prominent in legislative bodies and in positions of political leadership. British Prime Ministers Thatcher and Lloyd George were lawyers; so too were US Presidents Woodrow Wilson, Calvin Coolidge, Franklin Roosevelt, Richard Nixon, and Bill Clinton; and Australian Prime Ministers Robert Menzies, Harold Holt, William McMahon, Gough Whitlam, and Bob Hawke (see Sexton and Maher, 1982: 138, 142-3). Lawyers have dominated American politics to a degree unequalled in any other country, constituting at times more than three quarters of the Senate, and usually more than half the Congress. Richard Abel observes that lawyers have lost political influence in other countries following the rise of labour parties and the emergence of technocrats with more seemingly useful expertise. The US has no labour party, and its lawyers have retained influence by acquiring competence in economic analysis. (Abel, 1989: 175.) Almost all those convicted of criminal charges in the Watergate scandal of the mid-1970s were lawyers, mostly members of the President's personal staff (Sexton and Maher, 1982: 142-3).

Limitations of Lawyers

Only careful empirical study will reveal the extent to which legal education and legal practice affect the way in which lawyers in public office influence government agenda-setting. Their political or bureaucratic role and other influences may affect their behaviour more than their legal background, but the latter can have a very limiting impact. It can result in thinking that it is possible to resolve questions without reference to overriding goals and values and therefore their thinking is short-term and reactive (Sexton and Maher, 1982: 154). Understandably lawyers in politics tend to emphasize stability and the status quo.

In recent years, most countries of the Commonwealth of Nations have established law reforming agencies, following the United Kingdom's lead in 1965. Lawyers are typically in control of these reform commissions, and their very name implies the intention to improve or change for the better laws and the legal system - presumably in terms of human well-being. The agenda of the Australian Law Reform Commission is provided by the Federal Attorney-General, on the assumption that elected politicians will know social priorities better than non-elected lawyers and resultant reports are then more likely to get onto Parliament's own agenda for action by the government of the day. (Kirby, 1983: 7, 51, 54-5.)

Michael Kirby, first chairman of the Australian Law Reform Commission, acknowledged that it was rare for any law reform body in Australia, or elsewhere, to canvass at length the fundamental values that have led its members to a particular conclusion. Commissioners were 'lawyers brought up in the pragmatic legal tradition of solving the day's problems and working towards any higher principle by aggregation of decisions in particular cases.' (Kirby, 1983: 22.) 'Typically, they have not the time nor inclination nor the training to ruminate upon basic values that may be motivating their ultimate decision'. Yet, Kirby argued, coherent lasting and pervasive reform depended upon more attention being paid to fundamental values such as the proper limits of the law and legal intervention, the fundamental rights of man, and the basic objectives of legislation. (Kirby, 1983: 24.)

Questions of Justice

A commitment to the prime value of human well-being will entail putting on the ethical agenda questions about the distribution of harms and benefits between people where this can be constructively changed, and questions about punishment and compensation and retribution when one harms another. These are questions of justice - distributive, compensatory, and retributive. In what sense is 'justice' a basic value? The word comes from 'jus' meaning 'right', and 'justice' can mean conduct which is morally justified, that is, made right by relevant supporting argument in which the interests of all the persons involved are duly considered and weighed. Here it refers to a procedure. Moral justice entails this procedure, but even when this procedure is followed genuine moral disagreement may result because there is no consensus on justificatory needs and desert criteria and/or what weight to give to them. It is not surprising that much of the political process consists of argument about these matters, for all government intervention has distributional consequences, intended or not. If any person, group, nation, or generation has more than its fair share of harms or benefits this is reason enough to get their situation on the ethical agenda, not only of government but of all the relevant institutions.

Social Workers' Commitment to Social Justice

The 'International Declaration of Ethical Principles of Social Work' adopted at the General Meeting of the International Federation of Social Workers in 1994, reaffirmed the commitment of the social work profession to social justice. Eight of the twelve principles are related to the concept:

   - Every human being has a unique value, which justifies moral consideration of that person.
   - Each individual has a right to self-fulfillment to the extent that it does not encroach upon the same right of others, and has an obligation to contribute to the well-being of society.
   - Each society, regardless of its form, should function to provide the maximum benefits for all of its members.

- Social workers have a commitment to principles of social justice.
- Social workers are expected to provide the best possible assistance to anybody seeking their help and advice, without unfair discrimination on the basis of gender, age, disability, color, social class, race, religion, language, political beliefs, or sexual orientation.
- Social workers are expected to work in full collaboration with their clients, working for the best interests of the clients but paying due regard to the interests of others involved. Clients are encouraged to participate as much as possible, and should be informed of the risks and likely benefits of proposed courses of action.
- Social workers generally expect clients to take responsibility, in collaboration with them, for determining courses of action affecting their lives. Compulsion which might be necessary to solve one party's problems at the expense of the interests of others involved should only take place after careful explicit evaluation of the claims of the conflicting parties. Social workers should minimize the use of legal compulsion.
- Social work is inconsistent with the direct or indirect support of individuals, groups, political forces or power-structures suppressing their fellow human beings by employing terrorism, torture or similar means.

According to their code of ethics, American social workers have a responsibility to promote the general welfare through elimination of various forms of unfair discrimination; through ensuring access to resources, services and opportunities for all, with special regard for people who are disadvantaged or oppressed; through respect for cultural diversity; through advocacy of changes in policy and legislation to improve social conditions and promote social justice; and the encouragement of informed public participation in shaping social policies and institutions (Wells, 1986: 160-1).

Limitations of Social Work

Whatever its declared values and aspirations, the social work profession has not been prominent in influencing the agenda of government, even in its specifically 'social welfare' areas. It is true that Clement Attlee the Prime Minister of the social reform British government after the Second World War had a social work background, and so too did Harry Hopkins, a key adviser to President Roosevelt during the New Deal period. Wilbur Cohen headed the US Department of Health Education and Welfare in the 1960s, and Mitchell Ginsberg and James Dumpson headed the Social Welfare Department of New York City, one of the world's toughest bureaucratic assignments. Prime Minister Gough Whitlam who headed a social reform Australian government 1972-75, was married to a social worker! The head of the ill-fated Australian

Social Welfare Commission (see Coleman, 1976) was a social worker, and occasionally in Australia, state community welfare departments have been headed by social workers.

The most remarkable example of social work influence on a government's agenda occurred in Britain with the establishment of local authority Social Services Departments in 1970, arising from the Seebohm Report in 1968. It was especially remarkable because it reflected more the idea of a united, coordinated, broadly educated profession, than any reality. Although the Act had medical and other powerful opposition, social workers united in successfully lobbying for it. (Hall, 1976.)

The new local authority department was expected to provide 'a community based and family oriented service', available to all. It would 'enable the greatest possible number to act reciprocally, giving and receiving service for the well-being of the whole community'. (Seebohm Report, 1968: 11.) In the event, the reorganized service remained crisis-oriented. It also led to continuing debate on the place of the generalist and specialist education and skills in a social work service, and of the social worker's role in society. Should social workers concentrate on helping individuals and families to adjust to their situation, or should they concentrate on trying to change their situation through effective social action? (Hall, 1976: 128-9.)

Given its declared commitment to social justice, the social work profession wherever it is operating might be expected to place major emphasis on trying to achieve morally justified social arrangements. It has become particularly sensitive to the accusation that too often social workers have just helped people to adapt to an unjust society. The profession's impact on government agenda-setting has, however, been limited by many factors which will vary to some extent in different countries and at different times within the same country - for example, the continuing preponderance of work at the individual and family level, the employed status of most social workers which can produce divided loyalties, the shift away from a focus on social disadvantage when social workers move into private practice, the still relatively small numbers compared with the longer-established professions, the slowness to move into administrative and policy-making positions and a general reluctance to engage in what is described as 'indirect' practice, relatively weak research traditions, the profession's association with low-status clients, the difficulty of developing cumulative social work theory especially at the more macro levels of social relationships, the sometimes sharp differences of emphasis and ideology between those intervening at the individual and family level and those intervening at group, organizational, community, and societal levels, the breadth of the profession's social concerns, the lack of a long-term career commitment of many who qualify to practise social work, the limited collective resources for lobbying government, and the relative absence of social workers in political careers.

The continuing preponderance of women in the social work profession is obviously linked with many of these factors which have restricted the profession's impact on government agenda-setting. However, as women increasingly make a commitment to a long-term professional career, and take advantage of a full range of professional opportunities, a continuing preponderance of women could well give this profession new political opportunities for agenda-setting. Certainly it is particularly well placed to select and identify situations which have significant implications for human well-being and about which something constructive can be done by government. Of all the so-called 'helping' professions, social work has the broadest ethical frame of reference, in that it has a general commitment to social well-being, that is, the well-being of people living in a society governed by principles of social justice.

Lawyers' Justice

But at present it is the legal profession, not social work, that tends to be associated with the basic value of 'justice'. Arthur Seldon comments: 'No single section of society in Britain has been so successful as propagandists as the legal profession in representing themselves as specialists in 'justice''. The laity is led to believe that they administer justice, not the law, an impression reinforced by the names given to the various courts and their officers. (Seldon, 1987: 13.) Seldon insists that law and justice are two entirely different concepts, but are confused by governments and lawyers trying to give legitimacy to the laws they make and administer (Seldon, 1987: 7). Legality and morality are obviously related concepts in a democratic society, but all law is not morally justified, nor are all moral rules legal rules (see Benn and Peters, 1959: 59-62). Lawyers as such have special expertise in relation to legal systems and questions of legal validity (Benn and Peters, 1959: 72-87). Unless they also have substantive knowledge and value commitments relevant to the various aspects of human well-being, they cannot justify morally their intrusion in human affairs in the name of justice, or anything else. The legal profession has not been notable for placing justice on the agenda of governments. Given its strong representation especially in the US Congress, but also in British and Australian Parliaments, it has been extraordinarily well placed to do so.

In a nation with a federal constitution, the sovereign powers of government are divided between the national government and state governments, with the Supreme Court in the US and the High Court in Australia, determining disputed areas. Michael Kirby acknowledges that the Australian Constitution inhibits bold reforming measures; in almost every task the Australian Law Reform Commission has had to work within constraints imposed by the Constitution. The concept of a 'welfare state' is much simpler to apply in a nation with a unitary system of government.

Having a written constitution which requires interpretation, and especially when it includes a bill of rights as in the USA, gives the legal profession considerable work and political power. The judicial arm of government is in fact virtually monopolized by the legal profession. Lawyers typically use the language of 'justice' and 'rights' in the description of their activities and, especially in the United States, are encouraging citizens to use the courts to achieve 'justice'. 'Blaming the victim' (Ryan, 1971) is still a cultural phenomenon in many cases of rape and unemployment, but individuals and groups are now being encouraged to see themselves as victims of one kind or another (see Hughes, 1993) and to seek legal redress for the injustice they have suffered often in the form of monetary compensation. And so much the better if the money comes from people 'who can afford it' or from insurance companies or other organizations who can pass on the cost to other members of the community without them knowing it.

Lawyers are clearly greatly involved in agenda-setting for the judicial arm of government - in influencing what situations come before the courts, or alternatively are dealt with out-of-court. They are putting their legal knowledge to use which inevitably reflects value commitments. They are obviously not just neutral, disinterested observers. Indeed, in the adversary system of legal justice in countries influenced by Britain, lawyers are expected to pursue the interests of their particular client, within legally prescribed limits. But judges inevitably must make choices which reflect values of one kind or another. That is what is entailed in judgment of any kind. The question, then, is not whether judicial judgments are value-free, they cannot be, but what and whose values are operating. This is what the so-called 'realists' in the USA have insisted about judicial decisions since the early 1920s. A judge's choice of legal principles is often determined by his own broad social and political values, and judges can arrive at opposite conclusions by selecting different starting principles, as is clearly illustrated by split decisions in the highest court of the land. (Sexton and Maher, 1982: 4.)

Lord Radcliffe declared in 1966:

> There was never a more sterile controversy than that upon the question whether a judge makes law. Of course he does. How can he help it? ... Judicial law is always a reinterpretation of principles in the light of new combinations of fact... Judges do not reverse principles once established, but they do modify them, extend them, restrict them and even deny their application to the combination in hand. (Quoted in Seldon, 1987: 69.)

Sometimes a decision by the highest court in the land will set a new socially-constructive direction - for instance, the recent Mabo decision of the Australian High Court on Aboriginal land rights, and the successful civil rights cases for black citizens of the USA in the 1960s. In a democratic society, however, the primary legal rule-making body should be the elected legislature. Judges are a tiny, unrepresentative minority, and cannot be expected to be other than socially conservative, although there are notable exceptions such as Lionel Murphy in the Australian High Court.

More and more human situations are subject to litigation or threatened litigation, which gives work to the lawyers and the courts, and insurance companies. But how this relates to ethical agenda-setting for government is by no means clear. Certainly the courts use the power of government to force people to take part in their proceedings and to accept resultant decisions, but as already mentioned, the legal justification for dealing with a situation and the ethical justification are not the same. Given such factors as court delays, high legal costs, inability to afford legal representation, emotional costs, the adversarial system, uneven legal representation, and variable and often narrow judicial standards, parties to a dispute may well decide to avoid entanglement with the court system and the lawyers.

At a launching in 1994 of a legal rights information kit for students, Justice Michael Kirby, then President of the New South Wales Court of Appeals in Australia,[1] is reported to have said that legal action against teachers was an 'inevitable development', just as lawyers and doctors were held accountable to the courts for their professional performance. This evoked a number of critical responses. A spokesperson for the Federation of

---

[1] In 1996, he joined the High Court of Australia.

Parents' and Citizens' Associations said lawyers would be the only beneficiaries of legal actions against teachers for educational malpractice. It was the worst possible way a parent could pursue their concerns about teaching quality. The president of the New South Wales Teachers' Federation warned that the threat of legal action would dissuade teachers from trying new approaches and may even turn people away from teaching. The Department of School Education would more likely be sued than teachers, because 'lowly paid teachers have little they could be sued for'. (Lewis, 1994: 1.) A newspaper editorial agreed with these responses, and pointed out that teachers were already subject to scrutiny from the school principal, head of department, state departmental officers, parents and the community. A legal 'remedy' would not resolve any problem with teaching standards. This must be resolved elsewhere. (*Sydney Morning Herald*, Editorial, 31/8/94.)

Education and the Influence of Teachers

Every government must give serious attention to the education of the members of its society. The various stages, levels and forms of education and training are a major interconnected set of items on the agenda of modern government and continuing political pressures aim to keep it this way - pressures from parents, students, community groups, employers, occupations dependent on particular types of education and training, and those engaged in teaching and research.

There is no one teaching profession covering all aspects of education and training. Organized occupational groups of teachers have developed in connection with pre-school, primary, secondary, tertiary and continuing, technical, and adult education, with further groupings according to government or non-government employing institutions, subjects taught, and administrative responsibilities. Every established profession has an organized educational arm which usually consists of people who identify at least to some extent with the profession of university teaching as well as the profession associated with their particular subject. University teaching, however, still does not require a teaching qualification, although such qualifications are becoming evident and all university teachers are being expected to have a better explicit understanding of educational processes than in the past.

The extent to which each of the various groupings of teachers can successfully influence a government's agenda-setting for education and training will vary according to its size, organization, political interest and sophistication, and complementary and competing interests both inside and outside the educational sector. Educationalists take an overview of the educational institutions and processes of society, but they are not organized as a separate, identifiable professional occupation. As consultants, and in their research and writing, they can perhaps help governments to identify what ought to be on the educational agenda. They can point to lack of coordination between the various stages of education, between professional and technical education systems, and between education sponsored by government and non-government education. They can identify gaps and distortions in educational provision and alert government to unfair limitations on educational opportunity. They can point up the social consequences of making educational provision primarily responsive to economic values rather than a full range of human values. They can research and publicize strategies that maximize educational attainment.

There is no question that education is seen by many as *the* most important item for an ethical agenda for a government concerned with the general welfare. Only through education, it is argued, can people understand themselves and the world they live in, so that they can act constructively as responsible human-beings. You cannot have a concept of 'education' without human beings; the word itself relates to them both as learners and teachers. Who is educating whom? is always a relevant question when the concept is used, except when 'self-education' is being referred to, and even then the educator is obviously using the knowledge and insights of others.

The 'Education' Concept

The concept 'education', like 'justice', refers to a process. In this case the process brings out or develops a person's potential so that the person is capable of new levels of achievement, but achievement in whose terms? For educators, education is a purposive activity with goals and objectives against which the learner's progress is measured. How those goals and objectives relate to human well-being is the ethical challenge to be confronted by an educator, the students, and the institution within which the educational process is proceeding. But governments also cannot avoid this question, especially when so much of the functioning of modern society, including governmental functioning, now depends on an educated workforce, educated consumers of goods and services, and an educated citizenry, and when educational expenditure is a substantial component of the national budget.

We tend to assume that education is good by definition, and perhaps it is if it entails some notion of ethically responsible use of validated knowledge about the world we live in. The concept is, however, often used for situations which are difficult to justify if human well-being is the prime value. A so-called 'educated' person may use their knowledge and skills only for personal or sectional advantage and have little regard for the well-being of others, using them as means to their selfish ends. The knowledge acquired in the 'educational' process may in fact have been invalid; or it may have once been valid but has become less so under changed conditions. The person's 'education' may have been highly specialized, so they know a great deal about certain things, but are ignorant about most others. The 'educated' person may enjoy high social standing and competitive advantage over others, but the content of their education may bear little relationship to their actual work and conduct.

Educated people may know a great deal about situations, but lack the skills to change them. The strength of professional education, from an ethical justification viewpoint, is that it tends to be concerned explicitly with values and skills, as well as knowledge. This is in contrast to education in non-professional subjects where the focus is on analysis and description, and possibly prediction. How the learner might use such knowledge to intervene in the world is not the prime focus.

This contrast is not always sharp, however. The learner may be headed for a research career in the subject in question, and will be expected to learn not only the appropriate research skills, but also what are considered to be the relevant ethical standards for research. In addition, professional education is not always very clear-headed about the values at stake, even though a code of 'ethics' helps to typify the occupation in question. Technical 'education', by definition, concentrates on skills and is often more comfortably described as 'training', but again the distinction between professional and technical education can become blurred when the former in fact has primarily a skills focus and the latter becomes concerned with ends as well as means. Some of the most renowned educational institutions are actually called institutions of technology, for example, the Massachusetts Institute of Technology in the USA.

Because of its significance for human well-being, the educational arena is one of the most morally significant areas of government but much of what is described as education has considerable moral ambiguity. Educationalists can assist in helping government and the community in general to have greater understanding of these matters, and can suggest what educational issues might be on the ethical agenda given certain values that they believe would enhance human well-being. The final choices cannot rest with the educationalists. Ultimately it is the people themselves, whose lives are at stake, and the governments that claim to represent them, who must make the basic educational decisions in a democratic society - bearing in mind that educational processes are never value-free, and that there are limits to the amount of personal and collective resources that can reasonably be devoted to education.

The 'Health' Concept

As with education, we tend to assume that health is also good by definition. Indeed, just after World War II, The World Health Organization (WHO) of the United Nations described it as 'a state of complete physical, mental and social well-being and not merely the absence of disease or infirmity' (Bates and Lapsley, 1987: 227). In other words 'health' and 'human well-being' were made virtually synonymous. This would mean that the Prime Ministers or Presidents would in fact be Health Ministers or Secretaries of State for Health, and that all professionals performing ethically justified work would be '*health* professionals'. There is the further implication that the pre-eminent health profession, the medical profession, would have hegemony over the professional system of society. This is, of course, fanciful nonsense, and could be easily dismissed as conceptual grandstanding were it not for the prestige of its source and its widespread usage. We do now use 'health' and 'sickness' language in relation to a wide variety of social phenomena, like the economy, bank balances, and social institutions of various sorts, but these are metaphorical usages, extensions from the original biological use which relates essentially to a sound or unsound body and/or mind.

When the WHO Assembly in 1977 decided that the principal social target of governments should be for all citizens of the world to attain 'a level of health which will permit them to lead socially and economically productive lives' (Palmer and Short, 1989: 183), this at least acknowledged that good health is usually a prerequisite for the attainment of other values essential to human well-being. Special pleading for the health cause is, however, still apparent in the notion that this should be the principal social target of governments.

The Escalating Costs of Health Care

In industrial western democratic countries like the USA, Britain, and Australia, what is called 'health care' has become a major agenda item for governments to have policies about and to provide and/or pay for. Even in the United States, government is responsible for more than 40 per cent of health care expenditure. This compares with over 90 per cent in Britain, which has had a salaried national health system since 1948. Australia, with its national health insurance system supporting largely fee-for-service payments, lies between the two, with 73 per cent of total health expenditure provided by government. (Bates and Lapsley, 1987: 174-5; Palmer and Short, 1989: 14.)

By the mid-1980s, health expenditure constituted nearly 10% of the Gross Domestic Product of the United States, compared with about 8% in Australia and less than 7 per cent in Britain. This reflected the different degrees of government control over cost increases in the respective countries. (Bates and Lapsley, 1987: 176-7.) By 1992, the US proportion had escalated to 14 per cent, and unless reform could be achieved, would rise to 19 per cent by the year 2000. Already by 1990, more was spent on health care than on education and defence together. Yet the US still ranked low amongst economically developed countries on health indicators such as infant mortality rates (19th), life expectancy for men (21st), and for women (16th). (White House, 1993: 7-8.) It was scarcely surprising, then, that reform of the health care system was a major objective for President Clinton in his first term. His high-profile lawyer wife had the tough assignment to report on needed reforms

The resultant report to the American people claimed: 'No other health care system exceeds our level of scientific knowledge, professional skill and technical resources'. Yet health coverage is not a right of citizenship, as it is in other nations, where coverage is provided for all at lower and more stable costs and with higher levels of consumer satisfaction. More than 37 million Americans have no insurance cover and a further 25 million have inadequate cover. (White House, 1993: 1, 2, 10.) The report identified six major problems with the system: growing insecurity, with the threat of financial ruin because of inadequate insurance cover; growing complexity, with escalating administrative costs; rising health care costs which impact on the budgets of workers, families, businesses, and governments alike; decreasing quality, with no clear sense of what treatments work best, and neglect of preventive care; declining health care choices; and, finally, growing irresponsibility, with insurance companies excluding the sick and the elderly, pharmaceutical companies sometimes overcharging for prescription drugs, doctors and hospitals engaging in expensive 'defensive medicine' in response to the threat of lawsuits, and an estimated annual cost of $80 billion of health care fraud. (White House, 1993: 2-15.)

Small wonder the President stated a need to 'get the system under control - and put people first'. (White House, 1993: October letter.) Yet Clinton's proposed Health Security Act insisted on expanding the current employer-based health insurance system, rejecting any kind of broad-based tax to pay for a government-run system. Costs were to be contained by a new emphasis on preventive care, the encouragement of competition among health providers, and a cracking down on health care fraud. (White House, 1993: 81, 84.) Even these rather limited proposed reforms proved to be politically unacceptable.

Health Politics

As with the education of the members of a nation, every modern democratic government cannot avoid giving serious attention to the health of its citizens. It is under considerable political pressure to do so from people suffering from chronic and acute illnesses, from occupations involved in health care, from hospital boards, from employers who want a healthy workforce, and from research interests. The title of Sax's book *A Strife of Interests* captures the reality of politics and policies in Australian health services (Sax, 1984). Again like 'educational' activity, much of what is described as 'health care' has considerable moral ambiguity. The term is used to cover a wide range of activities which have very different justification status if human well-being is the prime value.

'Care' Language

'Health care' is apparently a useful political label, but 'care' terminology is not appropriately extended to all health-related activities. If it means 'caring about' people's health, that is morally desirable - provided it leads to health improvement. 'Care' in this sense, however, is a way of talking about moral concern and should obviously not be confined just to health concerns. 'Care' in the medical and nursing context, usually means 'caring for' or 'taking care of' a sick person, but this has come under increasing moral scrutiny because of the dangers of unnecessary paternalism.

The only other area of government policy where 'care' terminology is used is 'child care', where parents and others are seen as 'looking after' children, supposedly in the children's best interests. There is no appropriate parallel in the provision of health services to adults - except in carefully limited circumstances when a person is no longer able to take responsibility for their life because of particular physical or mental illness. 'Service' language is morally preferable to 'care' language anyway. This is because strictly it entails an assessment of outcome in terms of human well-being - something was 'of service' - and not just reference to attitude or intention, and especially an attitude or intention that runs the risk of unnecessary paternalism.

Inappropriate Priorities and Inefficiencies

The current government agenda on what is called 'health care' reflects the outcome of historical and contemporary argument between the people who make a living from providing a 'health' service, the politicians, and the public/s whose health they claim to serve. The interests of the major players interweave in complicated patterns; a host of justification issues are raised by present arrangements and trends, and each of these has implications for a justifiable health agenda for government. Despite mounting criticism, present 'health' systems are still overwhelmingly focused upon dealing with individuals suffering from an acute illness. That is the prime focus of most of the 'health' activity endorsed and resourced by government. It is where the high status, intellectual challenge, publicity, and profits lie, for the 'health' providers, in contrast with disease prevention, environmental health, occupational health, and health promotion. (Bates and Lapsley, 1987: 228; Palmer and Short, 1989: 182-3.)

The rising cost of acute care, associated with expensive changing technology and specialists' fees, is forcing governments to examine more explicitly the effectiveness and efficiency of its 'health' policies and expenditure, with equity issues becoming increasingly evident in the process. Governments are now extensively involved in determining who shall receive what kind of health service, from whom, at what cost, and how cost is to be met. Within the political arena of health, governments must try to understand and weigh up the interests and claims of people grouped by socio-economic class, gender, geographic location including urban or rural circumstance, ethnicity, age, genetic endowment, acute illness, chronic illness, type of physical disease, type of mental disease, and people with various degrees of risk of illness and other trauma.

Good health is a universal value, but access to it depends on one's heredity, luck, environment, socio-economic circumstances, and to some extent on one's own efforts (Bates and Lapsley, 1987: 228). It is assumed that governments can influence what health outcomes are achieved, but they must do this, bearing in mind the claims of other areas of government, as well as claims within the health sector. The 'new public health movement' insists anyway that the health of the public requires intersectoral collaboration, health promotion, and community involvement, which goes far beyond the current exaggerated emphasis on curative medicine (Palmer and Short, 1989: 48-50). Beyond all this again, are the decisions made in the capitalist economic system, which determine the health of whole populations, but over which governments, let alone health professionals, have little or no control (Willis, 1989: 216).

The Health Professions

As with education, there is no one health profession, but medicine is clearly dominant. It is now common to refer loosely to the 'health professions' when referring to the various occupations providing health services. In Australia, 24 distinct health occupations have been recognized by government through registration boards which set educational and other requirements. In each case government has given legal power and legitimacy to the occupation in question, supposedly in the public interest, yet through its membership of the registration board, the occupation usually retains substantial control of its members' destiny within its prescribed territory, although, in New South Wales, the medical profession has at least one place on every board (Bates and Lapsley, 1987: 203).

With recent government emphasis on a need for competition between and within professional occupations, and on 'self'-regulation by professions, the option of registration by government is no longer available to new occupations wishing to preserve and protect their occupational position. The existing legally entrenched positions remain, however, with the medical profession pre-eminent, with its exclusive authority to hospitalize patients, to prescribe drugs, and to order laboratory tests, and its almost exclusive right to government health insurance payments for its services (Palmer and Short, 1989: 44).

The Dominance, Organization and Influence of the Medical Profession

From about the middle of the nineteenth century, a nationally organized medical profession has emerged to a position of economic, political, social, and intellectual dominance in the health division of labour in western industrial countries like Britain, Australia and the United States (Willis, 1989; Starr, 1982; Bennet, 1987). Palmer and Short argue that health policy is distinctive for three reasons. (They are obviously interconnected.) First, is the medical profession's role in shaping and constraining government policy; second, is the complexity of service provision and inability of consumers to assess its quality; and finally, there is the possible involvement of life and death. (Pàlmer and Short, 1989: 25.) In his historical account of the emergence of medical dominance in Australia, Willis pays due regard to class and gender dimensions, as well as to the ideological and scientific aspects of medical knowledge (Willis, 1989: 13-26). These various dimensions are obviously relevant not only to the profession's relations with other health occupations and patients, but also with governments.

An important part of the explanation of the political success of the medical profession has been its organization in a national general professional association which has claimed to be concerned about the profession as a whole, and its generalist educational strategy prior to any specialization. The scope and complexity of modern medicine has, however, encouraged a medical division of labour as well as a division of labour between doctors and other health workers, and additional education and training and separate colleges or associations are associated with each of the main medical specialties. In Australia, a college of general practitioners has been formed to protect general practice from increasing specialist competition. In the United States, government funding policy has reinforced the trend towards medical specialists producing what the Clinton report calls an 'unhealthy mix' of 2/3 specialists to 1/3 primary care (or general practice) (White House, 1993: 68). In Australia, still less than 1/3 are specialists (Palmer and Short, 1989: 124), and patients are expected to be referred to a specialist through their general practitioner. The pattern of medical specialization does not follow any consistent logic; specialisms may be developed around particular age groups, bodily organs, bodily systems, gender, mental functioning, technical procedures, environmental concerns.

The medical profession is becoming far more heterogeneous in Australia, and elsewhere, not only because of the development of specialization, but because of changes in its gender, class and ethnic composition. In addition, new medical groups like the Doctors' Reform Society and the Private Doctors' Association of Australia, are now politically active in trying to influence in very different directions the government agenda for health (Palmer and Short, 1989: 41). The Australian Medical Association has had a reputation of being the most effective trade union in the country, because of its success in protecting the autonomy and interests of doctors, and is usually associated with conservative politics. A recent President, Brendan Nelson, provided a dramatic change in professional leadership by focusing attention in the media on government and professional neglect of Aboriginal health, the unemployed, and youth. With tobacco smoking the leading cause of preventable illness and death, the AMA is now playing its part in the anti-smoking movement, which has persuaded governments to restrict cigarette advertising and promotion and led to the banning of smoking in public places (Palmer and Short, 1989: 195-8, 212-14).

Regulation of the New Medical Technology

The development of new medical technology is raising difficult new questions for government, not only in relation to the financial costs involved and how these should be borne, but also whether adequate guidelines and regulations are in place to safeguard the public interest. Organ transplants, reproductive technology, genetic engineering, and life support systems all raise questions about human existence and human well-being which call for guidelines and possible regulation by government. The immediately involved professionals may see this as unnecessary outside interference or they may welcome it as providing a justification framework within which they can proceed with their work. Governments cannot, however, continue to ignore these matters, whether these developments be financed from the public purse, are driven by the financial profit motive, or are mainly the product of rampant technical curiosity.

Changes in Nursing

By far the largest of the health occupations is nursing. In Australia in 1986, it constituted nearly 70 per cent of health care professionals, compared with the less than 13 per cent who were doctors. Because of their subordinate relationship to doctors, their limited hospital-based training, and their gender, nurses have traditionally experienced low professional status, poor working conditions, and low pay, with the small group of directors of nursing being the only possible exception. Improving the condition of nursing has been forced on the agenda of government by militant industrial action by the nurses themselves, and by the continuing shortage of nurses associated with a higher proportion of seriously ill patients in hospital and greater responsibilities expected of nurses. (Palmer and Short, 1989: 124, 137-141.)

An Australian federal government inquiry (the Sax Committee, 1978) laid the foundation for shifting all nursing education to tertiary institutions by 1993. A 1988 state-level inquiry, significantly chaired by a former Commissioner of Equal Opportunity, examined the underlying causes of the 1986 Victorian nurses strike. (In 1983, members of the Royal Australian Nurses' Federation had voted to remove the no-strike clause from their constitution.) Nurses claimed they were often expected to use new technology without adequate preparation, and their emphasis on 'holistic' care clashed with a focus on a patient's 'medical' condition. (Palmer and Short, 1989: 137, 143.) The occupation is undergoing a radical transformation, including the recruitment of men, which will change its relationships not only with the medical profession, but with other occupations and with patients and their families.

Competition over occupational territory is inevitable as nurses take a more expansive view of their role and are educated to do so. For example, this can occur between new 'nurse practitioners' and general medical practitioners, and between community nurses and social workers. Through health and education policies, governments are caught up in these developments.

The Emergence of a Health Administration Profession

Health administration is emerging as a new identifiable occupation which is playing a significant role in the control and coordination of health resources, although it constitutes only about 3 per cent of the health workforce in Australia. Currently health administrators have had diverse backgrounds. Those with qualifications and experience in health professions such as medicine or nursing, at least will have had direct clinical experience dealing with health problems, and are therefore likely to have credibility with clinicians and patients. Such experience may, however, be out-of-date and distorting for administrative judgments. In any case, modern human service management obviously requires additional knowledge and skills, covering both organizational and resource management matters, and how the organization relates to its social, political, and economic environment. In Australia, a College of Health Service Administrators is moving towards developing health administration as a separate health profession with a distinctive educational preparation and occupational territory. (Palmer and Short, 1989: 145-7; Bates and Lapsley, 1987: 206-9.) The importance of modern health administration is apparently beginning to attract larger numbers of good quality medical graduates.

An alternative vision would be to develop health administration as a specialization within a new human services management profession, which would cover the various fields of social service administration. Both governments and the public could benefit if key administrators were professionally linked at least across the fields of health, education, and welfare.

National Security - Defence Against External Threats

War, the Threat of War, and Destructive Technology

Like health, the security of the nation provides a necessary condition for the attainment of the other human values which make life worth living. No government can ignore either external or internal threats to the security of the nation, and periodically, in times of war, nothing has higher priority. Even when a nation is not at war, its government may use a great deal of its economic and human resources in the nation's defence forces, both as a deterrent and in preparation for possible war. During the Cold War, the superpowers, with the technical help of scientists and defence professionals, set up systems of threatened destruction which not only diverted resources from other uses, but led young people to lose a sense of having a future. In 1980, roughly a quarter of the entire world expenditure on scientific research and development was for military purposes (Report to the Secretary-General, 1983).

The sudden, dramatic collapse of the Communist bloc since 1989, has demanded a re-thinking of defence strategy, including a scaling down of defence expenditure and a new emphasis on UN security initiatives. The terrifying destructive power of nuclear weapons, and increasingly of conventional weapons, remains, however, as an unprecedented moral challenge. In just a day or two of nuclear exchange, far more people would be killed than in the First and Second World Wars which lasted a total of nine years and cost 75 million lives; and the aftermath could well be even worse (Fotion and Elfstrom, 1986: 174). As early as 1945, Bernard Brodie, an American defence strategist declared: 'Thus far the chief purpose of our military establishment has been to win wars. From now its chief purpose must be to avert them'. (Fisher, 1985: 2; O'Connell, 1989: 296.) But could the use of weapons of such destruction ever be justified? Yet if they are never to be used, what is the point of developing and maintaining them, and how can they act as a deterrent?

Although nuclear war has been avoided, conventional war has continued. Between 1945 and 1983, 130 military conflicts were fought, almost all in 90 developing countries, and largely with weapons and technological know-how imported from the so-called developed countries. The loss of life exceeded that of the Second World War. (Report to the Secretary-General, 1983.) The continuing resort to violence and the threat of violence in trying to get one's way in international affairs is, of course, not new. What is new is the completely unprecedented destructive power of the weapons involved, thanks to 'advances' in science and technology. Humans now have the technical capacity to destroy their species many times over. It is ironical when the so-called security forces of a nation have become the main source of 'insecurity', both for its own citizens as well as for other nations. With the end of the Cold War, the threat of an accidental or even deliberate nuclear conflict between super powers has receded, but national security concerns remain as conventional weapons become more deadly, and more countries develop a military nuclear option. By the early 1980s, at least ten countries were believed to have a military nuclear option (Eban, 1983: 291).

Defence Professionals and Their Justification

War or the possibility of war is a continuing item on a government's agenda, and professionals of various kinds are clearly involved - at the political and public administration levels, in the permanent armed forces, and in the scientific community. Given the scope and seriousness of security issues for human life and well-being, it is not surprising that ethicists are turning their attention to military ethics. (See, for example, Fotion and Elfstrom, 1986.)

Their discussion is of obvious relevance to the justification of the conduct of the 'defence' professionals.

For pacifists, however, the very concept of 'military ethics' is a contradiction in terms. How can any human conduct which entails the deliberate destruction of human beings and their property ever be justified? Alternatively, realists see war as unavoidable but of such a violent character that moral standards are irrelevant and anything goes. Fotion and Elfstrom reject both of these extreme positions, using utilitarian arguments adapted from Hare (see p. 16) (Fotion and Elfstrom, 1986: 10-21). For them, human well-being is clearly the prime value. States do not have a moral standing in themselves: their actions must be justified in terms of their contribution to human well-being. The means, practice, and justification of war, as well as the use of military force must be weighed in terms of their contribution to the well-being of all the people involved. In the present world, states have special responsibility for the people residing in them, but they need to take account of the interests of all who will be affected by particular actions and policies. (Fotion and Elfstrom, 1986: 22-4.) There is no doubt in the minds of the authors that the use of military power raises a host of moral issues - in peace-time, immediately prior to a war, during a war, and at the end of a war; for a variety of groups of people; and for enemy and third-party states as well as for one's own state (Fotion and Elfstrom, 1986: 29-280).

Spying

One issue not raised is the justification of so-called 'intelligence' services, or spying, both in peace and in war. I can recall a rather bumbling effort by the Australian Security Intelligence Organization (see McKnight, 1994) to recruit a group of us at Oxford University in the mid-1950s! Its secretive, deceptive, and non-democratically accountable nature had no vocational attraction for any of us - as far as I know. But these very features have made such work a regular source of creative writing and films, especially in the period of the Cold War.

Peter Wright's internal account of Britain's MI5, which the British Government attempted to suppress, indicates the extent to which traitors and double-agents can undermine such a public 'service'. According to Wright, even a former Director-General of MI5, Sir Roger Hollis, was a Soviet agent (Wright, 1987: 372-81). In 1994, Aldrich Ames, head of the counter-intelligence branch of the Soviet division of the American Central

Intelligence Agency, was discovered to have been spying for the Russians for nine years (Weiner, 1994). Also, a former chief of the KGB's counter-intelligence division disclosed that from 1977 to 1980 someone in the Australian Security Intelligence Organization sold 'top-notch' intelligence information to the Soviet Union (Wright and Seccombe, 1994: 1). Such spectacular security failures have brought into question the efficacy of intelligence services. There is obviously a real danger that intelligence services will become a law unto themselves, even though they are a government agency.

The people who staff intelligence services require technical skills, strong patriotism and loyalty. Peter Wright clearly saw himself as belonging to a profession, but one with peculiar features. He wrote:

> The profession of intelligence is a solitary one. There is camaraderie, of course, but in the end you are alone with your secrets. You live and work at a feverish pitch of excitement, dependent always on the help of your colleagues. But you always move on, whether to a new branch or department, or to a new operation. And when you move on, you inherit new secrets which subtly divorce you from those you have worked with before. Contacts, especially with the outside world, are casual, since the largest part of yourself cannot be shared. It is built into the very nature of the profession, and everyone who joins knows it. (Wright, 1987: 67.)

Although MI5 expected its officers to remain 'loyal unto the grave', it did not necessarily offer loyalty in return. Wright was shocked to find Peter Ustinov's father, a former MI5 recruit, in retirement without any pension. (Wright, 1987: 67-70.)

Like the professional leaders in the military (see Fotion and Elfstrom, 1986: 50), the leaders of intelligence services can become isolated in their thinking about military and political matters, and can adopt selfish or paternalistic policies. They are, however, far less accountable than the military, even in a mature political democracy.

National Security - Defence Against Internal Threats

The Criminal Justice System

Not only must the political arm of government establish, maintain, and control military forces and an intelligence service to provide security against external threats, it must also establish, maintain, and control a police force to provide security against internal threats. The most serious internal threats against people and property are called crimes, and they are committed by fellow citizens over whom the government claims legitimate jurisdiction. The legislative body decides what is criminal activity. Through its police force, a government can stop, detain, and/or arrest any person suspected of a crime, and can use force if necessary, even deadly force, in certain circumstances. Through the judicial arm of government, the guilt and punishment of offenders is determined, and a government's correctional service carries out the punishment.

There can be no question that human well-being is seriously involved in the part of a government's agenda which deals with what is called the criminal justice system. By definition, a crime is conduct which is sufficiently socially harmful to use the power of the state to detect and punish the offender. Legislators must determine what categories of conduct should be classified as crimes, and what is the appropriate level and type of punishment, while the judicial process determines the level of guilt and punishment in each case. Taking into account exonerating or mitigating circumstances is relevant in both tasks. These will not affect the harm that has been done, but will influence the extent to which the perpetrator is considered guilty. Since punishment entails the deliberate infliction of some form of harm by the state on one of its citizens, it always requires moral justification, and this is especially the case with those forms of punishment which massively harm the life and life chances of the person involved. In the past, the most extreme form of punishment has been to be deliberately killed by the state, but no longer is capital punishment morally acceptable in most civilized societies. Restriction of liberty in prison continues, however, as a frequently preferred punishment option for modern governments, yet rarely does the prison experience lay the basis for a future law-abiding, socially useful life. Making a person 'pay for their wrong-doing' by imprisonment, with little regard for the effects on the person, their family, the cost to taxpayers, and future harm the person is likely to cause, makes no sense if human well-being is the prime value.

Criminologists

The study of the prevention, control, deterrence, and treatment of crime is the province of the criminologist. According to Stanley Cohen, 'As reformers, advisers and consultants, criminologists claim for themselves not merely an autonomous body of knowledge, but the status of an applied science or even a profession'. However, he admits that the major schools of criminological thought are divided on quite basic issues. (Cohen, 1987: 31, 33.) Criminologists by definition share the basic values of scientific inquiry, but whose and what values are they pursuing when 'applying' their knowledge? Unless this is clear and they have a reasonable degree of consensus, they cannot become effectively organized on professional lines. The specialized knowledge of criminologists needs, however, to be increasingly available to governments and the public to counteract tendencies for the media, politicians, and the public to give exaggerated attention to crime. For example, a 1994 survey for the New South Wales Police Department revealed that almost 60 per cent of the population believed they could become victims of crime; almost half feared being murdered. Yet according to criminologists the incidence of major crime had either dropped or remained stable. The Director of the New South Wales Institute of Criminology declared that people had more chance of falling out of a bus than being murdered in Sydney. 'Surely politicians and the media (had) a responsibility to tell the truth and keep telling the truth'. (Morris, 1994; Totaro, 1994: 21.)

The Police Force

Crime and its policing are favorite topics for television series, films, and books, whose prime purpose is entertainment, not enlightenment or information. The incidence of homicide in Jessica Fletcher's Cabot Cove or Inspector Morse's Oxford far exceeds any possible reality. An engaging story with some moral to it is typical fare; rarely is the culprit not eventually caught. Serious study of actual police work and its development as an occupation with professional aspirations is relatively recent (Elliston and Feldberg, 1985: 1-10). Yet the nature of at least some of the police work required in a modern society calls for well-educated, skilful police with high morale and firm commitment to public service. Without sufficient numbers of such police, organized crime, corporate and other white-collar crime, and computer fraud, go unchecked; police aspects of crime prevention are weak; domestic and other disputes are not handled constructively; traffic congestion can become unbearable; crowds can get out of hand; various emergency situations lack immediate, authoritative intervention; and so on. In 1996, the new reforming New South Wales Police Commissioner, Peter Ryan, said he would appeal to the professionalism of police to rebuild the police service (*Sydney Morning Herald*, editorial, 12/6/96), but the absence of such professionalism was his main problem.

Achieving a respected, effective and efficient police force which serves the general public interest is, then, a significant item on the ethical agenda for modern government. It is ironical when the policing function of government itself becomes a major source of ethical concern - because of police corruption, questionable methods involving various forms of deception, invasions of privacy, and/or the misuse of deadly force (see Elliston and Feldberg, 1985).

Urban Living Conditions

One of the key concepts used to typify the development of modern society is 'urbanization', the growth of cities and towns as places to live for a large proportion of the population. By the mid-1980s, 91 per cent of the 56 million people in Britain; 86 per cent of the 16 million in Australia; 76 per cent of the 26 million in Canada; and 71 per cent of the 241 million in the United States, lived in urban environments (Stonehouse ed., 1987). Australians are particularly heavily settled in cities that serve as political capitals of states and as industrial, commercial, cultural and educational centers. The size, shape, visual appearance, and functioning of urban settlements have great influence on human well-being, as well as on the natural environment of the land, air, water, and flora and fauna.

Trying to regulate urban growth and change in ways that improve overall human well-being and protect the natural environment for future generations, and in its own right, are vital ethical tasks for government. Non-government agents do not have the democratic legitimacy and/or scope of concern, to determine overall, longer-term objectives of urban development and to coordinate policy directions. Yet for a variety of reasons, urban planning has had a checkered history as an ethical agenda item for government in liberal democratic societies (Sandercock, 1977).

Professionals' Involvement in Urban Living Conditions

Most professional groups will be influenced by the urban location of their activities. Cities and towns provide them with the facilities and job opportunities not available in sparsely-populated rural areas. These professionals, and the services they provide, in turn shape the quality of urban living for the populace at large. A number of the professional groups concentrate specifically upon the physical infrastructure of the city - the design and construction of its roads, bridges, tunnels, railways, dams, waterways, airports, means of transport, waste disposal systems, telecommunication systems, power plants, buildings, and parks and recreation areas. Engineers of various kinds but especially civil engineers, and/or architects have played a central role in the design and supervision of such projects, but unlike doctors and lawyers, they have no government-determined monopoly of their functions. They may compete with each other and other professionals like lawyers, accountants, and general managers, and with various non-professionals. Although many are employed directly by government, typically they operate in non-government, profit-making organizations which may be on contract to government for a particular project. It has been said that an engineer's priorities in a project are viability, function, economy, and aesthetics, in that order, whereas an architect's are aesthetics, function, viability, and economy (Francis, 1990: 38).

The Influence of Engineers

A 1991 discussion paper to the Australian Prime Minister's Science Council claimed Australia had a high reputation for the quality of its public infrastructure; there had been few significant failures of major engineering systems (Fell, 1991: 5). Industry leaders believed, however, that Australian engineers were frequently too narrow in their vision and did not have sufficient understanding of commercial considerations to be good managers of technology. The profession had relatively low public esteem. University deans of engineering agreed that engineers had a poor national image - in contrast with USA, Japan, and Europe. Engineers were seen as despoiling the environment, having little regard for social issues, and being irrelevant to society's needs. (Fell, 1991: 14.) Yet an Australian textbook on engineering design claims that the objective of engineering activity is to use scientific principles to develop devices or facilities which are of value to human society. Engineering is seen as an activity which integrates both physical requirements and societal objectives. (Svensson, 1990: 3.) The stages in the book's problem-solving model are similar to those found in other rational action models.

At a 1990 international conference sponsored by seven national engineering professional associations or institutions, the focus was on quality, responsibility and liability. A number of the papers discussed the emergence of legal liability as a dominant influence in contemporary engineering practice. For example: A past president of the Canadian Society of Civil Engineers declared 'Today engineering endeavors appear to be driven by fear of liability, and no longer by constant striving towards exceptional and/or innovative solutions'. (Revay, 1990: 4.) A former president of the American Consulting Engineering Council also stated 'By having to think about liability at all times, we think first about the safe solution, rather than choose what may be the best and highest quality solution'. (Poirot, 1990: 18.) Yet he admitted that because of the current litigious atmosphere, his own firm now does far more research in negotiating a contract -

> We evaluate the potential client to determine compatibility with our goals and objectives... We evaluate the project for unusual risks... We evaluate our resources to be sure we can meet the client's needs. And... we negotiate a contract with a scope of work, financial terms, insurance and other legal requirements that are acceptable to all parties. (Poirot, 1990: 14.)

These would all seem to be ethically justifiable steps and not just ways of avoiding legal battles 'that could delay and add cost to a project'.

Legally determined standards for engineers, and others involved in the construction industry, have then become a significant item on the agenda of modern government. The current emphasis, however, on professional liability can lead to over-cautious, self-protective practice, at a time when engineering knowledge and skills are badly needed to develop new environment-friendly urban systems and devices. A major branch of engineering, civil engineering, has civic purpose built into its name. In a sense, all engineering endeavor needs to share a civic purpose if it is to be ethically justified.

The Architectural Profession

The field of building is often associated in people's minds with architects, perhaps because 'architecture' can mean building, but in fact much building is controlled by engineers, developers, and building contractors. In the USA, only about 1 in 10 houses, and 1 in 4 non-residences involves an architect (Blau, 1984: 4, 150). But even in these instances, architects will have been commissioned by others - individuals, corporations, governments - to design a building within specifications of location, function, cost, and legal requirements, which need to be mutually agreed upon. Cuff states: 'Very often, the architects' clients are an intimidating lot: they are powerful, wealthy, and able to go elsewhere for service.' (Cuff, 1991: 40.) How much influence an architect has in the design and construction of any particular building will vary not only according to the power and knowledge of a client, but also will be affected by the involvement and influence of other professionals, both architects and others.

Judith Blau draws attention to a three-way split in modern architecture - a prime commitment to design and art; serving the best interests of the client; and designing for the users of buildings (Blau, 1984: 8-9). She observes that architects have never agreed upon the profession's core or specialized domain. The profession is eclectic and interdisciplinary. It resists definition of its boundaries and internal specialization, and its conceptions about design, function and scale undergo frequent change. (Blau, 1984: 6, 7, 134-5.)

The American Institute of Architects stated in its 1972 Handbook: 'No longer is the Architect committed solely to the interests of the client; he is as much concerned with the best interests of the community, the people and the land.' (Cuff, 1991: 106.) This declared commitment to general human well-being, by the organized profession, if taken seriously, could lead to services of architects becoming available to the whole community and not primarily to the rich and powerful. But governments and the public at large will have to be convinced of the value of their particular aesthetics as well as their functional utility and cost. Britain's Prince Charles has been an outspoken critic of the aesthetics of contemporary architects, but in turn has been criticized for his conservative taste.

Artistic Enterprise

Liberal democratic governments have moved cautiously in the area of having an arts policy. Government leaders, like the former Australian Prime Minister Paul Keating, may see the encouragement of creative artists as essential to the national spirit and national pride. For him, this was clearly a significant item for the ethical agenda of government. Instead of artists having to depend only on private patronage, the marketability of their works, and/or teaching, some can now receive sustaining government grants, presumably because their work is, in some sense, in the public interest. But the relationship of artistic enterprise in its various forms - the visual arts, creative writing, films, musical composition, and the performing arts - to human well-being is complex and often controversial, and may be made even more so by heavy government involvement. Generally the arts have relatively weak occupational organization, although the various arts traditions have developed education and training courses and occupational associations, which may act as pressure groups on government.

The Limited Influence of City Planners

The twentieth century profession of city or town planning - sometimes just called planning - is an occupation that is directly employed by government, frequently at the municipal level. Taken literally it might be expected to cover the planning of all activities which take place within a city, but in fact it has been much more confined in its scope and influence. The scope of planning has been broadest when governments have been able to manage urban growth from the outset - as with a British 'new town', or a Canberra - and when planning has been for the future growth of existing cities. However, when urban renewal has been attempted, the vested interests of the existing property-owners and rate-payers, of industrial and commercial enterprises, of government departments and corporations, and of elected local bodies, have constituted limiting political realities. (Parker, 1972: 29.)

Modern cities, apart from Singapore, are not city-states. Because they are integral parts of broader political, economic, and social systems, it is difficult to achieve a coordinated focus on the city as a whole, despite its significance for human well-being. In Australia, city planning is a state government responsibility, and only Brisbane has metropolitan-wide local government. For a brief period in the early 1970s, the Whitlam Labor Government tried to adopt a national approach to urban development, through a Department of Urban and Regional Development (Alexander, 1981: 145). Federal government involvement in US urban renewal programs (Gans, 1972: 83-5) provided an example. In his 1972 policy speech, Whitlam asserted:

> No amount of wealth redistribution through higher wages or lower taxes can really offset the inequalities imposed by the physical nature of cities. Increasingly, a citizen's real standard of living...(is) determined... by where he lives. (Troy, 1981: 17.)

Reflecting the history of city planning (Gans, 1972: 70-95; Parker, 1972: 29), and often the engineering and architectural backgrounds of the planners, planning has concentrated on the regulation of land use and of a city's physical structures. Preparation of city master plans has been a feature of urban planning since World War I, but according to Gans, no master plan has ever become a blueprint for the development of a city because it assumes environmental or physical determinism. This is the notion that people's lives are shaped by their physical surroundings and that the ideal city could be realized by the provision of an ideal physical environment. (Gans, 1972: 75.) Unless physical planning is integrated with economic and social planning, its actual effects on human well-being can be negative.

To be an item on the ethical agenda of government, urban planning needs to be able to demonstrate that it can be pursued in the general public interest and not just in the sectional interests of private property owners, developers, bureaucrats, particular professional groups each with its own bias, political parties, or local government. The damage caused by processes of urban growth without government control in a laissez-faire capitalist environment has led to political pressure for government to become involved in the processes. Government urban planning, while it obviously must include highly technical knowledge, is at base a political process which allocates the human costs and benefits of urban growth. In a democratic society, it cannot be left to technocrats. Scholars have drawn attention to the inequitable outcomes of existing urban planning. (See Troy, ed., 1981.) Urban planning is, then potentially a very important ethical item for government, but in practice has often reinforced social division and social inequalities.

Population Studies and Forecasting

If governments are to have human well-being as their prime value, an important contribution is made by those who chart the vital features of human populations. This task has increasingly been done by demographers, in conjunction with official agencies staffed by statisticians. Societies that are well served by such occupations have a necessary basis for ethically justified decision-making not only in relation to population policies, but a full range of policies that depend upon accurate population statistics. Censuses, registration of births and deaths, migration records, and sample surveys are the main methods used to chart populations. A variety of disciplines - sociology, economics, biology, history, psychology, public health - contribute to the wider field of population studies where the focus is on what brings about population changes. The extent to which these are organized on professional lines will vary, but most will at the least adhere to the norms of scientific inquiry in one form or another. Government planners must inevitably make assumptions about the size and nature of future populations. Demographers are often called upon to assist with population forecasts, but tend to confine themselves to making population projections based on various assumptions. (Keyfitz, 1987: 34-40.) The longer the time period generally the more hazardous the exercise.

Population and Environment Pressures

Governments are beginning to realize that the need to limit the world's population growth is already the most urgent and vital item for the human agenda, if human well-being is the prime value. By 1600, the estimated world population was fewer than 500 million; by 1750, it was about 700 million. There will be a projected 6 billion human beings by the year 2000, and a projected 8 billion twenty years later. An especially worrying feature of the population projections is the ever-widening gap between the industrial countries, with stabilized and ageing populations, and the young and prolific Third World countries. (Peccei, 1982: 31, 36, 37.)

It has been estimated that the Earth's present inhabitants will consume more natural resources during their lifetimes than all their ancestors have consumed (Peccei, 1982: 44). With the recent development of Third World economies like that of China, this process will be even faster. Increasingly, issues relating to the preservation of the environment and the conservation of natural resources are being placed on national and international agendas, with the 'green movement' and Greenpeace at times having substantial successes. Compared with the size and extent of the problems involved, current governments are clearly giving completely inadequate attention to these matters. (See Toyne, 1994.) Immediate political and economic interests tend to predominate over the future interests of people, and especially of those not yet born.

Professionals and Environmental Concerns

Professionals of various kinds are involved in researching the effects of pollution and the destruction of flora and fauna. Professionals are also often heavily involved in the processes that lead to these results, whether as professional managers, professional politicians, engineers, professional economists, corporate lawyers, and others for whom the advantages are seen to outweigh any disadvantages involved. Given the seriousness and complexity of the issues, a new professional occupation of environmentalists could well develop, with its own specialty groups. In time it could play a significant role in ensuring that environmental issues are always on the government agenda, and given due significance. The education of such an occupation would need to be broad and underpinned by an ethical understanding of environmental issues as they operate globally as well as locally. An important aspect of environmental issues is that they often cross national boundaries and require international action. The ethical framework for a developing environmentalist profession may well extend to the claims of all sentient beings and not just humans.

Economic Development

Closely related to concerns about population and environment, are concerns about 'the economy'. This concept is the product of economists who, both directly and indirectly, have had a major recent influence on western industrial societies (see pp. 138-41), and in the economic development efforts in traditional societies. A rapidly growing interdependence between national economies has seen the emergence of a world economy. The nations with developed market economies make decisions on monetary and trade affairs which determine the overall fate of the world economy, even though they account for only 18 per cent of the world's population. Almost all the huge transnational corporations are based in these countries. A large and complicated ethical issue is the significance for human well-being of what is called economic development.

Information Technology

A feature of economic development since World War II has been both national and global extensions of information technology, much of it coming from transnational corporations (Lyon, 1988: 30-5). The overall effects on human well-being are mixed, and often far from clear, but liberal democratic governments have been increasingly forced to give more explicit attention to them, not only in relation to their own citizens, but also as member states of the United Nations. The debate in UNESCO on the proposed establishment of a New World Information and Communication Order brought into focus, in the early 1980s, the extent to which the rapid development of the new information technologies dominated by companies located in the United States, Japan, and Western European countries, is threatening the economic and cultural autonomy of many countries (Lyon, 1988: 118-20). Totalitarian political regimes can use information technologies for surveillance and manipulative purposes, but so too can dissidents.

The production, storage, distribution, and use of what is called 'information' occupies much of the time and energies of people living in a modern democratic society. Indeed, some commentators characterize it as an 'information society' because it is so dependent on the information made available through its information technology. (See Lyon, 1988: vii.) To the earlier technologies of the printing press, telephone, and telegraph, have been added films, radio, television, cable television, satellites, photocopying, facsimile machines, tape recordings, compact discs, and computers. In isolation, but also increasingly in various combinations, these now constitute the information technologies of modern society. David Lyon has emphasized the importance of military, commercial and government factors in explaining their development, and insists that only careful social analysis will expose the effects and available choices for future developments (Lyon, 1988: 26-41). Four reasons are given for government involvement in information technology. It gives the country economic and political strength; commercial development of the technology requires coordination; national economic and cultural autonomy need to be retained; and the example of the Japanese Ministry for International Trade and Industry.

Because human understanding and effective human decision-making depend on having relevant information, it seems reasonable to expect that a modern democratic government concerned with human well-being will include on its ethical agenda, the development and equitable distribution of information. It is, however, an item with many dimensions and often considerable moral ambiguity.

The 'Information' Concept

The concept of 'information' seems to imply relevance and effectiveness - that a significant message has been imparted to someone who can now be described as 'informed', at least in relation to that matter. Strictly, as with the concept of education, information is always person-specific. Also it needs to be subject-specific - 'informed about what? Further, the information needs to be accurate, otherwise it is 'misinformation' or 'disinformation'. A host of factors will affect how much any one person is informed and about what. They include the person's cognitive capacities and learning habits; the person's direct life experience; interests, values and responsibilities; the person's basic and continuing education; access to, use of, and confidence in, the various 'information' media (books, newspapers, magazines, journals, radio, television, computers and in particular the Internet), and the data contained in them; and the person's learning from direct contact with other people with relevant knowledge.

The Moral Significance of Information

The moral significance of information does not come from the information itself, but from the way in which the information shapes, or gives form to, the informed person's understanding of his or her world, and what they can do about it. Information does not determine its use, only human purpose and choice can do that. If human well-being is the prime ethical value, moral assessment of information requires linking the use of the information to improvement of the human condition. The world abounds with examples of informed individuals, groups and nations using their knowledge for narrow sectional purposes without regard to the impact on others, or actively trying to harm others classified as enemies or even just competitors.

A Government's Ethical Information Agenda Item

The development and distribution of information for ethical use should be a major item on an ethical agenda for government. It would have a number of overlapping components - the information aspects of the education systems, the professional system, the research systems, the information storage and retrieval systems, and the mass media.

The Education Systems

To enhance human well-being, the society needs education systems that impart information relevant for ethical use; that encourage curiosity and capacity to seek out and assess relevant information; that develop a critical capacity to assess the validity of information provided in its various forms; and that develop capacity for moral reasoning to guide the use of the information. The teaching occupation in its various professional segments (see p. 150), whether employed in government or independent institutions, is centrally involved in these issues.

The Professional System

The society needs professional groups that take responsibility for the organization of occupations, that develop and use specialized information in the public interest, and not just to protect their own interests, and that work in a cooperative coordinated way in the public interest, both internally and with other societal institutions. Government-created occupational monopolies can lead to restrictions on knowledge development and distribution. A professional may, however, make relevant information available to a client which extends the client's understanding and respects the client's autonomy. Provided the client uses the information in an ethically justifiable way, and there are not major impediments to people seeking relevant professional assistance, this can be a major way of ensuring that relevant information is used by citizens. Professionals may also make information available in suitably understandable form in the media, and not rely on client-specific situations. Recent developments in information technology are beginning to have a significant, but as yet uncertain, influence on the professional system.

The Research Systems

New important information can come from systematic research. An ethical government wants research systems which tackle subjects of relevance to human well-being, which build on existing knowledge, which use valid, reliable and ethical research methodology, which undertake both pure and applied research, which operate in an open, cooperative, but critical environment, and which make research findings accessible through effective publishing systems. The institutional review boards in the United States, established by federal regulation since the 1970s to provide 'ethical' reviews of researchers' government-funded projects, demonstrate a particular model of government action. They are, however, dominated by research interests.

The Information Storage and Retrieval Systems

Unless a society has adequate systems of information storage and retrieval, its educational, professional and research activities are in jeopardy. Librarians have become professionally organized and have often taken the lead in developing public libraries and archival collections, and in the use of electronic storage and retrieval. However, as employees they operate within the financial and policy restraints set by their employers, and they do not have substantive knowledge of the information they help to store and retrieve.

The Mass Media

An ethically responsible government wants mass media which are not concentrated in too few hands; which report news accurately and fairly, and separate reporting from commentary; which make clear in editorial policies what are their news values; which cite their sources, except in ethically justifiable circumstances; which respect the privacy of people and organizations unless a sound public interest argument is made; which give fair coverage to a range of views when dealing with controversial issues; which give more than just brief, superficial, and transitory handling of issues; which report on, and critique the media themselves, and rectify their own mistakes; which are not heavily influenced by the interests of advertisers; which separate commercial advertising from reporting; which carry only ethical advertising; which do not concentrate only on bad news; which do not just reflect the interests and values of the media proprietors, or of the majority of the population, or of particular powerful groups, including the political party in power; which do not manipulate the news to effect political change; which avoid sensationalism; which do not concentrate on violence and criminal behaviour; which indicate to people the nature of their content so people can choose not to view or listen; which pay due regard to the age, ethnicity, culture, and sex of the users; which stimulate informed political debate; and which do not concentrate only on political leaders and their images. (See Hurst and White, 1994; Goodwin, 1987.)

In recognition of the problems of having the media in the hands of commercial interests, governments may set up television and radio channels, independent of commercial pressures, to balance the media choices of the population and act as possible standard-setters for the media. The commercial-public 'balance' differs greatly in the United States and in Britain, with Australia being somewhere between the two. Standard-setting bodies may be set up for various parts of the media, by government or by commercial media, and/or by professional groups working in the media. The recent emphasis on government deregulation, for the media and other areas of public responsibility, has led to greater focus on 'self'-regulation by media organizations, both separately and together. (Hurst and White, 1994: 18-24, 252-9, 270-97; Atwan, Orton and Vesterman, 1986: 75-114.) Widespread concerns about the increasing irresponsible power of the media are likely to lead to a greater monitoring of media performance and possibly greater direct government involvement.

The Power, Responsibility and Limitations of Journalists

One particular professional group which might be expected to have a positive ethical influence in a democratic government's handling of media issues is journalists. Traditionally known as the Fourth Estate, they have claimed a special responsibility to keep people informed about relevant developments and events, and to act as a watchdog not only on government, but on all of society's institutions. The Code of Ethics of the Society of Professional Journalists, Sigma Delta Chi, in the United States, refers to 'the freedom and responsibility to discuss, question and challenge actions and utterances of our government and of our public and private institutions' (Goodwin, 1987: 368). Part of the First Amendment to the Constitution - 'Congress shall make no law... abridging the freedom of speech, or of the press...' - has been used to assert this sort of implied responsibility. But it has also been used to resist the development of any general standards for journalism or the media, whether by government or by journalism itself. (Goodwin, 1987: 5.)

A Canadian empirical study of news sources - in courts, police forces, legislatures, public bureaucracies, private corporations, and citizens' interest groups - has demonstrated how 'sources and journalists join together socially, culturally, and on beat locations as interdependent participants in knowledge production and use' (Ericson, Baranek and Chan, 1989: 395). Clearly the nature and amount of publicity vary greatly according to the context, purposes, power, level of trust, and organization of the parties involved (Ericson, Baranek and Chan, 1989: 377-98).

Despite the claim that 'the public's right to information' is an overriding principle for all journalists (see Hurst and White, 1994: 270, 14-15; Goodwin, 1987: 9-11), every person and every organization requires 'a workable level of privacy' (Ericson, Baranek and Chan, 1989: 8). Although the sources in the Canadian study complained about 'superficiality, distortion, inaccuracy, and lack of content' in the communications of the news media, they still felt bound to cooperate with them because of the perceived power of the media in the political process, and the potential costs of non-cooperation (Ericson et al.: 243). The dilemma is particularly acute for politicians who depend so heavily on media publicity, particularly on television whose format tends to emphasize image and brief rhetoric rather than substance (Ericson et al.: 172-258, 305: Windschuttle, 1988: 307-27). The development by organizations of public relations units, staffed often by former journalists, can effectively control journalists' access to an organization.

Although journalists are strategically important in the production and distribution of information through the media in a modern, democratic society, they are not strongly organized as an occupation, let alone as a professional occupation. The great majority are employed in media organizations which are basically commercial enterprises, and which must pay regard to their financial profitability. They have complex relationships not only with their sources, as already indicated, but with their editors and their publics. Editors need a journalistic background to achieve credibility with their reporting staff, but as editors they may not be members of the professional association of journalists or be bound by its code of ethics.

Media employers have been slow to accept professional education for journalism, or even to see need for university-level general education (Goodwin, 1987: 46). The quality press often now employ specialist reporters to cover various fields which cannot be easily covered by generalist reporters. However, given the breadth of scope of the media, and their constraints of format, resources, time, and sponsorship, the occupation of journalism obviously does not operate from a basis of shared knowledge and values which could give some consistency to ideas about 'the public interest' (see Hurst and White, 1994: 15-16), when government media policy is being debated.

Satisfying Employment for All

The media play an important role in keeping the public informed about the general employment situation, in advertising job opportunities, and in shaping attitudes to those who are unemployed. The changing nature and significance of paid employment for human well-being and the commitment of government to the maintenance of conditions of full-employment have already received some discussion in Chapter 3 (pp. 57-8). An earlier generation with memories of the Great Depression of the 1930s placed full employment on the ethical agenda for government, and was concerned increasingly with not just the availability of work, but the quality of the work experience. The idea of a living wage was established as a feature of Australia's arbitration system early in the twentieth century.

By the 1990s, the commitment of government to full employment has become uncertain. With the pressures of technological change, and the claimed economic gains from deregulating labour markets and becoming effective competitors in the international economic system, increased levels of unemployment have become politically acceptable and regarded as inevitable even by socially concerned governments like the recent Australian Labor Government. In her 1993 book, sociologist Jocelyn Pixley provides the case against developing 'alternative work' in an 'informal economy,' and guaranteed income schemes, as meaningful options for people 'disqualified from social and political life by unemployment'. She argues convincingly that, in place of these 'post-industrial dreams,' 'the only progressive solution to contemporary joblessness lies in genuine employment opportunities for all who want them.' (Pixley, 1993: 302.)

Modern democratic governments have an enormous impact on the work opportunities of the people who live within their boundaries - through their population policies, their attempted overall management of their society's economic system, their direct employment of large numbers of people in government programs, their subsidization of the employment of people in non-government organizations, the industrial relations system, the health and safety regulations in work settings, the education and training opportunities, the registration system for selected occupations, anti-discrimination legislation, employment exchanges, and the social security policies. Because of the continuing central importance of work for people living in a modern society, it is scarcely surprising to find democratic governments so heavily involved in the employment system. The ethical challenge for government is to make that involvement fruitful for human well-being.

Professional groups are, of course, an integral part of the employment system. Their work is often said to have inherent interest, but because they claim to be performing important functions for the society and not just for themselves and/or their employers, the groups expect government policies to reflect this. However, governments may, in fact, give very different levels of recognition to the claims of the various groups. This may reflect historical responses, a current pragmatic political response, or it may be the outcome of a careful, informed assessment within a public interest framework. Since each professional group is necessarily more limited in its human well-being frame of reference than a democratic government, no matter how reasonable a profession's proposals may be for a society, they still have to be coordinated with the claims of other professions and other functions and placed in priority in relation to the society's available resources.

Professional groups, like doctors, social workers and psychologists, may express their concern to government about the human cost of unemployment, and social workers in particular may emphasize the social injustice of it, but there is no one professional group that has made human employment its central, ongoing concern. Vocational counsellers and some modern managers try to match individual capacities and interests with job possibilities, and some labour economists have taken a special interest in the human aspects of their subject, but no occupation has an overriding value of satisfying employment for all and is professionally organized accordingly.

Income Security

Dating from the Elizabethan Poor Law in Britain, government has accepted some degree of responsibility for its destitute citizens. In nineteenth century Australia, this took the form of government subsidy to private charity, to avoid the hated British poor law tradition. In the circumstances of a modern, democratic, industrial society, government responsibility for destitute people was transformed into government income security systems which came to typify what was called 'the welfare state'. As we have seen, however, an ethically-conscious government will have human well-being as its prime value for all of its agenda items.

The income security item which has been traditionally described as 'welfare' is a large, complex, and sometimes controversial area of government, and it can be even more complex in a society with a federal system of government. Because of the significance of market transactions in modern society, every citizen needs at least a minimum income to lead a decent life and to meet unexpected or additional responsibilities. Thanks to the striking advances in economic productivity, affluent societies can achieve this if they have the political will to do so. But decisions must be taken which balance the interests of beneficiary groups (people who are aged, young, women, men, disabled, sick, unemployed, indigenous), contributors (if the system is based on the so-called 'social insurance' principle), taxpayers (if the system is financed from general government revenue, or is subsidized from general revenue), employers (through paying earmarked taxes, or establishing work-based income security systems), and all those affected by the government's management of the economy (the income security system's influence on savings, investment, and inflation). Decisions about levels, conditions, and administration of payments, 'benefits', can greatly directly affect people's well-being. Also it is obvious that a wide range of other ethical agenda items, such as health, education, and employment, link with the income security item.

The existence of an effective national income security system has radically changed the context and nature of work in the 'helping' professions such as social work and medicine. Although social workers have held senior policy and administrative positions in social security departments in the United States and sometimes in Australia, and there have been attempts in the United States to link income assistance with the receipt of professional counselling, income security is not the province of any one profession. It is, however, a major field of public administration. Economists have been active in research and discussions of 'poverty lines', income redistribution, and the relationship between income security and taxation systems. Various professionals and social scientists have engaged in discussion of the need to extend the notion of poverty, beyond just financial poverty.

The subject of this chapter is intimidating - for citizens, politicians, government officials, professionals, and scholars alike. The ethical challenges of a modern, democratic government are immense and complex, and the patterns of professional organization and involvement in government agenda-setting are variable and often morally ambiguous.

Earlier generations identified more and more human situations as items to place on the agenda of government because, either directly or indirectly, governments were seen to have the capacity to do something constructive about them. They were assumed to have a 'public interest framework', a democratic legitimacy, a coordinating capacity, relevant expertise, and legal power, unmatched by any other institution of society. The dramatic failure of the Communist bloc's socialist experiment with totalitarian government, a re-emergence in liberal democracies of a political philosophy which emphasizes freedom from government interference, and concerns about government rigidity and inefficiency and government inequity, have all contributed to reduced confidence in government as an ethical institution, that is, one which has human well-being as its prime value. Unless, however, the ethical legitimacy of democratic government is reaffirmed by a reforming process, rather than government being dismantled, a society will have no over-arching agenda, let alone one that can be used for ethical purposes.

7 Collective Non-Government Ethical Agendas and Professionals

People live their lives not just as individuals, but as members of a variety of collectivities, each of which has an agenda of significance for human well-being. The previous chapter has already discussed the central importance of an ethical agenda for government in modern society, but what about ethical agenda-setting in the host of other collectivities which impact on our lives? And again, are professionals a help or hindrance? Although there are few clear-cut answers, the prime value of human well-being continues to suggest the terms in which the answers might reasonably be sought.

Both in law and in everyday speech, we often personify collectivities, talking as if they were persons with human characteristics, purposes and will. Also, we can become emotionally attached or loyal to an ideal image of a collectivity, which may be based at least partly on past experience and which psychologically induces continuing commitment. We can talk of *the* firm, *the* family, *the* agency, *the* union, *the* profession, and so on, as if it is a living body with a life of its own, and to which we can relate in the same way as we relate to any other person. Yet by definition, a collectivity consists of a number of human beings, and sometimes, in a mass society, a great number. Certainly, sociological accounts of collectivities can see them persisting beyond the membership of particular individuals, but the concept of human well-being never makes sense apart from the well-being of particular human beings.

In fact, a collectivity can only act through people who are authorized by its rules, and because people perform many roles, we need to know in what capacity they are acting before we can know whether their action is a duly authorized action of any particular collectivity. (See Benn and Peters, 1959: 235-44.)

A prime concern for human well-being calls for understanding of the basic biological facts of human life, for obviously these are the realities and conditions within which humans must live their lives, and they explain why they are social creatures living in collectivities.

Families

Human life begins when a sperm which contains the genetic material of a male fertilizes an egg which contains the genetic material of a female. This sets in train a process of growth, development, and change, which passes through various biologically-based phases - embryonic, infant, child, adolescent, young adult, middle age, and old age, covering roughly 70 to 80 years in societies where social, economic and political conditions have enabled people to live out their full biological life spans.

Like other animals, humans have reflexes and also general drives for food, water, and sex, but unlike other animals they lack instincts, that is, fairly complex chains of behaviour in which an animal moves toward a goal without much prior learning (Goode, 1982: 21). Because they lack instincts and take many years to mature (much longer than any other animal), young humans need both care and instruction over a long period of time if they, and the species, are to survive. Their saving grace is a complex brain, which gives them a capacity for symbolic and abstract thought, and enables them to learn, initially through transmitted cultural solutions, how to live and to flourish as a human being with their particular biological inheritance and circumstances.

There are many reasons why some of the most morally significant rules and values in any society relate to the creation and rearing of children, and there are many legal rules which can shape people's conduct in these matters. Children come into existence as a result of the actions of others and may be wanted or unwanted, expected or unexpected. As has been mentioned, they are especially dependent on others for opportunities to grow and develop, but they are vulnerable to being hurt by others because of their inexperience, size, and lack of resources. Their needs and vulnerability give them special claims on those who are rearing them. Because their carers are usually highly involved with them emotionally, they can be a source of great satisfaction, but also at times of deep distress. Finally, the future well-being of the society can be placed in jeopardy if children are created and then not successfully reared to take their place as responsible adults in the society when it is their turn. Child creation and rearing is both a highly personal matter and a matter of considerable social responsibility.

The collectivity most centrally associated with the creation and bringing up of children is, of course, the family. When the Australian Federal Government established an Australian Institute of Family Studies in 1980, the Institute was expected to focus on 'factors affecting family and marital stability..., with the object of promoting the protection of the family as the natural and fundamental group unit in society' (Australian Institute of Family Studies, 1994: 8). From 1993, it has reported to a Minister for Family Services. 1994 saw widespread discussion about the concept of family, stimulated by the United Nations' International Year of the Family. At least some now insist that the concept should cover all the various primary group living arrangements now common in western industrial societies, which links the concept with the word's origin in 'familia', the Latin word for household. Others insist, however, that the term is generally understood to refer to kin relationships, and especially those which arise from the procreation and rearing of children.

Every individual has male and female biological parents, and is also biologically related to others produced by their mating. This produces a set of persons immediately biologically related to each other. Another additional and overlapping set of biological relationships is formed, when the individual mates and has children. (Harris, 1985: 290.) The vast majority of individuals mate and have children, and increasing numbers do this more than once in the course of their life. These sets of biological relationships form the basis of family or kinship groups, but what rights and duties biologically-related individuals have to each other is determined by cultural, social, and individual choice. What rights and duties they *ought* to have requires moral reasoning which takes into account the interests of all the people involved, both inside and outside the group.

In modern society, individuals have simultaneous membership of many distinct groups or collectivities. This can give them a rich and varied existence, but at the same time it makes living a human life a complex and sometimes difficult undertaking, especially if the person is to develop a sense of identity and integrity, and is to operate on a moral basis paying due regard to the claims of others as well as themselves. Rights and duties arising from the various memberships can be in competition with each other, and can, in fact, actively clash.

A person may cope with pressure or conflict by resigning from membership of one of the collectivities, or from a particular position in the collectivity, so they are no longer involved in its rights and duties. But one type of collectivity a person cannot resign from is family, although under special circumstances a child may now try to legally 'divorce' his or her family. A person is embedded in family rights and duties by convention, sentiment, law, and moral argument in various ways throughout life. The relevant family collectivity is never static; it develops and changes as the person and associated family members move through their life cycles. It makes sense to talk about moral agenda-setting in and for families, because how they operate has a great influence on human well-being, but the idea requires clarity about who belongs to the particular family in question, in what ways this family membership impacts on the well-being of each of the members, and how the family's operation affects non-members.

There is often reluctance to undertake a moral analysis of family relationships, because they are seen as bound by love and intimacy, not by rights and duties. It is remarkable that a book published as recently as 1982 could still claim to be 'the first philosophical study to offer a general theory of parenting' (Blustein, 1982). Its author concedes that the notion of duty might not be very prominent in the way people normally think about parenting. Nevertheless, natural affection is not always strong enough, consistent enough, or well-enough informed in all circumstances, for talk about parental duty to be pointless. (Blustein, 1982: 103-4.)

There are various family forms (see Sussman, 1977), and a particular person often will experience a number of them, in the course of their lifetime. The great majority of people start life and spend their childhood in an immediate family group, consisting of their biological parents or parent, and other offspring, because those who procreate are expected to take special responsibility in the rearing of those they have brought into the world. The adult members of this group usually have a marital relationship to each other, which is recognized by law, and they jointly have parental responsibility for their children, which in the modern world often involves seeking the assistance of others such as teachers, doctors, social workers, school and vocational guidance counsellors, community nurses, and the rest. But why should all the procreators have this over-arching responsibility? Successful child rearing clearly requires knowledge and skills, and resources. Surely children reared by parents who do not have these are being unfairly treated, both in absolute terms and in comparison with other children in the same society. A major reason for the development of public social services has been to make more equal the opportunities of all children in relation to their health, education, recreation, basic shelter, and food, but families still need knowledge and skill to use these effectively.

Preparing people with relevant knowledge and skills for successful parenthood has never been a major societal service, although at times the need for it has received serious attention by both politicians and professionals. For instance, in Britain in 1972, the Secretary of State for Social Services, Sir Keith Joseph, drew attention to what he called 'a cycle of deprivation', the persistence of problems from one generation to another, and suggested that a policy of 'preparation for parenthood' might play a part in breaking it (*The Family in Society: Preparation for Parenthood*, 1974: 5-7). This led to consultations with professional and other organizations, and a seminar of experts from many disciplines, which served to warn the government against 'over-simple and under-sensitive reactions' to 'the problems (perceived) in families struggling to cope with multiple deprivations'.

The seminar of experts realized they were treading on delicate ground. First, despite government assurances to the contrary, they did not want attention to be diverted away from the underlying social and economic difficulties of families. Second, they were aware of the need to be explicit about the value assumptions in notions of 'good and bad parenting' and possible lack of consensus on some aspects of these. Third, interventions in family matters involved subtle and complex feelings and had to take fully into account the individuality of the persons involved and their situations. (*The Family in Society: Dimensions of Parenthood*, 1974: 106-7.) During the consultations, 'a new cadre of professionals' was proposed, either specially recruited and trained, or drawn from the ranks of existing professions, with some additional skills. Perhaps this would eventually have led to a societal service. Instead, however, all professions and services in a position to identify those 'at risk' were urged to take part in the task of preparing them for parenthood. (*The Family in Society: Preparation for Parenthood*, 1974: 21-2.)

In the opening paper to the seminar of experts, Joan Cooper, the Director of the Social Work Service of the Department of Health and Social Security, suggested that a family home was functioning effectively when it:

- offers adequate shelter, space, food, income and the basic amenities which enable the adults to perform their marital, child-rearing and citizenship roles without incurring so much stress that anxiety inhibits a confident and positive performance;
- secures the physical care, safety and healthy development of children either through its own resources or through the competent use of specialized help and services;
- acknowledges its task of socializing children, encouraging their personal development and abilities, guiding their behaviour and interests and informing their attitudes and values;
- offers the experience of warm, loving, intimate and consistently dependable relationships;
- assures the mother support and understanding, particularly during the early child-rearing period, and provides the child with a male/father/husband model which continues to remain important through adolescence;

- offers children an experience... of group life, so extending their social relationships, their awareness of others and intellectual development;
- responds to children's curiosity with affection and reasoned explanations, and respects children through all developmental stages as persons in their own right, so securing affection and respect for others within the family circle and wider social network;
- cooperates with school, values educational and learning opportunities, and encourages exploration and a widening of experience;
- supports adolescents physically and emotionally while they are achieving relative independence of the family, personal identity, sexual maturity, a work role, relationships within society and the testing out of values and ideologies;
- provides a fall-back supportive system for the young marrieds during their child-bearing period. (Cooper, 1974: 12.)

Blustein observes that adoptive parents frequently have a clearer idea of the care and attention their child will require than biological parents and are less likely to misjudge their desires and capacities to rear (Blustein, 1982: 145-6). In order to maximize the probability that children will be raised by competent and willing parents, he suggests two distinct forms of marriage. A licence for parental marriage would only be granted to couples who met certain genetic, economic, and psychological criteria relevant for parenting, and had already spent time in an initial marital union, which would have given them opportunity to deal with problems of mutual adjustment before becoming parents. (Blustein, 1982: 241-3.) In a parental marriage, divorce would be made more difficult, but would be less necessary anyway.

Although Blustein presents strong ethical arguments for his proposal, its achievement would be impossible in a society with a strong liberal democratic philosophy, because it smacks of 'Big Brother' and 'social engineering'. Also, there is the serious worry that the idea could be used to restrict unfairly access to parenting for already disadvantaged people, and take away from them one of life's most fulfilling possibilities, given adequate resources and supports.

Trying to achieve Joan Cooper's suggested attributes of an effective family becomes difficult and sometimes impossible - if the parents do not maintain a committed, long-term and loving relationship, if they do not have an equitable division of labour in terms of their tasks and talents, if they do not have adequate financial and other resources, if they do not have a fulfilling life beyond the confines of the family, if they split up, if they are sole parents, or if they must divide their attention between children of a former marriage and those in a current marriage.

Many anxieties have been aroused by changes and instability in family living. It is significant that the Australian Institute of Family Studies was established under the Family Law Act 1975, which introduced 'no-fault' divorce as well as a counselling service attached to the Family Law Court. Older patterns of maintaining a loveless, bitter marriage 'for the sake of the children', or because of religiously-sanctioned marriage vows, have little to commend them ethically, and the radical change in many family arrangements towards female members having equal moral consideration is long overdue. Further, the development of moral education for children and the encouragement of their moral autonomy can complicate family processes, but it is likely to produce a greater capacity for understanding the normative complexities of the world in which they are living.

One way or another, professionals of various kinds and at various levels of professionalism, can be heavily involved in family matters - in officiating at a marriage ceremony, in pre-marital and marital counselling, in sex therapy, in family planning, in fertility counselling, in genetic counselling, in attendance at childbirth, in preparation for parenthood, in prenatal and postnatal care, in adoption counselling, in family social casework, in family therapy, in child abuse counselling, in paediatric medicine, in general medical practice by the self-described family doctor, in pharmaceutical practice by the self-described family chemist, in providing child care, in the education of a family's children, in the design of the television programs that children view, in passing and administering legislation relating to families and their resources and environments, in representing couples in divorce proceedings, in mediation work, in financial counselling, in family research, in preparation for retirement, and in geriatric medicine.

Family therapists are one professional group who view each family system as a whole and are concerned about making family functioning more equitable and effective (see Grunebaum, 1985). However, they assist only a tiny proportion of the population, they focus primarily on intra-family functioning, and typically they are involved only at one period in a family's life cycle. Also, it seems odd to use 'therapy' language for what they do.

Family agenda-setting is influenced by cultural and social class factors, and by a general political climate which will differentially emphasize the interests of men, women, children, the family as a whole, the economy, and the nation (greatly emphasized in time of war). But whatever the general influences, actual family agenda-setting will always be specific to the time, place, circumstances, and individuals involved. Agenda-setting for this kind of non-government collectivity is of vital human significance in modern, mass society. Inevitably it raises questions of justice within families and between families. Because of the particularity of family relationships, their long time-span, and the open-ended nature of commitments based on love, friendship, and gratitude, it is not surprising that family agenda-setting is such a complex, slippery and often controversial subject.

For-Profit Organizations

After the family, the most common non-government human collectivities in modern society are business, 'for profit', commercial, or market-based organizations. These constitute the private or free enterprise sector, where the organization is owned and operated by private individuals as opposed to government-owned ventures. The term private is also used to signify that they are entitled to maintain secrecy and to be free to do whatever they want to, provided they stay within the law. This means that despite their great impact on human well-being, they can escape close external scrutiny whether it be by government authorities, politicians, research scholars, or the media. It may also help to explain why neo-classical economists have concentrated on deductive abstract models of economic behaviour, rather than empirical study of actual behaviour in business organizations. (See Toohey, 1994.)

By definition, making a profit, or paying regard to what is often simplistically referred to in the media as 'the bottom line', is a necessary item on the agenda of 'for profit' organizations, but in itself it is not an ethical agenda item. Financial wealth is not an end in itself, although it can give access to many things which are valuable to human well-being, and it can be gained through a process which provides people with goods and services for sale, and jobs and incomes. Also financial wealth can, of course, be used for harmful purposes, it can lead to excessive concentrations of power, and it can be gained in ways that hurt people - by exploiting them in the production process, and by ignoring the interests of people and the environment external to the immediate transactions. An ethical agenda for business cannot, then, consist of just the one item, the maximization of profit.

The private sector is very diverse in size, legal forms and patterns of control. Some of its collectivities are huge - for example in 1984, Exxon had sales of $91 billion and Citicorp had assets of $150 billion, and in 1983, General Motors employed almost three quarters of a million workers (Green and Sutcliffe, 1987: 20). Most small companies are owned by families, small groups, or individuals, while the majority of big companies are owned by stockholders. Only a small proportion of the population are stockholders - about one tenth of the adults in the United States and in the United Kingdom owned more than nine-tenths of the shares in the mid-1980s - and only a tiny proportion of the population has most of the holdings. (Green and Sutcliffe, 1987: 24.)

A modern trend of special significance for the examination of the role of professionals in agenda-setting in business organizations is the development of what are called 'professional' managers who now control such organizations rather than the owners. Indeed the Harvard School of Business has as its motto 'To make business a profession' (Grace and Cohen, 1995: 64). With the proliferation of business schools, it is obvious that knowledge and skills relevant for the management of business is systematically being identified, researched and taught, laying the basis for claims to professional status, in more than just the simple sense of doing it for a living. Until, however, the occupation can demonstrate that its knowledge, skills and behaviour are informed by morally justifiable values, it does not have the grounding necessary for an autonomous professional occupation worthy of the name. Business managers do not combine in professional associations which claim a public service ethos and develop sanctioned codes of ethics for their members. Some of them take leadership in the development of codes of conduct for their organization, or combine with morally sensitive others in developing industry-wide codes, but these are not professional codes, and may be developed primarily to prevent government intervention or to increase profitability for the firm or the industry, rather than to make their activities ethically justified.

Depending on the type of business, the managers may have a professional qualification - in engineering, accountancy, law, architecture, medicine, nursing, pharmacy, journalism - which gives them relevant substantive knowledge and skills, and they may have also undertaken general management courses and/or management courses specific to their original disciplines. Their particular professional background may give them legitimacy both internally and externally when such knowledge and skills are seen to be relevant. The essential value components of professionalism can, however, raise complex and often difficult issues for professionals in a business context - particularly when different professions are involved in the same organization, when some people have more than one professional commitment, and when the organization's ethos is in conflict with that of one or more of the professions involved.

The first tenet in the Code of Ethics of the Australian Institution of Engineers boldly asserts: 'The responsibility of engineers for the welfare, health and safety of the community shall at all times come before their responsibility to the profession, to sectional or private interests, or to other engineers.' (Grace and Cohen, 1995: 177.) Are business managers with an engineering background members of the engineering profession, members of a business management profession, members of both, or members of neither, in the sense that they have no active commitment to either? To some, the innovative and risk-taking functions of business would become unduly restricted if it were to become the preserve of professional elites (see Grace and Cohen, 1995: 187-8). Others would argue that already the managerial group tends to operate with its own career interests in mind, and that genuine professionalism would encourage a public interest framework for their work.

A major reason for the lack or ambiguity of professionalism in the occupation of business management, and in the work of various professionally qualified people in a business context is that the moral status of business organizations themselves is far from clear. It tends to have been viewed differently at different times and in different places, and in accordance with the size and type of organization involved and the nature of its products.

At one extreme, have been the recently collapsed socialist societies of Eastern Europe where, inspired by Marxist theory and ideology, such organizations were viewed as against the interests of the people and were made illegal altogether. In these societies, a wave of unexpected political revolutions has replaced an often corrupt, totalitarian, closed, communist regime of low economic productivity but high environmental damage, with an open, liberal democratic political regime and a new market economy. Max Charlesworth has commented, 'Those who see recent events in Eastern Europe... as a triumph for the market capitalism, ought also to recognize that it represents the triumph of one state supported economic system over another' (Charlesworth, 1993: 202). He insists that the market cannot function outside of the context of commercial law and morality, and in support quotes an American book by Solomon and Hanson:

> Business is not a world unto itself and, indeed, needs a power greater than itself to protect its very existence. This is true not only in those transitory and much-debated areas such as protection from low-cost foreign competition, government subsidies for research, and selective tax breaks for certain industries. It is true of the nature of the business game itself. Business could not exist, for example, without respect for and when necessary, the enforcement of contracts. Government regulation, in this sense, is as basic as the civil law itself. It is not

an imposition on business but the foundation that makes business possible. (Charlesworth, 1993: 199.)

But this is not, of course, the extent of the interdependence of business with a modern society's other social institutions - even in the United States. Governments and a host of not-for-profit community organizations, as well as families and other informal social groups are making their respective contributions to the well-being of the population, making them a more productive work-force for business, trying to deal with human harm done as a result of for-profit activities, and dealing with those who cannot obtain a living from selling their labour or investing their capital.

The cold war in fact always represented antagonism between two extremes, communism and capitalism, neither of which represented a way of life which could be morally justified if human well-being is the prime value. Freed from the ideological straight-jackets imposed by membership of blocs dominated by each of the extreme super-powers, societies now have far greater opportunity than ever before to address moral issues raised by business activity and the operation of markets. The recent political climate in the western democracies with widespread distrust of governments and acceptance of deregulation and privatization, has made the task even more urgent, because the current generation often has no knowledge or memory of why, morally, government regulation and government enterprises were developed by earlier generations.

Just a generation ago, when H.B. Acton undertook his ethical exploration of markets, he observed that the free market economy was morally condemned by a large part of the population. This was for five main reasons. It exulted the vices of selfishness and avarice to the rank of virtues. Its competition was a source of strife which should be replaced by cooperation and public service. Competition anyway led to private monopoly and subsequent tyranny. Capitalist entrepreneurs and workers were in the grip of an impersonally operating system which took no account of justice or morality, and lost sight of the satisfaction of human needs which should be the purpose of the production system. And finally, it was held that the competitive market economy was chaotic and unjust by comparison with planned economies. (Acton, 1971: 1, 9.)

The recent popes of the Catholic Church, including the present John Paul II, have been strong critics of the capitalist societies because of their treatment of the poor, their encouragement of excessive consumption, their failure to provide adequate work opportunities, their growing economic inequality, their environmental degradation, and their 'hyper-development'. Yet, perhaps remarkably, in a recent encyclical, John Paul II can still see the free market as 'the most efficient instrument for utilizing resources and effectively responding to needs'. (Langan, 1993: 59.)

Through market operations most of the economic wealth in a capitalist society is generated, most of the paid jobs are provided, most of wealth accumulation opportunities are available, and most of what economists call 'goods' and 'services' are produced and sold. The market system as a means of maintaining a whole society is a relatively modern, revolutionary idea, given its first impressive articulation by a moral philosopher, Adam Smith, in *The Wealth of Nations*, published in 1776 (Heilbroner, 1980: 40-72.) Although the contemporary world is vastly different from that of Adam Smith's day, his views are still being used to justify minimal government 'interference' with the market, and 'market solutions' to a wide range of problems are urged especially by economists and by politicians of the New Right. Milton Friedman (see, for example, Friedman and Friedman, 1980) is the latter-day Adam Smith and his ideas seem to have been highly influential with various governments in the 1980s - the conservative Reagan government in the United States, and the Thatcher government in Britain, and the Hawke Labor government in Australia.

The basic idea of the market theorists is incredibly simple. Each person should do what is to their best monetary advantage; the interplay of one person against another will result in the necessary tasks of society getting done. In the words of Robert Heilbroner, 'In the market system the lure of gain, not the pull of tradition or the whip of authority, steered each man [sic] to his task' (Heilbroner, 1980; 18). He points out that the profit motive as we know it is only as old as 'modern man'. 'A general struggle for wealth diffused throughout society' is peculiar to recent societies organized on capitalist lines. (Heilbroner, 1980: 22-3.) It was an economic revolution brought about by the emergence of national political units which developed common laws, common measurements, and common currency; by the gradual acceptance of merchant activity by Christian leaders, particularly Protestants; and by various material changes such as the development of towns, road systems, accounting devices, and a host of inventions even before the industrial revolution. Further, it is only in the modern era that the basic means of production, land, labour and capital, have been conceived as 'impersonal, dehumanized economic entities'. (Heilbroner, 1980: 31-4, 25.)

Max Charlesworth has recently observed deep 'cultural' differences between business practitioners and ethical theorists (Charlesworth, 1993:

187). Amongst practitioners the idea that business is amoral retains a great deal of force, and practitioner concern for an ethic of 'enlightened self-interest' is hardly moral (Charlesworth, 1993: 191-3). He urges an institutional development within business of various devices, as has happened in medical ethics and bioethics, to encourage greater dialogue between business practitioners and those who reflect on ethical dimensions of business and commerce (Charlesworth, 1993: 203-5). There needs to be a 'revised and enlarged' view of both business and ethics. Many in the business community have been put off by 'simple-minded moralism'. Ethical reflection clearly requires more than application of ethical principles, just as business needs to be understood in terms of its context and the variety of human relationships involved, not just market relationships. The central myth in the sub-culture of business is 'the market' seen as a self-regulating mechanistic device, with ethical considerations irrelevant to its functioning. (Charlesworth, 1993: 193-9.)

If human well-being is the prime value, what, then, are the kinds of things likely to be included on the agenda for business organizations, and what influence should professionals have, particularly in a changing world of rapidly increasing, but changing expertise? Items for the agenda may be reflected in and suggested by mission statements and industry-wide and organizational codes of conduct, and may be derived from items in a corporate planning document. Again, however, as with individual choice, the agenda - literally the things to be acted upon - is morally relevant only because the agenda items are based on actual conditions in the real world, and it is considered something constructive can be done about them in terms of human well-being. 'Doing' is always time-, place-, resource-, purpose- and agent- specific. The items are not part of an ethical agenda if they are not intended to be acted upon, or if they have become obsolete because of changed circumstances or changed purposes.

Brief reflection on the business system suggests the multiple ways in which it affects human well-being, and an ethical business agenda would need to show awareness of this. The interests of shareholders, directors, employees, suppliers, consumers, and society can all be involved in complementary and/or conflicting ways.

Shareholder Interests

A business organization of any size must attract and retain shareholders to invest in the company. The interests of shareholders should be served by accurate information about a company's prospects and its performance, but how a company's profits should be divided between shareholders, re-investment, and wages and salaries is often contentious and can fracture the organization in industrial disputes, and disputes between shareholders and directors. The interests of shareholders can receive some protection by regulation of stock exchanges and government Securities Commissions.

Limits may be set on the proportion of shares held by any one person, to limit their power and to spread the benefit of membership of the company. As already mentioned, however, widespread shareholding amongst citizens has not yet been achieved, although this is one of the avowed purposes of recent privatization of public enterprises. Those who do invest are often advised by financial consultants, but this is not in itself a professional occupation even though accountants, lawyers and others often engage in it. Occasionally investors may be urged to avoid 'unethical' firms, but at present few would have the relevant knowledge and perhaps inclination to act accordingly. Unlike medieval times, it now seems reasonable that a person should benefit from lending his or her savings to a commercial venture (see Benn and Peters, 1959: 166-7), but the system can open up wide economic inequalities and consequent social divisions between those who can save easily from large incomes and those who need most of their income for current consumption. Also income derived in this fashion, especially from speculative activity which contributes nothing to the production of needed goods and services, is often seen as less socially valuable than income derived from personal exertion. Depending on the tax system, and their actual tax paying, influenced by their professional advisers, the wealthy can, however, make a disproportionate contribution to government activities through their taxes, and they may use some of their money to support voluntary welfare activities and the arts.

The Interests of Directors and Managers

How much directors should receive in fees can be contentious, and conflict of interest can occur when a director has other interests which affect or are affected by the operations of the company (see Costigan, 1993: 125). People with professional backgrounds may serve as company directors especially when their particular knowledge is seen as relevant for the company. Are they doing this in a private capacity, or as a member of their profession, or is this irrelevant because they are legally required to fulfil their responsibilities as directors anyway?

Business managers tend to be well placed to look after their own financial interests, as is indicated by their remuneration packages that are large, sometimes huge, in comparison with senior management in the public sector, and wages in their own companies.

Incorporation and limited liability, privileges granted by the state, have allowed concentrations of economic power that would have horrified Adam Smith. These need to serve 'wider purposes than the aggrandizement of those who head these organizations' (Sampford and Wood, 1993: 21).

Employee Interests

An ethically justified agenda for a business organization would include concern for the well-being of its employees. The well-being of an organization's employees can be affected by many factors - the availability of alternative work, the organization's hiring and firing practices, anti-discrimination legislation, health and safety legislation, superannuation legislation, the cooperation or otherwise with government regulators (see Gunningham, 1993), the profitability of the organization, the particular expertise of employees and their contribution to the organization, the extent of unionization and the way unions operate, the systems for setting remuneration for the different types of employees, the amount and type of remuneration, job security, promotion prospects, and the nature and extent of company-based and community-based welfare provisions.

A long-standing concern about the well-being of employees is that in large, bureaucratic settings, they have become separated from the purpose and product of their work. The work has little intrinsic interest and no personal point for the worker except that it gives him or her what is ironically called 'a living', even though it occupies much of a person's time in a 'soul-destroying' fashion. An ethically aware firm would be expected to be organized so that its workers can 'live' while working and not just act under orders and in response to economic incentives.

Management theorists in the 1980s have emphasized the development of corporate culture as a means of enhancing managerial control. In the words of Amanda Sinclair, 'Through a sense of purpose, a shared set of meanings and a sense of involvement or ownership, organizational culture (can) directly enhance organizational effectiveness'. The culture can be moulded to ethical ends by two different approaches. In the first, management creates a strong, unitary and cohesive, organizational culture around core ethical values. The methodology for this is well established, and Johnson and Johnson is cited as an outstanding example. But, say the critics, this in fact reflects the ethics of the managers, it offers no real answers to the ethical dilemmas faced by people in the organization, and the ethics are not genuinely internalized by much of the organization. Further, a strong, cohesive culture can be undesirable. People can become too devoted to the organization and unresponsive to its environment, and the organization can lose its capacity to cope with conflicts of interest and dissent. (Sinclair, 1993: 134, 138-40, 147.)

The second approach tries to understand the value differences of subcultures within an organization, and points to potential consensus. For example, instead of 'imposing corporate-derived ethical values', the managers are here expected to understand and unleash the moral commitment towards goals which are consistent with those of the organization. This is especially relevant for organizations which employ various kinds of professionals. According to Sinclair, it is this subcultural approach that offers most ethical promise. It 'requires a role for management which supports and advances just organizational norms, while recognizing the importance of debate and devolution of power in their devising and ongoing enforcement', but 'it ultimately relies on individual, rather than institutional processes, to produce better ethics'. (Sinclair, 1993: 141-3, 148.)

Consumer and Public Interests

Johnson and Johnson acknowledge 'responsibility to all... who use our products and services' (Sinclair, 1993: 137). A claimed virtue of the market system is that the consumer is king. It is the consumer's 'demand' expressed in the purchase of products and services of business organizations which supposedly drives the system. 'Demand' has an imperative ring about it, yet what purchases consumers can make is obviously conditional on many things - how much money or credit they have, the consumers' knowledge of the product, guarantees attached to it, their need for it, their desire for it, other needs and desires, the costs of production, the profit margins sought by the supplier, the asking price, how many are interested in the same product, their market strength, and so on. Consumers can learn about products and services from other consumers, from seeking the advice of professional experts, from information provided by consumer organizations, or from government consumer departments. The great bulk of consumer information comes, however, from businesses which are trying to persuade people to buy their products, and a huge advertising business has arisen, with special links to the business media (see pp. 178-80), to help them do so. These both stimulate and shape consumer demand. They are certainly not disinterested sources of information.

Standards in advertising are not safeguarded by codes of professional ethics, for advertising is not organized along professional lines. However, government, citizen, and industry concerns can lead to the development of advertising codes. For example, until its abolition in 1996, the Advertising Standards Council in Australia examined complaints from individuals or organizations in terms of an advertising code which contained fifteen rules. According to these, advertisements must be assessed in terms of their probable impact; must comply with the law and not encourage unsafe or illegal behaviour; must not be demeaning or discriminatory; must not cause serious community offence; must not be deceptive; must be distinguishable as such; must disclose their source when they are controversial; must not exploit superstition or play on fear; must not disparage competitors or their products; must not harm children or urge children to pressure parents to purchase products; must not use misleading or irrelevant data; must only use honest testimonials; and guarantees or warrantees referred to in advertisements must comply with the law. (See Grace and Cohen, 1995: 109-10, for the full code.)

The sponsorship by commercial organizations of sporting competitions and events, is an insidious form of uninformative advertising, and commercial media interests have begun to take over control of what were originally community-based sporting competitions. Winning players now routinely thank commercial sponsors, corporate officials speak at the conclusion of a competition, and the corporation's name is attached to the name of the competition. The winners can receive huge monetary rewards subsidized by sponsors, and can in turn enter into lucrative contracts with commercial organizations to endorse their products. The commercial organization has no particular interest in the sports or the individuals involved, yet its advertising interests are being allowed more and more to intrude. The hypocritical example of sponsorship of sport by tobacco companies is just an extreme example of the way commercial organizations are increasingly insinuating their presence and their products into the public consciousness. Paying for their products to appear in films and television shows is another strategy.

Increasing numbers of people can make a living from sport - as players, usually for only a small part of their adult life, as coaches, commentators, journalists, and administrators. Sporting occupations are, however, usually sport-specific. They may be unionized, but are not organized on professional lines, and rarely produce countervailing public interest arguments when corporate money helps to support their particular sport.

Subsidizing welfare organizations and the arts has been a long-accepted practice by commercial organizations, particularly in the United States, and especially when it is tax deductible. It is usually without strings attached, and the donor's name does not get attached to the organization but is acknowledged in annual reports. This corporate giving may be justified in the name of 'good citizenship', although it is an odd reason because 'citizenship' implies political membership of the state, and corporate motivation can be to support 'voluntary' organizations as a positive alternative to state provision. Some claim business fulfils its general social responsibilities by paying its taxes, and any other payments should be seen as outside the proper role of business.

Environmental Interests

Another set of concerns for an ethical agenda for a business organization relates to its impact on the environment - in the pollution of the planet's land, air and water; in using up non-renewable resources; and in the destruction of plant and animal species. These actions diminish the current quality of life, and reduce the life options for future human generations, as well as ignoring any claims to consideration which other parts of the natural world might have. Although these concerns have quickly become politically significant in widespread public concern (Grace and Cohen, 1995: 152), in an active Green movement, and some Green parliamentarians, the response of governments and companies has not been as dramatic as would be suggested by the claimed size and urgency of the problem. Companies have now been encouraged to act before government does. 'Self-regulation, it is argued, is more likely to be knowledgeable and effective than government regulation.

The Valdez Principles, developed after the *Exxon Valdez* ran aground in 1989 in Alaska, commits signatory corporations to protect the biosphere; to a sustainable use of natural resources; to reduction and disposal of waste; to wise use of natural resources; to reduce risk to employees and the public; to marketing safe products and services; to provide compensation and repair environmental damage; to disclosure of environmentally harmful incidents and protection of whistle-blowing employees; to appoint directors and managers qualified to address environmental issues; and to assessment and annual audit, made public, of compliance with the principles. (Grace and Cohen, 1995: 159.)

'Principles of Environmental Management', developed by Australian corporations, and endorsed in 1992 by the Business Council of Australia, indicate an acceptance of the international idea of 'ecologically sustainable development'. (See Burnup, 1993: 184; and Grace and Cohen, 1995: 162.) However, consumers are not yet willing to pay for the full cost of the products they consume; further, if prices reflected full costs, only the more affluent could afford them.

The Commercialization of Modern Life

A feature of modern life has been its increasing commercialization, where more and more things are 'commodified' for sale and can be purchased if you have the requisite money. Yet everything does not, and should not have a price. Love, family relationships, friendship, loyalty, votes, national security, body parts, human freedom, human life are, or ought to be beyond the reach of the market. In its pursuit of profits an ethical business will not run rough-shod over these central aspects of human society. Yet, often indirectly, market activities can impact on them.

Not-For-Profit Organizations

What remains to complete this discussion of the main components of the moral action universe is consideration of agenda-setting for that part of a society which is formally organized like government and commercial bodies, but unlike government is based on freedom of association, and unlike commercial organizations is not primarily engaged in making a profit. Depending on context, ideology, and purpose, these organizations are variously described as 'voluntary', 'non-government', 'community', 'not-for-profit', 'non-profit', 'private', or 'third sector', or some combination of these. The notion of them belonging together in a 'sector' is common in macro social and economic analysis, but it is a meaningless notion unless it is related to the whole of which it is claimed to be a part, and it is evident why this particular 'cut' or classification makes sense.

Moral and political analysis requires that not-for-profit organizations be differentiated in terms of what they intend to achieve and what they actually achieve for human well-being. In these terms they are very diverse indeed. What they all share is their dependence on voluntary initiative and commitment. They have formal independence from government, but government may be heavily involved in setting limits on their activities, in providing their members and their office-bearers with legal safeguards, in regulating their fundraising activities, and even providing financial subsidies which can take various forms, and may or may not have strings attached (see Horsburgh, 1980: 20-9).

It is not always clear in whose interests voluntary organizations are operating. Membership organizations are intended to further the interests of the members, but these in turn require ethical assessment, and organizations of any size need to rely on governing groups, office-bearers, and employed staff, whose interests may displace those of the members. Welfare organizations are intended to provide benefits or service to others. This is the rationale for their existence. They may have members who identify with the organization's objectives, and they will have governing groups, office-bearers, staff and often voluntary helpers, but the organization's purpose is not to serve the interests of these people, except to the extent that this fulfils the service mission of the organization. The 'welfare' objective itself, again requires ethical assessment.

Voluntary Welfare Organizations

A basic ethical as well as organizational problem in welfare organizations is often the lack of clarity in the objectives of the organization. Objectives may not be stated at all, or if they are they may be 'generalized public relations objectives' or 'over-generalized "soft" objectives' (Stein, 1962: 22-4).

There are many advantages in a welfare organization having defined, clearly stated objectives. They provide general direction and purpose for the organization. They set down guidelines for organizational activity. They identify short and longer range goals for the organization's programs. They constitute a source of legitimacy for the organization's existence and particular activities. They support bids for the use of scarce community and organizational resources and gain general sanction for specific agency activities. They establish for sponsors and clientele expectations of what the organization aims to achieve. They provide standards against which the effectiveness and efficiency of the organization can be assessed. They provide a basis for its accountability to its clientele and sponsors. They help the organization remain primarily service-oriented rather than reflect the organization's own needs. They make possible more effective planning of coordinated community service systems. They provide a basis for comparative evaluations between agency programs and of the same programs over a period of time. And they provide a basis for those connected with the organization gaining a better defined sense of purpose and of achievement. (Report of the Objectives Committee, 1981: 2.)

Rough estimates in the first national empirical study of non-government welfare organizations in Australia, undertaken in the early 1980s, revealed 'an industry of some considerable magnitude', even when many organizations in the education and health fields were not included. Tens of thousands of organizations were operating with a total income of some billions of dollars, over a third of which came from government, and with the possibility of almost a million employed staff and 1.7 million volunteers (these were the highest estimates). (Milligan et al., 1984: 13, x-xi).

Given the large number of organizations, serving on the governing board or management committee of a voluntary welfare organization is a fairly common experience, at least within some social groups. It has not, however, attracted much scholarly or government attention, partly because the field is so large and diverse, and partly because of a reluctance to scrutinize closely work done for the community on a voluntary basis. Yet because of its significance for human well-being, including the particular vulnerability of many of its clients, it can be argued that it should come under especially close ethical scrutiny. We need to be reminded of the historical diversity of motivations for providing welfare services. Dunham mentions, for example:

... religious concern or belief; philanthropy; a moralistic desire to 'make over' human beings; fear and repression; economic gain; self-expression or self-glorification on the part of donors and founders of charities; scientific investigation; humanitarianism; and the democratic notion of joint responsibility. (Dunham, 1958: 4.)

Whatever may be the individual motivations of board members, collectively they have continuing responsibility for agenda-setting for their organization. To do this in an ethically responsible fashion is a complex, difficult, and sometimes thankless task, and one that they cannot accomplish successfully without the full cooperation of the employed staff of the organization and especially its chief administrator.

Voluntary or non-government welfare organizations can contribute to human well-being in many different ways. The British Wolfenden Committee describes replacement, relief, and reinforcement roles in relation to the informal system of family, friends and neighbours (Wolfenden Committee

Report, 1978: 22, 41-2). In relation to the statutory or governmental system, a voluntary organization can act as a pressure group on government, as a pioneer of new services, as a provider of complementary, additional, or alternative services, or as the sole provider of services (Wolfenden Committee Report, 1978: 43-9).

According to British social policy scholars Kathleen Jones and her colleagues, voluntary social services have eight main justifications - they have an initiating role; there is need for continuing partnership between them and statutory services; there are jobs which statutory services cannot do; there is virtue in diversity; they are socially cohesive; all needs cannot be met by the state; they offer a critical dimension; and the public needs information (Jones et al., 1983: 87-9).

In his comparative study of voluntary agencies providing services for disabled people in the Netherlands, England, the United States and Israel, Kramer identifies four roles traditionally ascribed to voluntary agencies - a vanguard role, an advocate role, a value guardian role, and a service provider role. He found, however, that the pioneering role was rare. The services tended to be more specialized than that of governments, but were more substitute services rather than complementary and qualitatively different. (Kramer, 1981: 9, 263.)

After thirty years' experience in voluntary welfare agencies, in Australia and internationally, David Scott differentiates a number of functions of voluntary organizations, some of which are also performed by government agencies. They fill service gaps. They provide people with a choice of service. They help people to use government services more effectively. They monitor and research both government and non-government services. They engage in community development. They share resources to help establish new programs. They act as mediating structures between the individual and the public sector. They engage in innovation. And they undertake social action to change social structures and social conditions. (Scott, 1981: 20-33, 77-97, 101-50.)

These various commentators indicate the wide range of agenda possibilities for voluntary organizations, and each organization has to decide where it stands amongst them, and where it ought to stand if its agenda is to be an ethically justifiable one. Obviously working collaboratively with other organizations who share the same basic values and purposes can greatly extend an organization's potential for human well-being, but to do this effectively requires considerable knowledge, and skill, and the more serious the attempted collaboration the more likely it is that value and policy conflicts may be exposed.

Coordinating Bodies

Many voluntary welfare organizations in North America, Britain, and Australia have membership of general coordinating or peak bodies called by a variety of names - councils of social agencies, community welfare councils, councils of social development, councils of social service. They may also have membership of more specialized bodies, which may in turn have membership of these general bodies. An Australian Industry Commission Report in 1995 described peak councils as an important element of the sector's structure, performing an intermediary role between the sector and government, and representing a resource to its members. A survey for its report discovered at least 188 peak councils. They had greatly increased since the 1970s, partly because of the expanded service provider role of the voluntary sector, deeper interest in consumer input to services, and increased government funding to the sector. (Industry Commission, 1995: 182.)

The 1995 Industry Commission Report differentiated five roles for peak councils - disseminating information, supporting members, coordination, advocacy and representation, and research and policy development. Individual peak councils gave these different priorities depending on their objectives and membership. Thirty per cent of the peak councils surveyed reported a national focus for policy interaction with government. The Commission commented that organizations may gain economies of scale and higher quality information from peak council membership, but they may disagree with the policy agenda set by the peak body. This can lead them to remain independent, or to group with agencies of similar character and policy position, or to represent their own policy position to government on a particular issue. (Industry Commission, 1995: 183, 186, 184.)

In terms of policy and functional focus, social policy peak councils take a broad perspective, aiming at social development goals for the whole of a community or social group; service development peak councils focus on service delivery in a particular field; and consumer peak councils focus on specific disadvantaged interest or client groups. Peak councils derive their representative status from their membership, yet many claim to speak on behalf of much broader social groups. The Commission commented: 'The source for such a mandate however is unclear, given that there is no formal accountability of the peak council to these broader groups'. Membership may include service provider organizations, other non-profit organizations such as peak councils, corporate bodies and individuals, depending on the policy and functional focus of the peak body. It is not clear, says the Commission, how the tension which emerges from having mixed memberships of organizations and individuals is reconciled. (Industry Commission, 1995: 186-7.)

Issues of coordination between welfare organizations are obviously complex.

> In Australia, as in other Western countries, social welfare organizations have arisen in a piecemeal, largely haphazard fashion. By definition they are all concerned with the personal well-being of individual community members - but which ones, in what locality, in what aspects of their lives, with what skill, and under whose sponsorship? Clearly every organization is specialized, and limited in its social welfare interest and scope. Whose responsibility is it, then, to coordinate the work of the organizations so that from a community point of view their efforts are most productive? If people answer 'the democratically elected government', which level of government and which authorities within government? In any case, would and should government intervention be tolerated by the non-government sector of social welfare? Structurally the situation is greatly complicated by the possibility of coordination according to any of the specialized bases on which the organizations are built - clientele, location, program, and auspice. (Lawrence, 1966: 36.)

Funding

Unlike the North American scene (see Murphy, 1977: 480-1), cooperative fundraising and associated local community planning has never become a prominent feature amongst Australian non-government welfare organizations. The Australian Industry Commission Report could only mention relatively few Australian examples of cooperative fundraising. It recognized significant advantages in the development of a combined approach to fundraising, but better coordinated welfare planning was not listed among them. (Industry Commission, 1995: 238-40.)

The Commission observed that Australians did not seem to be large donors to not-for-profit organizations. They gave annually about $A100 per capita, with 50 per cent from individuals, 28 per cent from business, 15 per cent from bequests and 7 per cent from trusts, compared with almost $A600 in the United States, with 83 per cent coming from individuals, 5 per cent from business, 6 per cent from bequests, and 6 per cent from trusts. The difficulties of making such international comparisons, when the tax and

welfare systems, the per capita incomes, and community expectations about
government and community organizations differed, were, however,
acknowledged. (Industry Commission, 1995: xxxvi, 229-30.)

The Commission noted the 'increasing professionalization of fundraising'
(Industry Commission, 1995: 221) and discussed the competition for
donations. The Fundraising Institute of Australia (FIA) is described as a
professional association which accredits fund-raisers on the basis of their
experience, education, and 'service to the profession'. In 1994, it had only
1048 members, but claimed that 80 per cent of community social welfare
organizations used the services of its members. The FIA expressed concerns
about judging levels of efficiency on the basis of fundraising cost ratios and
placing legislative controls on the costs of fundraising. The Commission
agreed that the latter was not desirable, and favored 'self-regulation, for
example, voluntary accreditation by a professional association' over state
licensing. It had heard concerns that many fund-raisers were untrained and
inexperienced, fundraising agent and consultant fees were not structured to
reflect their performance, and the public were often not aware of the
proportion of fundraising which went to fundraising agents and consultants.
(Industry Commission, 1995: 241, 237, 240.)

Government Funding

As governments have become interested in purchasing service from voluntary
welfare organizations, the focus has shifted towards payments for achieved
outcomes rather than on the basis of stated intentions, but the complexity and
multi-purpose nature of social service work often makes this problematic. The
more government insists on carefully prescribed monitoring and program
accountability which is increasingly expected when government funds are
being used, the more questionable becomes the voluntary status of the
organization. Whether receiving government funding or not, any ethically
conscious voluntary welfare organization might be expected to be more
conscious of its purposes and its achieved outcomes. If these coincide with
what the government is willing to provide funds for, then the organization's
capacity can be greatly strengthened, without its autonomy being seriously
breached.

In the United States, from the early 1960s, voluntary organizations
became progressively dependent on purchase-of-service by government so
that by 1980 private contributions accounted for only 33 per cent of the total
revenues of voluntary social service, community development, and civic

organizations. In 1983, Gilbert pointed out that any decrease in public social service expenditure would both heighten service demands on voluntary agencies and reduce their fiscal capacity to maintain even current levels of effort. (Gilbert, 1983: 132.)

New Emphasis on the Voluntary Sector

In a number of countries, including not only the United States, but also Britain and Australia, the prolonged period of persisting unemployment and recurring economic recession from the mid-1970s to the early 1990s increased the need for welfare services at a time when governments were trying to reduce overall expenditure and re-emphasize the role of the voluntary welfare sector and the family. Yet the changing roles of women in families and changing family patterns have made families often less capable of being service providers and more in need of services themselves. And the voluntary sector has not had the capacity to take up additional welfare responsibilities, because many actual and potential donors are themselves under economic pressure, many married women are in paid employment and no longer volunteering their services to community agencies, and new standards of effectiveness and accountability are expected of voluntary agencies by their clients, by professionals, and by public and private donors.

Enough has been said to indicate the complexities of agenda-setting for voluntary welfare organizations. On the face of it, because of their public commitment to the well-being of others, it is assumed that such organizations have ethically justifiable agendas, but in the complicated society in which we now live, it is often far from obvious on what situations a voluntary organization ethically should concentrate. Goodwill continues to be necessary to work for common causes, and to gain and retain legitimacy, but clearly it is not enough. It needs to be expressed in 'an overall ends-means framework' which covers all the work of the organization, which is coherent and intelligible to all who are associated with the organization, which has periodic review points and is sensitive to changing circumstances, which takes into account community needs not served by other organizations and needs in the constituency which the organization is currently serving, which takes into account the resources needed to accomplish its objectives and realistic constraints on the organization, and which has the commitment of those who work for the organization. (Report of the Objectives Committee, 1981: 1.)

Professional Involvement

The involvement of professionals in influencing agenda-setting for voluntary welfare organizations varies greatly between organizations, and can vary within the same organization at different periods of time. Gilbert and Specht have noted in the management of community affairs 'a continuing cycle of competition' between the values of participation, leadership, and expertise, with each value tending to be associated with a rather different view of the public interest. They warn against social planners just 'drifting on the currents of change towards whatever value happens to be in favor'. The planners should chart an independent course of action which keeps each of the values salient. In this way, both democracy and social welfare will be served. (Gilbert and Specht, 1974: 184-9, 196-7.) Generally, however, there is no one social planning profession which can undertake this role, desirable though it may be for human well-being.

Without employing professionals who can successfully identify examples of unmet needs and discover gaps in services, who can research these, and who can inform relevant people about the situation (see Gilbert and Specht, 1974: 16-18), a voluntary welfare organization is unlikely to have an agenda which is convincingly justified.

The administrative or managerial head of a welfare organization can be viewed as having the overall responsibility to ensure that each of the various stages of collective rational action for human well-being is pursued effectively and efficiently. This must include the agenda-setting stage as well as the later policy, program, and results stages. A governing board operating usually on a voluntary, spare-time basis does not have the capacity or the perceived legitimacy to undertake this necessary coordination function. It can, however, appoint a chief executive, administrator, or manager to be accountable to the board for such coordination.

Given the great expansion of welfare organizations, both government and non-government, since World War II; the increased complexity of the social environment, both in terms of the problems to be addressed and of the society's welfare response; and the development of knowledge relevant to the improvement of the human condition through welfare intervention, it might be expected that welfare administration would emerge as a recognizable professional activity. Certainly with its direct implications for human well-being, it is an occupation with a high moral significance. Generally, however, the occupation is fragmented. Welfare administrators do not have their own distinctive educational qualification, their own codes of ethics, or professional associations. Depending on their educational backgrounds and experience, they may belong to an established, broader professional association, for example, an association for social workers, or for psychologists, or for psychiatrists, or for doctors, or for urban planners, or for teachers. Within these, the administrators may form a specialized interest group, membership of which may or may not be associated with management education, provided by the profession's own schools or by general management schools. One reason for the occupational fragmentation is the contested nature of the welfare management role and whether it is best done by people trained in business or public administration, or with more welfare-specific education and training.

Rosemary Sarri acknowledges that there are many management technologies useful in all formal organizations - goal setting, resource allocation, personnel selection and control, assessment and evaluation, and staff training and development. She highlights, however, critical differences between a human service (or welfare) organization and organizations that pursue profit and individual goals. Because of these, the administrator needs to be fully cognizant of the opportunities and constraints so that he or she can act as 'expert-advocate' of the program managed. Administrators require knowledge about 'social service technologies as well as needs of clientele', and exert leadership in the promotion and protection of critical values. Sarri notes, however, the recent decline in the numbers of professionally trained social workers in management roles in the public social services in the United States, yet professional social work knowledge is necessary for the effective management of a human service organization. (Sarri, 1982: 19-30.) In 1983, Patti noted that in an increasingly conservative political and economic climate, many welfare management positions now went to generalist managers who had 'no substantive background in or demonstrated commitment to social welfare programs'. (Patti, 1983: 1-23.)

In 1987, Patti observed that service effectiveness should be the principal concern of management because 'changing people and/or the social conditions in which they live is the raison d'etre of the human service agency, not the acquisition of resources, the efficient utilization of resources, or the satisfaction and development of staff'. These may be important in their own right, and even instrumental in providing effective services, but they should be subservient to the agency's main objective. (Patti, 1987: 9.)

Rapp and Poertner have provided indications that the field of human service management in the United States is not client-centred. Agency and program goals are not stated in terms of benefits to clients. Agency information systems are dominated by productivity and financial data, rather than effectiveness data. Management or staff meetings rarely focus on 'how well we are doing' in terms of clients. 'These practices and a myriad of others manifest goal displacement whereby achievement of the mission of an agency is preempted by organizational maintenance'. The systematic monitoring of client outcomes is rare, in part, because of four myths - the outcomes are highly idiosyncratic, they cannot be measured, we cannot be held accountable for client outcomes, and monitoring outcomes will take too much time and resources. The authors cogently challenge each of the myths. To the authors, 'not to monitor client outcomes substantially and use that data to improve operations is tantamount to managerial irresponsibility, incompetence, and unethical conduct'. (Rapp and Poertner, 1987: 24-36.)

Despite this emphasis on service effectiveness, now being emphasized in the social work administration literature (see Patti et al, 1987), Harold Lewis points to the moral complexity of the manager's position (Lewis, 1987: 271-84). He observes that giving primacy to clients' interests is required by the code of ethics of the social work profession, but the typical manager is confronted with a plethora of clients whose interests she or he must consider if the organization's work is to succeed - not only the service recipient, but the staff, other administrators, the board, the funding body, and the wider community. The manager's tasks involve making moral choices, often in ethically ambiguous situations.

'Self-Help' Organizations

Recent years have seen a proliferation of what are often called 'self-help' or 'mutual aid' organizations. Professionals, like social workers and doctors, may have helped in their establishment because they can enhance people's autonomy, and because they may be more active advocates of their particular interests than are professions and traditional welfare agencies. Also, they may employ the services of sympathetic professionals as committee members, consultants or staff, although they are usually small with very limited financial resources. Some self-help organizations however, have a strong anti-paternalistic ideology, and are sharply critical of professionalism in any of its forms, and also of welfare agencies run by boards that are remote from the people and the conditions they are supposedly trying to assist. Having a particular problem or condition does not in itself equip a person to run a welfare organization effectively, or to provide help to others. The 'self-help' description can obscure new forms of paternalism. It is both patronizing and

214 Argument for Action

morally unjustifiable not to give these newer arrangements the same close moral scrutiny that all welfare organizations call for.

Client Participation

Since the 1960s, most welfare organizations have experienced pressure to include people who are their service recipients in various additional roles which can influence the service provided by the organization. Service recipients may provide information to an administrator, or a researcher, on their experience of the agency's service. They may participate in an agency committee or provide a consumers' viewpoint. They may become a member of the agency's governing board. Persuading them to participate usually must appeal to altruistic values, such as helping other clients of the agency, or more generally helping others with similar problems.

When there is evidence that a welfare organization may not be primarily focused on meeting the needs of its clients, consumer participation seems an attractive idea, but its feasibility will vary greatly according to the types of service envisaged and the nature of the clients - their age, their other responsibilities, their interest, their health, any disabling conditions they may have, and so on. For those who can and do participate in governing boards, there can be dangers of tokenism and/or being coopted by the non-client majority.

Welfare Accountability

Clearly there are no simple answers to ethical agenda-setting for voluntary welfare organizations, but organizationally, and morally, managing groups both individually and collectively should stay focused on an organization's welfare objectives and be held accountable in these terms. Welfare organizations that fail to do this are not worthy of the name, they bring other genuine welfare organizations into disrepute, and they encourage unjustified general cynicism about motivation of people who are genuinely engaged in trying to provide constructive help to others. There can, of course, be genuine ethical disagreement over an organization's welfare objectives. This should not, however, be confused with a situation where an organization is, in fact, primarily focused on meeting the interests of people other than those they claim to be primarily concerned about. Goal displacement, or goal deception, particularly to serve the interests of powerful, affluent others - whether they be board members, employed professionals, volunteers, private donors, or governments - is especially ethically repugnant in community activities which are ostensively designed to provide help to vulnerable and needy people. Using 'community', 'service' and 'welfare' language can obscure whose welfare is the actual primary focus.

Professional Collectivities

So far ethical agenda-setting has been discussed for various collectivities in which professionals have various degrees of involvement - in government, in families, in commercial organizations, and in voluntary welfare organizations. As we have seen, sometimes their involvement is strategic, in others it is much more remote, but never has it been a sole and complete responsibility. Professionals are, however, fully responsible for the agenda-setting for their own professional associations and professional schools, and for the agendas of their professional practice organizations if they are organized as independent practitioners.

As mentioned earlier (p. 31), in the 1960s and early 1970s, professions were amongst the many social institutions which were targeted to justify their activities socially, and therefore, morally. The idea of 'deprofessionalization' gained rapid currency, at least in some community circles, and has since been evident in various guises - demystifying the language used by professionals, emphasizing alternatives to professional help, not recognizing professional qualifications, and managerialism which focuses on skills and a flexible workforce used instrumentally for its purposes.

If human well-being is the prime value, why is it especially important for professions to be able to justify morally their actions? The brief answer is - because their knowledge and their skills place them in positions of considerable trust and power. Yet it is only reasonable to give them the trust and power if it is going to be used for morally justified purposes. A crucial feature of a profession is hence its so-called 'ethics' which supposedly guarantees that the profession serves rather than exploits the society in which it operates. Professional occupations claim professional status at least partly because of a community service ethic and because their members are said to be ethical in their behaviour. Their specialized knowledge and expertise is a social product acquired often very substantially at public expense, and they are expected to use it in socially justifiable ways. This is particularly the case if the state has guaranteed them an exclusive right to practise. It would be morally intolerable if a legally guaranteed monopoly were used primarily for

Code of ethics for a business

its own selfish ends, and especially if this is done masquerading as a community service.

What a profession professes or avows is typically contained in a written code of ethics. Ongoing open discussion of the content, application and moral justification of such declarations is a useful societal device for keeping the professions socially accountable. For the written code to be more than just a self-protective, public relations exercise, it needs to cover the most important responsibilities of the occupation; it needs to genuinely reflect the actual and normative behaviour of the profession; and it needs to be related to some general theory or theories which justify the behaviour being prescribed.

If a professional occupation has a genuine commitment to maximizing its contribution to human well-being, what sorts of concerns would be on its agenda?[1] These can be considered under four interrelated headings, each with its cluster of relevant questions - the worth of the professional product? who should benefit from it? who should practise the profession? and, how should the profession be organized? Since the focus is still on agenda-setting, no attempt is yet made to examine possible answers by allocation of responsibility, and subsequent policy and program responses. What is being suggested here are generic concerns which the members, leaders, and educators of an occupation which has or claims professional status, might be expected to take seriously, and about which they must make decisions.

1. The Nature and Worth of the Professional Product?

Without a worthwhile product, a profession is without any moral basis for its work. What is produced as a result of the work of the profession and how valuable it is are, then, obvious starting points. Typical concerns include:

- What are the relevant values, knowledge, and skills components and how do they interact to produce the profession's product?
- Is the production of the product the exclusive prerogative of the profession? Should it be? Should the situation be protected by law?
- Does the nature of the product require the length and type of education and training specified by professional bodies and educational institutions?

---

[1] What follows is based on 'Questions for the Practice and Education of Any Ethically Conscious Profession' in Lawrence, 1983.

- How can the quality of the product be maintained through continuing education?
- Is the product changed and improved in response to new knowledge and techniques?
- How much variation in product occurs from practitioner to practitioner? Is the variation harmful or helpful?
- Whose values are reflected in the nature of the product?
- What is the impact of the product on the lives of its consumers? What are the negative as well as positive aspects?
- Since no one profession can possibly provide all the specialized products needed for contemporary living, how does the profession's product get related to the other needed specialized products? Is this left just to the product consumers to do the best they can, or in its education and practice, does the profession give serious attention to inter-professional collaboration?
- Is the usefulness of the product regularly evaluated, taking into account the interests of the various interested parties - consumers, potential consumers, the general public, practitioners, employers, and governments?
- Are the members of the profession reasonably remunerated for the product, taking into account their skill, responsibility, length of education and training, the community needs they are meeting, and relativities with other occupations?

2. Who Should Benefit from the Professional Product?

Assuming that the profession's product is valued, and for good reason, a number of questions arise about who can and who should benefit from it.

- Do all the members of society have equal access to it according to their need for the type of product it is, irrespective of their socio-economic status, their age, their gender, their ethnicity, their religion, and where they live?
- Do the social, political and economic processes that distribute the product do this in ways that are seen to be equitable?
- What roles should be played by the various distribution mechanisms -. commercial or private enterprise, non-profit voluntary organizations, and government agencies at various levels?

- Does the development of specialized aspects of the profession's product reflect an overall concern to provide maximum benefit to society?
- Are the profession's resources equitably distributed across its various specialties in terms of society's need for these specialties?
- Should a profession give prime allegiance to its clients when this ignores the claims and interests of others?

3. *Who Should Practise the Profession?*

A third series of questions focuses on the people who can and should be responsible for the profession's practice.

- Are there sufficient numbers for the profession to produce a valuable product that can be equitably distributed throughout society?
- Do all members of society capable of undertaking the work have equal opportunity to become members of the profession?
- On what basis are people excluded when numbers exceed places available?
- Do members of the profession, and especially its leaders, manifest the virtues of justice, courage, honesty, and sense of tradition, that MacIntyre sees as essential to attaining standards of excellence in any human 'practice' as he has defined it (see p. 18)?
- How dependent are the members of the profession on external goods, like money, power and fame, compared with the standards of excellence or the goods internal to professional practice?
- Do the members of the profession have a prime commitment to it and see their adult life story as importantly bound up with the pursuit of their profession?
- How much do members of the profession identify with the profession as a whole as well as with particular aspects in which they are engaged, or sub-groups to which they belong?
- If members of the profession are not self-employed, do they give prime allegiance to their profession or their employer, in the case of conflict?

4. *How Should the Profession be Organized?*

A fourth and final series of questions focuses on the organization of the profession. It may seem odd to include these in the broad agenda-setting for a profession, but unless they are addressed the very existence of a profession as an identifiable occupation is in jeopardy. Unless the occupation has relevant structures that enable it to address effectively, both in its education and its practice, the kinds of questions and issues that have been raised under the previous three headings, it will not be able to provide ethical justification for its work.

National organization Given the continuing dominance of the nation-state in modern society, this provides the usual frame of reference for professional organization to address the issues that have been raised.

- Should the profession have an over-arching national body which has leadership, membership commitment throughout the nation, resources, linkages and professionalism, which will enable it to maintain and develop the profession in morally justifiable directions?
- Should there be separate, specialized professional associations? If so, what should be their relationship with each other, and with a more general professional association?
- How should the profession's educational institutions be organized? Should they be independent of other organizations or should they be a part of an educational institution containing schools for many different professions and academic disciplines?
- If they are located in technical institutions, does this mean broader knowledge and value questions are neglected? If they are located in universities, does this mean technology is relatively neglected?
- Should the profession's schools have an association of their own, and what should be its functions?
- How future-oriented are the profession's schools?
- What should be the respective roles of the professional association or associations, the educational bodies and employing bodies, in shaping the initial and continuing education for the profession?
- Does the organization of the profession's work enable it to pursue excellence in its practice?
- Is it too much in the employ of others to be sufficiently responsible for its actions and outcomes?

International organization It is difficult enough trying to address these questions in the context of each nation. Yet a significant aspect of a profession is its existence across national boundaries. At least initially, professionals are strongly influenced by the so-called professional literature and often by educators who have received some of their education from professional peers in other nations. The literature is obviously massively skewed in the direction of numerically large nations with resources to publish and sell their products throughout the world. What should be the attitude of a struggling professional group in a developing country, or of professionals in a smaller developed country, to professional literature that has arisen in a social, political, and economic context that is obviously different from one's own? But how different, and do you ignore it at your professional peril, and is it not a source of support and security to know that the concerns of your profession are not just local and peculiar, but shared concerns in other nations of the world? Each profession needs, then, to examine how it functions internationally as well as nationally.

- Do international influences help or hinder the profession's pursuits within each nation?
- How well organized is the profession internationally?
- Does the profession see itself as a world social institution and therefore as addressing the issues already raised, in a global context and not just within each nation?
- Should national professional groups devote a considerable amount of their resources to international affairs so that the development of their profession is more equitably achieved throughout the world, and not just within each nation-state?

8 When are Professionals the Relevant Moral Agents?

The last three chapters have focused on the contribution of professionals in identifying and determining ethically challenging situations for each of the main agenda-setting arenas in modern society - individuals, the government, commercial organizations, and not-for-profit organizations. If in the justification of human conduct, human well-being is the prime value, identifying situations that are most significant for human well-being and about which something constructive can be done is a necessary and ongoing human task, both individually and in various levels and types of social organization. By definition, the people who establish an ethically challenging agenda item expect it to be acted upon. It is more than a matter of interest or concern, it is something that someone can and should do something about because of its significance for human well-being. But who and when is it appropriate for professionals to be the responding agents? This is the focus of the present chapter. (It must be remembered that 'agent' here is *not* being used in the sense of acting on behalf of someone else. It refers to anyone capable of responsible action, that is, action for which they can be held accountable.)

No Relevant Agent

Each agenda item can be seen as providing a logical and practical starting point for a project, which will conclude when results from deliberate action have been obtained. Unless, however, someone accepts responsibility to do something about the situation a project will not proceed. Many factors can explain why an agenda item does not attract an appropriate responding agent - it is too vague or too general; there is basic disagreement over the nature of the situation and/or its implications for human well-being; the situation is too novel for relevant agents to exist; relevant agents exist but cannot be induced to give priority to new and different projects; there are not enough relevant agents; people are willing to respond but not in ways acceptable to the agenda setters; no-one is willing to accept responsibility to decide what to do; there may be legal restrictions on who can act as the responding agent; possibly relevant responders are not informed about the situation; possible responders contend for the opportunity to respond but their legitimacy is not accepted, either because of doubts about their efficacy and /or their values - on the part of clients and/or of those who control financial resources; and apparent agents are found but only at the price of redefining the situation in their terms.

Agent Commitment

The responding agent is the person or persons who accept responsibility to decide what ought to be done in response to the ethically challenging situation. Responding agents are responsible in more than one sense. They have the ability to respond autonomously; they can be called to account for what they do; and they have accepted duties or obligations in relation to the situation in question.

People can become responding agents responsible for deciding what shall be done, in a wide variety of ways, which can influence their level of commitment as a responding agent. There must, of course, be some level of commitment otherwise they cannot be described as 'responding agents'. But the commitment may be minimal, which means the project has low priority and little emotional significance for the agent and is accepted reluctantly. At the other extreme is the whole-hearted, enthusiastic commitment which fully engages the intellectual and emotional resources of the responding agent. The former type of reluctant commitment may arise when the responding agent has had little involvement in determining the original agenda item, is already over-loaded with other responsibilities, does not have the requisite resources or perceived legitimacy to deal with the task, is doing it primarily to please or placate others or to keep up appearances or just for the money or because he or she happens to be best placed to do something, or because no-one else is willing to accept the responsibility, or because the responsibility is shared, or because it is not shared, or merely because it falls within what is expected of a person occupying a particular social role, or because they have no special relationship to the people whose well-being is at stake in the project, and so on.

Obversely, strong commitment may arise when the responding agent has also had involvement in determining the original agenda item, welcomes the additional responsibility because it is congruent with other concurrent responsibilities of the agent, accepts the responsibility out of interest in and concern for the well-being of the people involved and a belief that something constructive can be done, welcomes autonomy within agreed limits, has the requisite resources and perceived legitimacy to undertake the task, and so on.

A reasonably strong commitment to a project on the part of the responding agent or agents is necessary for the project to proceed with any degree of confidence of success, but agent commitment does not guarantee that it will proceed in ethically justifiable directions. The responding agent/s may not be the most appropriate person/s to be deciding what should be done in response to this particular situation, and even if they are, their actual decisions in the case in hand and the criteria they use, cannot escape ethical scrutiny. The next chapter places under such scrutiny the decisions of the responding agents and the criteria they use, but first we need to determine *who* should be making the decisions if human well-being is the prime value.

The Moral Character of Agents

Decisions are always taken or made by particular people and are therefore inevitably influenced by the characteristics and concerns of the decision-makers, otherwise *they* have not made the decision. Yet some theorists in a liberal individualist tradition of thinking have mistakenly tried to ground ideas of social responsibility in so-called rational decisions taken by disembodied individuals who have no prior social identity (for example, Rawls, 1972). These are intellectual constructs, not thinking, feeling, and acting human beings, making reasoned decisions and therefore commitments about their world and their part in it. Because the decision-makers are seen, by themselves and others, to be responsible for the decisions they make, their decisions reflect the sort of people they are or aspire to be.

According to Aristotle and other early Greek philosophers, novelist Jane Austin, and contemporary moral philosopher Alasdair MacIntyre, human character as defined by associated virtues and vices should be the prime focus in ethical discussion (see MacIntyre, 1981). It has been claimed that the modern preoccupation with acts, and principles and rules to guide action reflects a diversion, induced by the need for regulation in modern, mass society, and also by misleading monolithic so-called 'rational' models which have aspired to define right conduct for human beings. The counter-claim to character being primary in ethics is that conduct is primary, and this is what allows us to have notions of character, that is, of continuing human traits, in the first place. Other theorists argue that the two are interdependent, and therefore neither is to be neglected in ethical discussion. Some of these have suggested a neat symmetry between character traits and prescribed courses of action, while others have rightly recognized that some character traits, like compassion, do not seem to give rise to parallel prescriptions of conduct, and virtues are valuable in themselves, and not only because they lead to the performance of certain kinds of acts. On this latter view, human well-being consists both in virtuous action and being a person of a certain character. (See Hudson, 1986.)

It is clear that we value the moral worth of agents as well as of their actions. If human well-being is the prime value, we cannot avoid the responsibility of making such assessments. The Christian biblical injunction of 'judge not lest you yourself be judged' may have served to encourage some people to try to avoid this responsibility. Others seem too ready to judge their fellow human beings, usually because they do not adhere to their own values and standards of conduct. Social work students are challenged not to be judgmental in this sense, and not to pre-judge people on the basis of superficial knowledge and single episodes of behaviour. Further, like Christians, and democratic philosophers, they are expected to respect each person's 'fundamental worth' and have some understanding of what this means. But like it or not, social workers as with everyone else have to make value assessments of people - of both themselves and others, as well as of human conduct.

Assessing people morally is particularly difficult and onerous in modern conditions when we often experience relationships that are brief, transitory, specialized, and superficial, and our knowledge of many others, especially those who are socially, culturally, and geographically distant from us, is at best indirect and fed to us through various media and other cultural screens. The size, complexity, and mobility of modern social living makes genuine character assessment often impossible except for those with whom we associate in families, friendships, small persisting groups, and some long-term occupational relationships, especially with professional peers. This gives considerable scope for cultural stereotyping - where the person is judged on the basis of a particular attribute (such as their gender, skin colour, age, or size) and single episodes of behaviour, as distinct from actual knowledge of the person's interests and capacities gained over a period of time across a range of activities. Other forms of cultural stereotyping occur when people, or a selected group of people are seen as inherently or 'naturally' evil or sinful, and hence to be 'converted' or 'controlled' or 'eliminated'.

Yet the nature of any particular human being is not, and cannot be preordained and therefore prejudged. A person's natural capacities and social, political, economic and cultural context will set limits on and influence that person's actual character, but each person has the inescapable responsibility of living their life and thus determining their actual character amidst the plethora of possibilities. How they live in relation to human well-being, their own and others', cannot be a matter of moral indifference if human well-being is the prime value. If they self-destruct, or they destroy others, or harm others, or refuse to help others when they are in a position to do so, or take more than their fair share of scarce resources, or do not develop and use their natural talents, their moral character is likely to come under ethical scrutiny. They are not seen as excelling as human beings.

A danger of stressing the importance of moral character is that moralists will try to pre-empt human choice by telling people that the ethically good life must take a particular form. There is, in fact, more agreement about what sort of human character is to be ethically condemned, than there is about the possible attributes of an ethically good person. MacIntyre observes that although versions of the traditional scheme of the virtues survive, there is no clear consensus as to which dispositions are to be included within the catalogue of the virtues or the requirements imposed by particular virtues (MacIntyre, 1981: 210). In western thought, a set of seven cardinal virtues has traditionally been delineated - wisdom or prudence, courage or fortitude, temperance, and justice, the 'natural' virtues of the early Greek philosophers, and the Christian virtues of faith, hope, and love. They are cardinal in the sense that they cannot be derived from one another and all other moral virtues are forms of them or are derived from them. Frankena and others, however, consider benevolence and justice to be the only cardinal moral virtues in this sense. If a disposition cannot be derived from these it is not a *moral* virtue. (Frankena, 1973: 64-5.) The values of benevolence and justice in turn can be seen as expressions of the even more basic value of respect for persons, so that if human well-being is the prime value, *the* cardinal virtue is to be respectful of persons. From this all other morally justifiable virtues flow, and moral vices can be identified. On the one side are the character traits which enhance human well-being; on the other are the traits which diminish human well-being.

Professionals' Moral Character and Intellectual Capacity

It will be recalled that for MacIntyre the virtues of justice, courage and honesty, together with an adequate sense of tradition, are necessary components of any 'practice' with internal goods and standards of excellence, and that their exercise is a crucial component of the good life (see pp. 18-19). Each occupation organized on professional lines can be viewed as a 'practice' (medicine and architecture are explicitly mentioned by MacIntyre) which requires its members to exercise these virtues otherwise it will not persist and continue to provide internal goods which are also good for the whole community who participate in the practice. (MacIntyre, 1981: 178.)

Beauchamp and Childress have observed that the 1980 version of the American Medical Association's professional code eliminated almost all traces of the virtues, except that physicians 'deficient in character and competence' were to be exposed. They contrasted this with its first code in 1847 which was based on the work of Thomas Percival who had arrived at conclusions about the physician's proper traits of character based on the premise that the patient's best medical interest is the proper goal of medicine. (Beauchamp and Childress, 1989: 381-2.)

It is evident that what are seen to be 'the proper' or most appropriate traits of character for a professional will vary according to the responsibilities expected of the professional, and these in turn will vary according to what is perceived to be the professional's role. As the expected role of a profession changes, so too will the appropriate character profile, or the weight given to particular elements in it.

A person's character consists of a number of elements which together contribute to that person's identity. When a person is deciding as a professional what ought to be done in response to an ethically challenging situation, the person's whole character is inevitably engaged, such is the responsibility and complexity of the choices being made. They must decide to take on the responsibility in the first place and on what terms, whether in collaboration with others or with sole responsibility, or they must decline to take it on, and decide whether or not to refer it to others, and if so to whom? Their professional education and experience will make them aware of the possibilities for an appropriate response to the situation by a member of their profession, and by them in particular. It may also have alerted them to the possibilities of working collaboratively with people outside the profession. They may, however, be genuinely unaware of the existence of other more appropriate responding agents or be antagonistic to them.

As clarified in Abbott's work (see pp. 85-6), professions and professionals compete in the workplace, public, and legislative arenas for recognition, jurisdiction, and reputation. Typically they lay claim to special expertise which their clients and others do not have, but their professional expertise is always a combination of values, knowledge and skills. The knowledge and skills only have relevance when related to the values and consequent purposes which professionals are trying to achieve. The very idea of professional knowledge and skills is instrumental to the purposes of the profession in question, and can have no independent existence.

What knowledge and skills are relevant to the profession are regularly under debate within the profession, and especially amongst its educators. Professional education cannot avoid normative or value issues, and they are now receiving more systematic and explicit attention with the developing interest in the teaching of professional ethics. The idea of the good professional has always, however, included normative features. People with personal characteristics seen to be unsuitable for the professional role have not been admitted into professional courses, or have been counselled out along the way, or have been failed in clinical or field work. And much reliance has been given to learning by example from appropriate role models in the profession.

Individuals, organizations, communities and whole societies are particularly vulnerable to exploitation by professionals because they cannot check the validity of their knowledge and skill claims, except sometimes by past results if these are available. This means that they must place considerable trust in the virtues and integrity of professionals when they are seen to be the most appropriate responding agents, and have at least some assurance that their values and purposes are ethically justifiable.

If human well-being is the prime value, professionals are, then, appropriately employed as responding agents to ethically challenging situations, when they are capable of ethical reasoning to justify their decisions, they have relevant knowledge and skills to decide what should be done, they are willing to be accountable for their decisions, have sufficient commitment to the task, others cannot do the task better, they are not primarily interested in the achievement of external goods, money, power, and fame, they are willing to cooperate with others when this is appropriate, and they do not respond in a routine, pre-determined fashion without independent assessment.

The development of so many different occupations on a professional basis or aspiring professional basis, has been the main way of institutionalizing expertise in industrialized countries (Abbott, 1988: 323). It is scarcely surprising that we turn more and more for help in deciding what should be done to people who are engaged full-time in particular areas and who have invested in acquiring the relevant expertise to make their way in occupational markets in private practice or government or non-government organizations. But it is only ethically justifiable if the professional is a person of good character and has been effectively socialized into a socially responsible professional role. Otherwise resort to professionals can lead not only to unjustifiable dependence but to morally outrageous outcomes, for example, when professionals are using clients to achieve fame and fortune without regard to their rights and interests, when professionals and clients are colluding to exploit others, and when professionals are making false claims about the efficacy of their work, or are unwilling to examine its effects.

Only empirical study will reveal the extent to which a particular occupation recruits people of reasonable moral character into its educational system, and suitably shapes that character as people learn to become practising professionals. If their upbringing and schooling has failed them in their earlier moral education and their professional socialization is too brief or concentrates mainly on technical and knowledge aspects of the job, and/or if they are mainly interested in the power, status, and money rewards expected from the job, they are clearly not relevant moral agents.

Is it reasonable to expect higher standards of conduct from professionals than from other members of society? Codes can provide certain minimum safeguards that can be used to prevent or at least limit, the most harmful forms of behaviour, but can they realistically go beyond this to specify ideals of conduct and character? If there is too big a gap between the reality and the ideal, either in terms of the numbers aspiring to it, or the degree of its attainment, a professional code can bring an occupation into cynical disrepute. Members of a professional occupation may keep a strict limit on its numbers and jealously guard its reputation, but at a cost of limiting community access to its services and demanding too many personal sacrifices of its members. Clearly balances must be struck between minimum and ideal standards, and how these relate to the numbers of practitioners, and what can reasonably be expected of the individual practitioner.

Bayles points to a number of possible ethical models for the professional-client relationship, each built upon a different view on where the responsibility and authority in decision-making ought to lie. He argues for a fiduciary model, which recognizes the professional's superior knowledge, but acknowledges that one or more of the others might be appropriate for certain specialized types of situations, or as the situation changes for a professional and a client. (Bayles, 1989: 69-70.)

In the agency model, the client should have most of the authority and responsibility for decisions, with the professional an expert acting at the direction of the client - in effect, as an employee. It is plausible for lawyers, physicians, architects, social workers, and engineers, but not accountants performing public audits. However, a professional's devotion to a client's interests is limited, because the professional has obligations to third parties, is not confined just to an advocacy role, has independence of judgment, and may usually be able to accept or reject specific clients, and may terminate a relationship with a client. (Bayles, 1989: 70-1.)

In the second model, the professional and the client should share authority and responsibility equally, dealing with each other either on the basis of a contract or a more personal relationship of friendship. In a contractual relationship, each is expected to have mutual obligations and rights freely accepted. However, says Bayles, the contracting parties in this instance do not have equal bargaining power. The professional has greater knowledge, although clients in fields like architecture, accounting and engineering may be reasonably well-informed. The client usually has more personally at stake than the professional. Professionals and clients have different degrees of freedom to enter relationships and to form new ones. Some authors have viewed a professional-client relationship as like one of friendship, and this justifies giving clients' interests more weight than those of others. Yet, says Bayles, it is a false analogy. There is no mutual concern for each others' interests, and the affective commitment of friendship is usually missing. Professionals, particularly specialists, do not get to know their clients well. Also, friendship cannot apply when organizations are clients. (Bayles, 1989: 72-4.)

Bayles's third main ethical model for the professional-client relationship is where the professional has the primary responsibility and authority for decision-making. But to what extent should someone decide what is in someone else's interests? The paternalistic view - more appropriately described these days as parentalistic - is that the professionals' knowledge and experience allows them to perceive better the advantages and disadvantages of alternative possibilities. Clients, it is argued, cannot give sufficiently voluntary and informed consent. Further, they will later come to agree with informed decisions taken in their interest. (Bayles, 1989: 74-5.)

Bayles suggests that reasonable people would allow others to make decisions for them only when the differences involved are trivial, when the decisions might require knowledge or expertise a person does not possess, or when he or she is or will be mentally incompetent. They would want some assurance, however, that the persons making judgments for them in the second and third situations had values similar to their own.

The client incapacity argument does not hold in most professional-client relationships, although it can in special cases. The other argument for paternalism, the superior knowledge and skills of the professional is flawed because many decisions require balancing the professionals' concerns against other client interests with which the professional is not concerned. Further, the choice of means as well as of ends has a value component. Professionals have not been trained in value choices, and says Bayles, even if they were they might not know a client's values well enough to determine what is best for them. Clients are 'capable of making reasonable choices among options on the basis of their total values. They need professionals' information to make wise choices to accomplish their purposes'. (Bayles, 1989: 76-7.)

Bayles argues the case for a fiduciary relationship, in which both parties are responsible for decision-making, but the professional's superior knowledge is recognized. They do not contribute equally but a client's consent and judgment are required, in relation to courses of action proposed by the professional. It is a relationship based on trust, trust that the professional will use his or her knowledge and skills in the client's interests. The more the client has knowledge about the subject matter for which the professional is engaged, the more the relationship can be close to 'a contract between equals or even agency'. The less a client's knowledge and capacity to understand, the greater are the responsibilities of the professional to the client. The paternalistic model is only appropriate in the case of clients not competent to make decisions, and even here a legal guardian should often be appointed, with the professional in a fiduciary relationship with the guardian. (Bayles, 1989: 77-9.)

According to Bayles, then, client trust is the basis for a professional-client relationship. For a professional to be worthy of such trust, he suggests and discusses in some detail, with the help of various authors, seven character traits - honesty, candour, competence, diligence, loyalty, fairness, and discretion. He argues that these are required for the professional to fulfil his or her professional functions. Competence is said to be probably the most crucial characteristic of a professional and generally the most reliable judgments of competence are made by other professionals. Clients, on their part, have three general obligations to professionals - to keep commitments they make to them, to be truthful in their dealings with them, and not to request that they act unethically. (Bayles, 1989: 79-99.)

Beauchamp and Childress observe a recent decline in trust in medicine, evidenced by 'the dramatic rise in medical malpractice suits and adversarial relations between health-care professionals and the public'. Factors like 'the loss of intimate contact between physicians and patients, the increased use of specialists, high charges for health care, conflicts of interest in referrals and investments in clinical centres, and the growth of large, impersonal, and bureaucratic medical institutions', have undermined the possibility of trust developing between professionals and patients. Trust is based on an assessment of character. When strangers interact, character will generally play a less significant role than principles and rules backed by sanctions. (Beauchamp and Childress, 1994: 470.)

However much stress is placed on the values and character of a professional agent, a person cannot become a professional and continue to be an effective and efficient professional unless he or she is operating at a reasonable level of intellectual capacity. Good intentions are never sufficient in professional work. They must be integrated with the capacity to abstract and generalize, to make cognitive distinctions, to think logically and to tackle and solve problems, and to understand, retain and apply knowledge. It will be remembered that some of the writers have emphasized the fundamental role of abstract knowledge in the very notion of professionalism.

Each professional occupation must recruit people with the requisite intellectual capacities, otherwise both practically and morally what it has to offer to clients, employers, and the community at large will be jeopardized. The greater the pool of talent from which a profession draws in terms of socio-economic class, gender, age, and ethnicity, the greater its chances of intellectual success. But the drawing power of professional occupations varies greatly depending on their length of establishment, employment expectations, expected financial rewards, social status, the inherent interest of the work, the demands of the professional education, and the demands of the job. If human well-being is the prime value, the intellectual talent of the society is not reasonably distributed amongst its professionalized occupations. Each occupation needs its fair share of intellectual talent, if the functions it performs are going to be performed well. Some occupations may be more intellectually demanding than others, but this may be more a reflection of occupational competition than functional necessity.

From a community viewpoint, it can be argued that Australian medicine has in recent years attracted more than its fair share of intellectually talented people, with a considerable social cost because their talents would have been more productively employed in other fields. Another example was the practice established after World War II of the then Australian Department of External Affairs successfully recruiting the best Australian graduates with first-class honors degrees, for Australia's diplomatic service.

In this chapter we are focusing on the question of when are professionals of one kind or another the most appropriate agents to respond to an ethically challenging situation. So far, we have examined why sometimes no ethically suitable responding agent can be found; the need for a reasonable level of commitment by a responding agent; the knowledge claims to special relevance by the professionals, and their consequent relationships with their clients; and finally, the moral character and intellectual character required for professional responsibility.

Judgments about whether professionals, either individually or collectively, are the most relevant ethical agents to decide what should be done in a situation obviously call for knowledge about the professionals who would be involved. A full range of the potentially relevant data for both individual professionals and professional collectivities has already been canvassed in the first part of Chapter 4, and will not be repeated here. How much or how little of this data is available when particular professionals or professional collectivities become the responding agents to an ethical agenda item is an empirical matter. How much the data ought to inform the choice of agent has both empirical and ethical aspects, which the decision-maker cannot avoid if they wish to select the ethically most appropriate agent, all things considered. Selection criteria of some kind are operating whenever a person or collectivity becomes an agent with responsibility to do something about the ethically challenging situation. They are needed as much by the potential agent, who may be volunteering his or her services, or applying for an advertised position, or deciding whether or not to accept an assignment, as by those who are on a selection committee, or are managers allocating staff. Questions of suitability for the task to be done inevitably arise when determining who ought to be the responding agent.

'Politically Correct' Selection Criteria

Ideas of fairness in a democratic society include equality of opportunity. In the last couple of generations, democratic governments have introduced legislation to try to ensure equality of employment opportunity, especially for people who have a characteristic which in the past has been used to ignore or at least discount their claims to employment - whether it be their gender, their race or ethnicity, their nationality, their age, their homosexuality, their religious faith, or some physical or mental handicap. Prejudice has many guises and can have deep psychological, social and cultural roots (Gioseffi,

1993). Some degree of stereotyping is occurring whenever some characteristic of a person is used to make a general judgment about what such people are like. It is prejudice when a judgment is made without examination of the basis of the stereotype and the extent to which a particular case conforms to the stereotype, and there is unwillingness to examine relevant evidence. The prejudice may be in favor of the person being judged, but more commonly the term is used for adverse judgments.

The attempt to eliminate the operation of prejudice typically uses the language of anti-discrimination, and a new set of 'politically correct' conventions have become established, sometimes with legal backing. How effective this is in furthering human well-being can, however, be problematic. Choosing a person to become responsible for ethical decision-making in employment must be based on discriminating, but not discriminatory, judgment. A discriminating judgment must be made between candidates, and to be ethically justified it must be related to the task in hand. People in previously disadvantaged groups should receive every encouragement and assistance to become relevantly qualified, not only in terms of their equality of opportunity with other members of their society, but also so that they will develop and use their talents to carry their share of ethically important tasks in the society.

If ideas of equality of educational opportunity are taken seriously, and historically disadvantaged groups take the opportunity to become competitive in selection for employment, should they, in fact, receive preferential treatment? Some argue that this is their due, given the history of their group. Others go further and argue that even when they are not as well qualified as their competitors, they should still be appointed provided they have a reasonable level of competence for the job. In both these cases, the individual applicant is not being treated solely on his or her suitability for the job, but on the basis also of an attribute which in the past would have been a negative factor for the applicant, but is now a positive one. So-called 'positive discrimination' has replaced negative discrimination.

Group after group, especially in the United States, with its emphasis on pluralistic, pressure group politics, has claimed victim status - unfair treatment (discrimination) at the hands of the rest of the society. (See Hughes, 1993.) The issues are complex and the process is often highly politicized with much use of moral language, particularly the language of inequality and rights. There seems to be a basic contradiction, however, in saying that attributes like gender and race ought to be irrelevant in making appointments and then using these as a basis for positive discrimination. Ethicists do not agree on the reasonableness of positive discrimination, at least partly because there are so many possible claims that could be made on the basis of past injustice. Every generation must decide what selection criteria to use when people are being employed. The process of ethical justification is not, however, advanced when free and open discussion is limited by ideas of 'political correctness'. Always an applicant for a position is a person with a large number of attributes, both personal and social. What that person can bring to the job in terms of human well-being should be the prime criterion for choice.

Selection Processes

Instead of choosing a responding agent who is most likely to make the most ethically justifiable decisions, a selector may give preference to someone who shares the selector's own prejudices or ideological position. Selection is often done by a committee so that checks and balances operate amongst the selectors as well as bringing to bear their collective understanding and experience. What should be the size and composition of the selection committee and how should it proceed in order to achieve the ethically most justifiable outcome?

Selecting the most appropriate candidate raises many questions if human well-being is the prime value. How widely and for how long should the position be advertised? Should it be advertised outside the country, and how relevant are experience and qualifications gained in a different culture? Should there be a search committee and 'head-hunting'? Should particular individuals be invited to apply? How do candidates get to know about what is likely to be involved in the position? Are the conditions of employment made clear to applicants - duties, line of accountability, remuneration and other rewards, working conditions, review points, length of appointment, termination arrangements, opportunities for advancement, and staff development opportunities? How confidential should their application be? When should references be asked for? How much should referees know about the prospective job and should the employer provide any guide-lines for a reference? Should referees attempt to make an accurate assessment of the person's suitability or be an advocate for the candidate? (From observation, British and American academic referees tend to differ on this point.) At least a short list of candidates is usually interviewed, yet according to Stuart Sutherland selection interviewing is 'not merely unhelpful, it can be harmful'.

It is 'one of the most curious acts of irrationality in the Western world'. (Sutherland, 1994: 284-6.)

When an individual or an organization employs a genuine professional to decide what ought to be done in an ethically challenging situation, the employer has at least some safeguards. The gaining of professional qualifications requires reasonable intelligence, and active membership of a profession calls for adherence to the standards of the profession in question. If, however, an employer disregards an applicant's professional qualifications and commitments, they must then try to make a completely independent assessment of the applicant's potential for the job. There are always, of course, questions about the relevance of an applicant's educational qualifications for a particular job, and the extent to which further learning on the job will be required. Some employers may deliberately not insist on particular educational qualifications or professional commitments, so that they can mould the employee through in-service training. This can have the advantage to a manager of locking employees into a particular organization, but it is difficult, if not impossible, for a single employing organization to have the educational and training capacity to match a society's educational institutions. By employing professionally qualified staff, an organization becomes embedded in a much larger educational, research and knowledge system, and avoids the narrow parochialism of organizations that rely completely on in-service training. Professional qualifications typically allow professionals to retain their professional identity while moving between organizations in government and non-government sectors and between organizational employment and private practice.

Selecting Professional Collectivities for Responsible Action

Depending on the size and nature of the ethically challenging situation, a professional responding agent may appropriately be an individual or a collectivity. As is indicated in Chapter 4, when it is a collectivity it can consist of members of the same profession or members of different professions. It is clearly a *professional* collectivity when the persons concerned meet the various conditions for membership of their particular profession when it is a single profession collectivity, or of their respective professions when it is a multiple-profession collectivity. This usually requires that they have the recognized educational qualification for practice, they are engaged in practice, they belong to the relevant professional association, and they have commitment to their professional obligations. (See pp. 101-2.) If any of these conditions do not hold in the case of a particular person, this raises doubt and ambiguity about the 'professional' status of the collectivity of which he or she is a member.

In deciding on the relevance of a particular collectivity to be the most appropriate responding agent, you need to know the qualifications of its members, their practice experience, their affiliations, and the extent of their commitment to their profession, as well as the nature of their involvement in the specific collectivity. You also need to know the terms of reference of the collectivity, its concurrent commitments, its structure and processes, and its 'track record'. If, however, the collectivity in question is being established specifically to undertake a particular task or project, it will not have a track record, but can be more carefully designed for the prospective project. Whether ad hoc or continuous (standing), much of the work of professionals is done through peer groups. How those groups are selected and operate, and are made accountable to the community as well as to their fellow professionals is a continuing ethical challenge. Larger groups will develop administrative structures and authority patterns which may sit uncomfortably with rank and file professionals.

The situation becomes more complicated when a collectivity contains people from a number of professional occupations. These collectivities may be dominated by one of the participating professions, or may be constructed on a team model of changing responsibility depending on the particular expertise required, or may be held uneasily together by a general administrator. The work of Huntington (see pp. 61-2) and others has indicated the difficulties of genuine collaboration between professionals in multi-professional collectivities. Strains between members of mixed work collectivities can be experienced at a personal level, although the basic problem can be that the respective occupations are at very different levels of professionalization, and have different structural and cultural elements.

When an ethically challenging situation is referred to a collectivity for action, the collectivity must decide who should deal with it. Should it be the collectivity as a whole, or should it be a sub-group? If it is a sub-group, how much autonomy should it have? Should it have the final say on what should be done, or should this rest back with the collectivity itself? Specialties within a profession can develop considerable autonomy, but to retain membership of the overall profession requires a specialty and its concerns to be placed within a broader professional framework.

Premature reference of a situation to a specialist collectivity can restrict the options that will be considered to address it. The same can be said, however, when a situation is referred to just the one profession, or even to a group of professions. What professionals can bring to the task of deciding what ought to be done is the particular knowledge and skills of their occupation, but since these are always selective and specialized, since no one occupation can develop expertise in everything, professionals' prescriptions are inevitably limited by their specialization, whether it be their specialization within a profession, or the specialization of their particular profession.

It is for these reasons that many have argued that professions and professionals ethically should be 'on tap, not on top'. They should not have autonomy either in determining ethically challenging situations or in determining what should be done about them, although they certainly should be involved because of their knowledge and expertise. This is because the prescriptions of professionals need to be related to, and coordinated with, prescriptions which take account of all the values and interests which further human well-being, and this can only be done by general citizens and governments which operate on their behalf. The main exception to this is when professionals are handling their own affairs as individuals, and as members of their own occupations for which they are directly responsible.

The Moral Relevance of Ethicists as Agents

One way in which professions and organizations are now trying to ensure that their work is ethically justified is to employ ethicists or ethical consultants, and to refer troublesome situations to them, or to ethics committees which include ethicists if they are available. Certainly there is an emergent group that are employed to undertake what is called ethical analysis for a living, and they are not confined to university teaching and research settings. The employment of ethicists would seem an obvious strategy in confronting an ethically challenging situation. Does this indicate a new emergent profession, already with various degrees of specialization, for example, bioethics, legal ethics, public sector ethics, business ethics? Is it instead, a new developing specialization within each profession? Is it a developing occupation which is not yet organized on professional lines, because there is not sufficient agreement on the values, knowledge and skills required for membership of the occupation? Just what is its domain?

Potentially, ethicists can operate wherever questions of ethical justification can be raised; which makes their domain virtually co-extensive with the choice aspects of human conduct and character. This means an almost endless proliferation of ethicists covering the human enterprise, with field after field being claimed by these new professionals in the name of expertise in 'the ethics of...'. Particularly in a democratic society, is this the most insidious form of claimed expertise, for how can 'experts' get any of us off the moral hook? As humans we cannot divest ourselves of the responsibility for moral choice.

Are these newly-appointed ethicists engaged in a new form of philosophy, which helps philosophical analysis and speculation, and especially moral philosophy, to be related to the real world, and gives philosophy graduates employment? The idea of philosophers controlling human society is as old as Plato's philosopher kings, but it sits uncomfortably with a democratic society and with the idea that morality cannot be a matter of authority. Moral justification must be based on good arguments, not on pronouncements made by moral authorities.

The more 'ethicists' move in and become decision-makers themselves, that is they make commitments amongst action possibilities, the more they can be expected to come under critical scrutiny as a professional occupation - from governments, from the established professions, from administrators, and from the public. In other words, what are the characterisic values, knowledge and skills of the members of this occupation? If an 'ethicist' is well-educated in moral theory, this does not necessarily mean personal commitment to achieve any particular values, although it may if the person finds some justificatory arguments more persuasive than others. It is as relevant to clarify and evaluate the ethics of someone described as an 'ethicist' as of anyone else - perhaps more so, since the label can give some degree of specious authority in justificatory argument.

As already noted, the substantive expertise of any professional carefully described is inevitably a mix of value, knowledge and skill. Value choices and their justification are pervasive in professional life, as much as in the rest of human living. Ethicists can help others to clarify their value options, but even such activity cannot be value-free, and they can only engage in more sophisticated justificatory argument for particular courses of action if they have the requisite substantive knowledge and skills relevant for the actual situation being addressed by an actual decision-maker.

I can well recall attending an important named lecture at Columbia University where the invited lecturer was an ethicist employed by a major

New York hospital. She had a legal background and had discovered in the name of ethics the various situations and courses of action which experienced medical social workers had had as their terrain for generations. I suspected her advantage to her employer was her legal qualification in an increasingly litigious environment.

A 1995 article notes that a number of professions - particularly medicine and more recently, psychology, business and law - have developed 'a cadre of ethics consultants'. They are described as:

> usually obtain(ing) formal training in ethical theory, applied ethics, and professional ethics, to supplement their substantive expertise in their respective professions. These are individuals who are trained to identify, analyze, and help resolve ethical issues. (Reamer, 1995: 6.)

Social work is urged to follow suit. It is acknowledged, however, that:

> ...there is some danger that practitioners will shed some of their own responsibility for thoughtful reflection in deference to the consultant's advice and opinions. In the end, practitioners themselves bear ultimate responsibility for sound ethical judgments and must equip themselves with the knowledge and skills necessary to make such judgments... Consultants are not of uniformly high caliber, possess their own biases, have ambiguous accountability, may not be sufficiently attuned to the clinical and practice dynamics involved in cases, and can intrude in the social worker-client relationship. (Reamer, 1995: 14.)

The Example of Bioethics in the United States

While ethicists are gaining employment in various fields, the field of bioethics in the United States has demonstrated the strongest development. This is scarcely surprising since decisions about life and death, procreation, health, illness, and disability directly impact on every human being, and are the focus of a vast and growing human enterprise operating at individual, group and societal levels, and driven by fear, love, hope, economic profit, and scientific curiosity. The bioethics movement in the United States gained momentum in the 1960s, stimulated by both a revolution in medical technology[1] which meant more could be done for and to people, but often at considerable personal and financial cost, and a social revolution which stressed people's rights, the value component of clinical decisions, and the capacity of lay people to make decisions. (See Veatch, 1993: S7.) Veatch has noted 'how many of the scholars and leaders in those early years were trained in theology, especially Protestant theology'.

According to Daniel Callahan, co-founder and long-term President of The Hastings Center which played a significant role in the development and acceptance of American bioethics,

> the great dilemma was whether the ethicist should be the prophet, the outside critic, the one who raises the hard and unpleasant questions against the establishment or whether those in ethics should be primarily collaborators, one more set of experts or specialists among the medical team trying to be helpful to resolve dilemmas.

In the gaining of acceptance of bioethics in the United States, Callahan mentions a number of factors. Religion was pushed aside, and language became fully secular. A focus developed on 'regulatory ethics', the creation of bodies to monitor and regulate, which according to Callahan, was the typical American way of dealing with controversial issues. Two national commissions sought to find common ground in dealing with 'controversial and delicate' issues.[2] Bioethicists were found to be helpful and not dedicated to

---

[1] Including ventilators, dialysis machines, transplants of human organs, chemotherapy, radiation, cardio-pulmonary resuscitation, oral contraception, and new abortion techniques, and more recently, developments like fetal research, organ transplants from animals to humans, artificial organs, and genetic engineering.

[2] The National Commission for the Protection of Human Subjects of Biomedical and Behavioral Research, 1974-87, developed federal regulations. Their implementation was left primarily in the hands of institutional review boards. Researchers dominated both the Commission and these boards. The President's Commission for the Study of Ethical Problems in Medicine and Biomedical and Behavioral Research, 1979-83, undertook studies of specified subjects, such as defining death and deciding to forego life-sustaining treatment. (Annas, 1994: 19.)

whistle-blowing. And finally, 'a factor of great importance... was the emergence ideologically of a form of bioethics that dovetailed very nicely with the reigning political liberalism of the educated classes of America'. (Callahan, 1993: S8.)

In a subsequent reflection, this time to celebrate the 25th anniversary of The Hastings Center, Callahan identified the field of bioethics as having two serious deficiencies:

> It has failed to pursue with sufficient imagination the idea of the common good, or public interest, on the one hand, and that of personal responsibility, or the moral uses of individual choice, on the other. By its tendency to reduce the problem of the common good to justice, and the individual moral life to the gaining of autonomy, it has left a moral void. (Callahan, 1994: 28.)

Another commentator observes that U.S. bioethics has focused almost exclusively on doctor-patient relationship issues, rather than broader health care system issues. He notes that economists, not ethicists, built the framework for a national health care plan. (Annas, 1994: 19.)

Under a heading 'The Newest Profession', the *Hastings Center Report* described the founding of the American Association of Bioethics in 1993. Its reported goals were '(1) to gather together the wide array of individuals and organizations now active in bioethics; (2) to help its members with their professional development by gathering and updating information on available jobs, grant opportunities, graduate education programs, and the like; (3) to sponsor an annual conference for the presentation of new research'. (Nelson, 1993: 2.) With organizational affiliates - from government and non-profit agencies and from the ethics committees of the health professions, it was certainly not a professional association in the normal sense, and its impact on existing bioethics organizations like the Society for Health and Human Values, the Society for Bioethics Consultation, and the American Society of Law and Medicine, was uncertain.

A milestone in the development of American bioethics was a 1983 national conference on institutional ethics committees, sponsored by the American Society of Law and Medicine. The opening paper traced the emergence of such committees, their benefits and functions, and the problems they raised. For example, it was claimed that they could ensure that all appropriate factors would be considered in confronting medical dilemmas, that they could link societal values with decisions being taken in institutions, and that they could help to clarify whether a consensus was achievable in particular situations. The three general functions of education, the development of policies and guidelines, and consultation and case review, were delineated. Before, however, an ethics committee could perform an educational role, the committee members themselves needed relevant education and experience. The multidisciplinary ethics committee was seen as especially suited for the development and revision of policies and guidelines - for example, in relation to decision-making for incapacitated patients, and in relation to problems such as the determination of death, orders to resuscitate, foregoing life-sustaining treatment, supportive care, and treatment of handicapped newborns. An ethics committee could provide consultation for staff, patients, and families, but the final decision usually rested with the patients, their surrogates, and/or with the responsible professionals, or in the exceptional case, with a court of law. (Cranford and Doudera, 1984: 9-13.)

A number of problems were highlighted. There was confusion about the name and functions of ethics committees, particularly when some were limited merely to confirming a patient's prognosis. Although ethics committees were supposed to be multidisciplinary, and reflect a diversity of views and interests, in fact one person, discipline, or point of view could prevail. Another problem was the lack of clear understanding or agreement about the authority of the committee. Finally, an ethics committee often lacked requisite resources such as time and experience and knowledgeable members. Research, information sharing and communication among the committees were seen as essential. Local and independent development was preferred over government regulation. (Cranford and Doudera, 1984: 14-16, 18.) Unlike the prescribed format for institutional review boards, the size, composition and functions of ethics committees varied greatly. They could include not only professional staff in various categories and ethicists, but also senior administrators, board members, non-professional staff, and 'community members' such as politicians.

A recent book[3] emphasizes that bioethics committees must have intellectual integrity, and pay close attention to the sensitivities of any group its decisions might affect. A high level of scholarship is required to avoid 'reinventing the wheel', and sound judgment which strikes 'an appropriate balance between the relevant rights and interests, disciplinary perspectives,

---

[3] *Society's Choices: Social and Ethical Decision Making in Biomedicine*, Washington D.C., National Academy Press, 1995.

and cultural traditions in a given society' (p. 155). A bioethics committee can be a disadvantage to society if an advocacy group gains sway over it, or if a committee attempts to seize a high moral ground of correctness when none is truly attainable. (See review by Palca, 1995: 7.)

In Australia, the process of hospital accreditation has encouraged a proliferation of ethics committees. The American development has provided a useful example and stimulus, provided its cultural limitations are understood. Modern technology has brought into sharp relief a host of ethically challenging situations both old and new, for which there are no clear-cut morally justified solutions. Who should be deciding what ought to be done is a complex, difficult issue not amenable to simple answers. Patients, families, health professionals, administrators, board members, lawyers, researchers, technicians, governments, political parties, taxpayers, citizens, investors, ethicists - all have interests at stake.

Because of their skill in moral reasoning, ethicists may be more successful than others in persuading themselves and anyone else who is amenable to persuasion, that some courses of action are more justifiable than others. But unless they and their audience share the prime value of human well-being, and the main values which constitute human well-being, they are caught in basic value conflict, which no amount of argument will resolve. For the reasons elaborated in Chapter 2, the present discussion is based on the assumption of human well-being as the prime ethical value. While many ethicists would seem to accept this, there would be others who would go beyond the human species or even the animate world, and there would be still others who would stay within the confines of particular human cultures.

The Moral Relevance of Researchers as Agents

It is apparent that much of the early bioethics discussion concentrated on the ethics of research, and especially the protection of human subjects. As mentioned this was the exclusive focus of the first national U.S. bioethics commission and resulted in institutional review boards which assess ethically research proposals that involve federal government funds. The moral appropriateness of government taking an interest in research has already been considered (p. 178), and it is evident that this must extend far beyond just government-funded projects in bioethics reviewed mainly by researchers themselves. In recent years the ethics of social research has attracted growing attention (for example, Diener and Crandall, 1978; Beauchamp et al. (eds),

1982); so too has research using animals. But how does all this relate to the ethics of professional conduct, the main focus in this book? In what sense are researchers morally relevant professional agents?

As we have seen, an occupation successfully organized on professional lines has a basis of specialized knowledge, which requires people performing research functions both inside and outside the profession. People inside the profession seek knowledge in order to use it for professional practice, teaching, or further research. Relevant knowledge is borrowed from outside and/or developed from within, with each of these two strategies having its strengths and weaknesses for the occupation. Wherever the research function is performed, it is addressed to descriptive, analytic, predictive questions.

Within our model of ethical choice, the researcher is the morally suitable agent only when the ethically challenging situation is one of rectifiable human ignorance and enlightenment about it is likely to improve human well-being, and the researcher has the relevant knowledge and skills to effect enlightenment. Unbridled scientific inquiry, irrespective of its human and other implications, is no longer an acceptable absolute value, although the implications of 'pure' research may be impossible to assess.

When enlightenment or understanding on matters of complicated empirical reality is the ethical challenge, researchers may well be the most appropriate moral agents. But knowledge can never determine its use. As soon as researchers start making policy prescriptions about the use of the knowledge, they are no longer confining themselves to the research role, although as researchers they may make prescriptions about further knowledge development.

Researchers can form a significant sub-community within a profession, even though research rivalry may hold it in check. As such, their work would be assessed in terms of that profession's purposes and structures. Alternatively researchers may be members of scientific occupations whose purposes are primarily knowledge development. Or researchers may be free-lancers selling their skills outside professional structures. Although almost all contemporary researchers are likely to be university graduates, a general profession of research has not developed. Research is fragmented as an occupation.

Enough has been said to indicate that, if human well-being is the prime value, this second step of determining *who* should be responsible for deciding what ought to be done in response to an ethically challenging situation, is vital in the process, and the involvement of professionals requires careful justification.

9 Criteria for Justifiable Policy Decisions by Professionals

The Policy Response by Professional Agents

Once a situation has been accepted as ethically challenging and a professional agent has accepted responsibility to respond, the agent must decide what ought to be done, when, why, and by whom. The whole point of having a designated responsible agent, whether individual or collective, is for them to decide what ought to be done in terms of the specific objectives to be achieved and the kind of action that will be needed to achieve them. This is the policy phase of the rational decision model. As already mentioned (p. 9), the term 'policy' can be used for a fairly specific guide to action, or as a composite term to cover a whole range of inter-linked guides to action. We are here focusing on the policy response of a professional agent who is responsible for deciding what ought to be done.

The following chapter examines the role of professionals in implementing policy responses in the program or implementation phases of projects. Although the policy and program phases are conceptually distinct, with one following and building on the other, in practice they may become so interwoven that it is difficult to distinguish between them. This will be particularly so once a project becomes a continuing enterprise with policy being developed from program experience, and when the same people are involved in both.

The Basic Criterion of Human Well-Being

With human well-being as the prime value, the professional (or anyone else in the responding role) is expected to decide what kind of action will be most likely to be effective and efficient for the human well-being at stake. For an agent with a commitment to human well-being, not only must the prescribed objectives be persuasive in term of the human well-being at stake, but also the prescribed means to achieve the objectives. Unless the agent pays due regard to, and balances the interests of all of the people affected, the policy response will be open to ethical challenge. Already in Chapter 2 (pp. 48-50), there is a general discussion of the decision criteria which an ethically conscious agent might be expected to consider in making their response. The present chapter extends that discussion, but with a specific focus on the criteria for policy decisions about objectives and ways of achieving them when professionals have the responsibility to decide what ought to be done.

Relevant Standards

A criterion is a principle or standard by which a judgment is made. The word comes from the Greek word for a judge. The judgment is a policy determination in the sense that it is a decision about a course or plan of action in response to the situation being addressed. Sometimes, people will use 'ought' when they have in mind some standard in terms of which they might be expected to behave in response to a situation. It is, however, important to clarify what the standard is and whether on this occasion, the agent has made a decision to adopt that standard and why. It is perfectly reasonable for someone to say, 'I ought to do this (according to some religious, legal, conventional, organizational, economic, professional, or personal standard), but I am not'. The responding agent will need to be fully aware of standards or criteria which might be applied to, or relevant for the challenging situation, but a decision must be made by the agent himself or herself for the best reasons he or she can muster; only then will the agent have made a morally justifiable decision. Religious, legal, conventional, organizational, economic, professional, and personal standards cannot be immune from critical assessment, if human well-being is the prime value.

Reasonableness and Communication Standards

The underlying standard is one of reasonableness related to morally justified purpose. Reasons include the desirable ends in the circumstances, and why these are desirable, and the best ways of attaining them, all things considered. To be convincing or persuasive in a justificatory reasoning process, an agent must rely on communication standards of logic, language, and culture. Unless supporting argument is clear, consistent, and able to be comprehended by its audience, adequate justification has not been provided. A professional agent must convince herself or himself and also be able to adapt justificatory argument according to audience. It would seem that the fullest justification can be entered into with professional peers, because of their cumulative experience in similar situations, their understanding of the technical possibilities, their shared technical language, and their increasing insight into the values at stake as they become better educated in this aspect of their work. Fellow professionals may, however, be unwilling and/or unable to examine action options outside their particular cases, their specialty, or their profession.

The ideas of informed consent in medicine, and acting under client instructions in law depend heavily on the capacity of professionals' patients or clients to understand options presented to them by the professionals, sometimes in situations of considerable stress. Each struggles with the complexity and difficulty of adequate communication standards in professional-client relationships, when lay understanding cannot match the professional's technical knowledge, but when it is the life of a patient or a client that is primarily at stake.

The Need for Explicit Rationales

As mentioned, in deciding what ought to be done, professional agents must convince themselves as well as relevant others. If they are in a position of unquestioned authority, they may decide to keep their rationale to themselves, merely telling people what ought to be done, without any justificatory argument, apart possibly from reference to their legitimate authority. Without any explicit available rationale, the point and purpose of the prescribed course of action is, however, unavailable for assessment. The responding agent is, by definition, expected to respond to an ethically challenging situation, but unless the policy response is reasoned in relation to that situation, its practical and moral status is uncertain. Indeed, it could be argued that unless the rationale behind a policy is known, it is not possible to assess its intended efficacy. People may support what looks like the same policy, but with very different rationales in mind. This is likely to become apparent in the following program phase and will certainly become obvious when results are being assessed. For instance, the same course of action, say the provision of employment to young people, may be intended to achieve social control, or to achieve equality of opportunity, or both. These are three different possibilities, each with different policy options once the underlying rationale is available for assessment.

The more a professional engages in an open reasoning process which solicits and examines the claims of the various interested parties prior to policy determination, the more chance there is that the agent will be able to provide a justified basis on which to proceed. Unless agents can convince themselves as well as other interested parties about a prescribed course of action, their sense of personal integrity and trustworthiness can be called into question. They may try to give a retrospective rationale which suits subsequent results, or they may deliberately conceal their actual rationale for political advantage, or they may provide a publicly acceptable rationale in which they do not believe, or they may be capable of self-deception. While professionals value their autonomy, and cannot be held to account if their autonomy is too circumscribed, the more isolated they are from the experience and views of others, the more idiosyncratic and limited are likely to be the professional agent's policy prescriptions.

Relationship to Extant Standards

Every time an agent makes a decision about what ought to be done, this is an instance of actual human conduct. Since every actual decision is time-, place-, resource-, and agent- specific, its relationship to extant standards requires careful clarification. It may reflect one or more such standards, in which case it may be characterized as an application, or at least an instance of the standard or standards in question. What seem to be relevant standards may, however, conflict in the particular circumstances, or they may be given different weight, or they may be amended to accommodate the circumstances which can establish a precedent for similar circumstances in the future, or the decision-maker establishes a new standard because existing standards do not seem applicable, or existing standards are stated at such a high level of generality that they provide little specific guidance to the decision-maker embedded in his or her specific circumstances. Further, standards may relate to basic and/or instrumental values, to knowledge assessed in terms of its validity and reliability, and to different types and levels of skill. Standards may also relate to matters of substance or to procedural matters.

One way or another, these are the constituent elements of moral reasoning which professionals must learn to handle in justifying and deciding what ought to be done. Adequate professional education will help professionals to engage in moral reasoning, and to develop and use various standards in the course of such reasoning, but responding and responsible agents are just that. They are the ones who must decide what ought to be done and be assessed accordingly. While each individual, each generation, and each collectivity must make their own way, in deciding what to do in response to their particular ethically challenging circumstances, it makes sense to learn from and build on the experience of others, provided their circumstances are sufficiently similar.

Professional Standards

Professionalism is an occupational device which develops and transmits shared practice standards, in terms of which professional decision-making can be assessed. The educators of professionals, and the professionals themselves supposedly belong to a critical tradition which keeps their professional standards relevant to their contemporary and expected situations. Through conferences, seminars, working groups, professional journals, peer review, and professional staff development, a well-established professional occupation can ensure that its members develop and maintain practice standards reflective of experience far beyond the experience which any one individual, organization, or country, could provide.

Components of the Basic Justificatory Standard

If the prime value for ethical justification is human well-being, what kind of standards might be relevant for a professional agent responsible for deciding what ought to be done in an ethically challenging situation? Justificatory standards may refer to values seen to be at stake, relevant rules to be followed, rights to be recognized which arise from the rules, and correlative duties or obligations under the rules. The values, rules, rights, and duties can operate at different levels of abstraction and different degrees of specification. For example, at the highest level of abstraction and most general level of specification, the interconnected justificatory standards could be:

primary value - human well-being
basic rule - when deciding what ought to be done in an ethically
    challenging situation, the responsible agent should determine ends
    and means that are most likely to enhance human well-being

> *basic right* - every human being whose interests are likely to be affected by a proposed course of action has a right for those interests to be given due consideration by the decision-maker
> *basic duty* - the decision-maker has a duty to give due consideration to the interests of all affected parties

These normative standards are primary and basic in the sense that there is no further justification beyond them. Because of their lack of specificity, there is, however, obviously need for a great deal of further justification within them. In coming to a justifiable decision about what is to be done, the responding professionals will need to determine, or at least make assumptions about, what is a human being, what constitutes human well-being (see p. 49), whose well-being is involved in the situation being addressed, what aspects of their well-being are at stake, and what are the advantages and disadvantages in terms of human well-being, of the possible courses of action.

If it is a familiar situation about which a great deal is known and there is a high level of consensus about the values involved, and the likely effects of different policy options, the policy maker may be able to act quickly and rely on pre-existing standards in relation to the various components in the task. The less these conditions hold, the slower and more problematic is the determination of what ought to be done. For example, modern medicine knows a great deal about handling medical emergencies to save lives, minimize damage to human functioning, and reduce human suffering, through the expeditious use of standardized (tested) drugs, equipment, and procedures. The situation can become more problematic, for example, when the professional policy maker is inexperienced, or has competing emergencies, or does not have sufficient of the requisite treatment facilities, or when the acute emergency situation is replaced by a more long-term, chronic situation and other values such as quality of life and cost to others demand consideration.

Whatever the conditions and the policy outcome, the decision by the professional agent is an instance of a professional's decision-making and can therefore be assessed accordingly by the professional's peers, and by others, including clients and third parties, whether they be client-related, employers, funders, governments, or the general public.

Human Existence Standards

In some situations, the professional must decide on operative standards for determining what is a human being, and therefore a source of moral claims or claims to consideration. When does a human come into existence - at conception, at some stage of fetal development, at birth? When does a human cease to exist? - when heart and lungs cease to function? when there is 'brain death'? And what about the claims of organisms that are so severely handicapped that they cannot ever function, or continue to function, as human beings? Various religious, legal, biological, cultural, and professional standards contribute to decisions about these matters. Much of the recent discussion in American bioethics has been focused on these kinds of questions.

Modern technology is forcing the various interested parties to become more thoughtful about definitions of human existence, at least partly because of their practical implications. Such definitions, for example, determine the moral status of frozen embryos in test tubes, or of bodies with no mental functioning kept alive on life-support systems. If, in the one instance, they are considered to have only potential moral status, and in the other, former moral status, they can be treated accordingly. Doctors, nurses, lawyers, judges, clergy, social workers, and politicians may be caught up in situations where these difficult, and often highly emotional definitional questions cannot be avoided. This is also increasingly the case for people in the final stages of terminal illness, for parents having difficulty to conceive children, for parents with profoundly handicapped, newborn children, and for relatives of profoundly and hopelessly damaged accident victims.

In Whose Interests?

If human well-being is the primary value, every human being impacted by the selected situation and by proposals to deal with it has claims and interests to be considered by the responsible agent who is responding to the challenge provided by the situation. Whenever feasible, the responding professional agent is well advised to find out from the people themselves how they see their interests to be involved, and what they would see as a reasonable policy response to the situation in question if their interests are to be reconciled with the claims and interests of others. But in various situations, people themselves may not be able to make claims to consideration - if they are too young, too incapacitated, too distant, too inarticulate, too ignorant, are unaware that policy decisions are being made about the situation, or they have not yet been born. Since no-one affected is beyond the moral pale, the ethically responsible professional agent must somehow pay due regard to all these human interests. Desirable as this may be, is this a hopelessly impractical prescription, especially in large-scale, complicated and changing situations?

It may eventually prove to be so, but as already indicated the situation in question has been placed on the ethical agenda and an appropriate agent has been chosen, precisely because it is anticipated that something constructive in terms of human well-being can be achieved. The responding responsible agent will often, however, need to engage in considerable further clarification and analysis of the situation to which they are expected to be responding, before they can decide what ought to be done.

Specification of the Situation

Without at least some assumptions about the scope, nature, and implications of the situation being addressed, notions of an ethical agenda and of responsible, professional agency would be meaningless. The moral significance of policy responses or of acts of agency is lost without reference to originating situations. These provide the context, scope, and point for human conduct. Situations expected to be addressed by professional agents, individual or collective, may be specified in general terms in duty statements, and terms of reference, and by particular clients. Typically, however, the responding, responsible agent will need to engage in considerable further clarification and analysis of an actual situation to which they are expected to be responding before they can decide what ought to be done in terms of feasible objectives and the best ways of attaining them.

An essential criterion for the policy response is, then, specification of the situation being addressed. Each agent does not have an open-ended, global responsibility to the billions of extant human beings and the countless numbers of future humans. The agent does, however, have responsibility for doing something constructive about a defined situation which they can influence for the betterment of the humans involved.

The situation may initially be too narrowly defined by a client or an employer for the interests and expertise of the responding professional agent, in which case the professional must decide whether and when to renegotiate the scope of their responsibility. On the other hand, the situation may be defined so broadly and vaguely that reasoned judgments about an appropriate response are impossible. If a professional agent is, in fact, concentrating only on part of a much larger situation, because of limited resources, limited expertise, and/or a limited mandate, this needs to be made clear, so that the action can be assessed appropriately and coordinated with action which addresses other parts of the larger situation. Professionals themselves may, however, be reluctant to designate limitations on the scope of their service, for theoretical, practical, and political reasons - theoretical, because of the abstract and shifting nature of their knowledge base; practical, because of their wish not to foreclose options; and political, because of their need to compete with other occupations claiming the attention of clients, funders, employers, and governments.

Professionals' Interests

In deciding what objectives should be sought and the means to attain them in an ethically challenging situation, the responsible professional agent must attempt to identify whose interests are at stake and what form those interests take. Since the professional's own reputation and livelihood are centrally involved, these are one set of interests for which the professional has an ongoing responsibility and which cannot reasonably be ignored. Like everyone else, professionals have the ethically challenging situation of a life to live. What is distinctive, however, about their occupational solution is that they have apparently made a personal commitment to and investment in the values, knowledge, and skills of an occupation organized on professional lines, which means commitment to a public service ethic, not just a personal advancement ethic.

It is important not to interpret the concept of 'interests' only as selfish interests. As social beings, the interests of humans are very much bound up with their social existence - with the well-being of their families, friends, colleagues, fellow citizens, and fellow human beings. But their communal interests do not just have an instrumental relationship to their individual well-being. They are an integral part of their interests and can lead individuals to make personal sacrifices which on no stretch of the imagination are in their personal interest.

Clients' Interests

Professionals are expected to serve the interests of their clients, otherwise at least voluntary clients would not continue to use their services. The situation may become ethically complex, however, when a client's interests are indeterminate, are internally inconsistent, are in conflict with the interests of others, are deliberately harmful, are not revealed, or when there are cultural, socio-economic, gender, and ethnic differences between professionals and their clients.

Further complications arise when a client is a collectivity and/or the professional agent is a collectivity. We tend to personify collectivities, but they in fact, by definition, consist of more than one person, and are both more and less than their composite members - more, in the sense that they persist as a corporate idea beyond their changing memberships; and less, in the sense that they incorporate only a part of each member's identity and commitment.

Organizational Standards

In addition to the practice standards of their profession, professionals increasingly are practising amid a plethora of organizational and legal standards, all apparently concerned with some aspect of what they should do as responsible decision-makers. Each of the three main organizational contexts of government, not-for-profit, and commercial, employ professionals, presumably to further the interests being pursued by these different kinds of organization, and all claim in a general sense to be concerned about the well-being of the population. Many interests are obviously being pursued in these organizations, but only some are in the context of a professional-client relationship.

Professionals may be engaged in managing the organization, in providing specialized services to its employees, in providing a specialized service to the public/s of the organization, or in research and development activities. They may have multiple clients, or none. As organizational employees, they are expected to adhere to organizational goals and objectives, and organizational codes, as well as to anti-discrimination and other legislation which applies to the organization. By definition, professionals are expected to adhere to professional standards as well as organizational standards. If they experience conflict or tension between the two, they may try to change one or both, they may leave and find employment that is more professionally acceptable, or they may 'sell out' on their professional standards and make a commitment instead to the organization and its standards.

Ethical Principles

With the increased attention in professional education to questions of ethical justification, professionals may now look to ethics textbooks or journals, general or specific to a profession or field of practice, for assistance in deciding what they ought to do in an ethically challenging situation. One approach in this literature has been to concentrate on widely-held 'ethical' principles. These can be justified by one or more ethical theories, even though the theories may be incomplete and may be in conflict. The principles are then used in discussions of practical situations. It has been common to refer to this as 'applied ethics', although the term is now described as an outmoded label because moral reasoning is more complex than this implies.

For example, Thiroux's general book on ethics deals with consequentialist and nonconsequentialist theories, absolutism versus relativism, and freedom versus determinism, before proposing a workable moral system built upon a number of basic assumptions and basic principles. He assumes that it should be based on reasoning, but should not disregard people's feelings; it should be as logically consistent as possible and yet allow enough flexibility to be applicable in the complexity and variety of human living; it should have general applicability; it should be able to be taught and promulgated; and it should be able to resolve conflicts among duties and obligations and among participants. He proposes and provides justification for five principles: the value of human life, doing good (promoting goodness over badness, not causing harm, and preventing harm), justice (the fair distribution of goodness and badness), truth telling or honesty (for meaningful communication and trusting relationships), and individual freedom (exercised within the framework of the first four principles). Thiroux observes that despite human differences, 'goods' on which humans generally agree include 'life, consciousness, pleasure, happiness, truth, knowledge, beauty, love, friendship, self-expression, self-realization, freedom, honor, peace, and security'. Ideas of 'good' involve pleasure, happiness, excellence, harmony, and creativity; ideas of 'bad' will involve the obverse. (Thiroux, 1980: 118-39.)

The five principles are seen as 'near absolutes', but can be violated with sufficient justification. The first two principles, however, are logically and empirically necessary for the others to operate. Priority among the principles is determined by the actual situation and context in which actions and decisions occur. The unity that humans need is provided by the basic principles, while the required diversity is provided by the individual interpretation and carrying out of these principles in particular situations. Morality or immorality occurs in particular situations or contexts which must be observed and analyzed carefully. (Thiroux, 1980: 144-8.)

Beauchamp and Childress (1994) describe and assess several types of ethical theory - utilitarianism, Kantianism, character ethics, liberal individualism, communitarianism, the ethics of care, casuistry, and principle-based common-morality theories - before concentrating on the last. They acknowledge that in another framework the principles might be developed as rights, virtues, or values. The principles are *prima facie* obligations, general guides that operate between more detailed rules and policies on the one side, and ethical theories on the other. Four clusters of moral principles are identified in the authors' search for considered judgments and coherence in biomedical ethics.

1. *Respect for autonomy.* [Action done intentionally, and with a substantial degree of understanding and freedom from constraint. The principle's precise demands remain unsettled in biomedical ethics. The current focus on disclosure should shift to a focus on understanding and effective communication. (pp. 123, 181.)]

2. *Nonmaleficence.* [Not causing harm or injury includes physical and psychological harm, and harm to reputation, property, privacy, or liberty. The many types of harm can be covered by more specific rules. The rules are negative prohibitions to be obeyed impartially, and provide reasons for certain legal prohibitions. (pp. 193-4.)]

3. *Beneficence.* [All action intended to benefit other persons. This covers preventing harm, removing harm, and promoting good by the provision of benefits or the balancing of benefits, risks, and costs. Since these rules require positive action and it is impossible to act beneficently towards everyone, there is a need to clarify and specify beneficence noting the limits of its obligations and when it is an optional ideal rather than obligatory. Obligations of specific beneficence arise from our relationships with our children, friends, and clients, but are we obligated to act impartially to promote the interests of persons beyond our limited sphere of relationships and influence? The more widely we generalize obligations of beneficence, the less likely we will meet our primary responsibilities to those to whom we are close or indebted, and where our responsibilities are clear. Specific beneficence may, however,

include an obligation under certain conditions to rescue strangers. (pp. 190-3, 259-66.)]

The idea of reciprocity, or making an appropriate return, provides justification for obligations of beneficence although it does not account for the full range of obligations (pp. 269-71). No pre-eminent principle exists in bioethics to resolve conflicts between respect for the autonomy of patients and professional beneficence (pp. 271-3).

Various informal strategies are used to help make decisions about costs, risks and benefits, including judgments by experts based on the most reliable data that can be gathered and analogical reasoning based on similar situations. Increasingly, however, particularly when public or institutional policies are being developed, techniques of formal quantitative analysis (cost-effectiveness, cost-benefit, risk-benefit) are being used. While these seem to be more objective, they are often criticized for not including all relevant values and options. (pp. 291-318.)]

4. *Justice.* [A group of rules for distributing benefits, risks and costs fairly in the light of what is due or owed to persons. There are several competing and complementary principles of justice each requiring specification and balancing in particular contexts. They include - to each an equal share, and to each according to need, effort, contribution, merit, or free-market exchanges. The formal principle of justice merely requires that equals must be treated equally, and unequals unequally, which means that people must be treated the same unless some difference between them is relevant to the treatment proposed. (pp. 326-34.) The fair-opportunity rule requires that people be given a fair chance in life when their disadvantages are not of their own making (pp. 341-3).]

These four clusters of moral principles receive further specification when the obligations of veracity, privacy, confidentiality, and fidelity, are discussed in the context of professional and patient or research subject relationships (pp. 395-453). Changes in the field of bioethics and a burgeoning literature have led to substantial revisions in each new edition of this book since its first appearance in 1979. The latest edition, in the context of a more sophisticated discussion of moral justification and of types of ethical theory, defends its continued primary focus on principles of common morality. (pp. 13-40, 100-9.)

Another example of a 'principles' approach is Munson's book on medical ethics (Munson, 1988). After a section on basic ethical theories - utilitarianism, Kant's ethics, Ross's ethics, Rawls's theory of justice, and natural law ethics and moral theology, Munson turns to five principles which would be endorsed as moral guidelines by the moral theories. It is acknowledged, however, that they are not complete, and may come into conflict. They are seen as expressing 'standards to be consulted in attempting to arrive at a justified decision...They provide a basis for evaluating actions or policies as well as for making individual moral decisions... By following them we are more likely to reach decisions that are reasoned, consistent, and applicable to similar cases'. (pp. 32-3.)

1. *Nonmaleficence*. [The way this is stated - 'We ought to act in ways that do not cause needless harm or injury to others' - requires acting with 'due care' as well as not intentionally causing harm. (pp. 33-5.)]

2. *Beneficence*. ['We should act in ways that promote the welfare of other people'. Whether or not this is a general duty, there is a duty of beneficence inherent in the role of all health professionals. Not only are physicians expected to provide appropriate treatment, they are expected to make 'reasonable', if not exceptional, sacrifices for the sake of their patients. (pp. 34-7.)]

3. *Utility*. ['We should act in such a way as to bring about the greatest benefit and the least harm' (pp. 37-8).]

4. *Distributive justice*. ['Similar cases ought to be treated in similar ways' is the formal principle of justice. The principles of equality of distribution, of need, of contribution, and of effort, are substantive principles. (pp. 38-41.)]

5. *Autonomy*. ['Rational individuals should be permitted to be self-determining'. Autonomous decisions involve freedom from duress, genuine options, and relevant information. We demand compelling reasons to justify restrictions on self-determination. These can occur to prevent harm to others and they may occur to prevent self-harm, to promote a person's good, and to provide benefits to others when this does not demand serious self-sacrifice. (41-6.)]

It must be evident, even from this brief sketch of some examples of a principled approach to decision-making, that each principle calls attention to important values which professional agents might be expected to take into account when deciding what ought to be done. None of the principles, however, can operate in isolation from the others. Both theoretically and practically they are interwoven in complex patterns, and it is obvious that they can overlap, be complementary, or be in conflict. For example, apart from the empty formal principle of justice, more specific rules of justice can be in competition with each other and must involve other principles such as autonomy and beneficence. There is, therefore, considerable ambiguity in calling each an 'ethical' principle in its stand-alone and highly abstract form, and when the list of principles is not related to agreed upon ethical theory or to an underlying general value.

For reasons already argued, this present discussion of justification of professional conduct accepts human well-being as its prime value. This means that any standards used by professionals in deciding what ought to be done in a particular situation require justification in terms of their effect on human well-being. In democratic societies, where a general concept of human well-being is supposedly taken seriously, it is only reasonable to describe a particular standard - whether it is expressed in terms of principles, rules, rights, or obligations - as 'ethical' if its use in a particular situation, on balance, enhances rather than undermines human well-being.

Conventional rights and duties based on traditional principles and rules may in fact be harmful and stultifying for many of the people affected and may not, therefore, be able to be justified. The same can apply, however, to new 'moral' conventions, for example in relation to the claims of 'minorities' (which may include the female majority of a population) which are typically expressed in terms of rights to give legitimacy to the claims. The vague term 'political correctness' has been used to refer to, and often to devalue, these newer conventions.

Ethicists acknowledge that at best the principles they discuss can only have *prima facie* status. The approach taken in this book is deliberately consequentialist. If human well-being is the prime value, one is bound to consider the consequences on human well-being of one's actions, difficult though this may be. The various standards - professional, organizational, legal, communal, personal - draw attention to important considerations for human well-being, but they can only serve as guide-lines. Only the responsible agent can determine or take an argued position about their relevance in particular real-life circumstances, and all actual decision-making and actual conduct is inevitably agent-specific.

Specific Objectives

Returning then to our professional agent responsible for deciding what ought to be done, the agent must pay due regard both to the situation and the various extant standards which may be relevant. Whether the agent is an individual or a collectivity, the policy stage must result in decisions about objectives in relation to the situation and how these are best achieved. As has been demonstrated, 'policy decision is essentially a matter not just of calculation, but of judgment, balancing short-term and long-term considerations, the claims of different people, competing and complementary values, costs and benefits both economic and other, and degrees of probability' (pp. 49-50).

The situation to which the professional is responding has already been defined as ethically challenging in the sense of having implications for human well-being. It is the responsible agent's task to clarify the nature of the situation and its possibilities for effective and efficient action for the attainment of human well-being. In order for the particular project to proceed, the responding agent must decide on specific objectives for the project and how these are to be achieved. Whatever form the initiating and first stages of the project have taken - getting the situation on the agenda and establishing responsible agency, and study, data collection and consultation, and diagnosis, where appropriate, by the agent - decision by the agent on specific justifiable and feasible objectives to be achieved in the situation is vital. Already, in the discussion of agenda-setting for a welfare organization, the advantages of having defined, clearly stated objectives have been listed (pp. 204-5). In fact, clarity of objectives is necessary for the functioning of any collectivity.

When a collectivity has been established *de novo* as the most appropriate response to a particular ethically challenging situation, that is the project in focus. The initial policy response has been to set up this collectivity with its specific objectives and an appropriate format and resources to meet those objectives. The objectives must relate appropriately to the situation of concern, and must be sufficiently specific to serve as a basis for an organizational structure, resource recruitment and allocation, client recruitment and participation, internal and external service coordination, and outcome assessment.

Concurrent Projects

When the responding agent is an already established collectivity handling a number of projects, it is important that both existing projects and any new project have clearly stated specific objectives and that these are congruent with the organization's general purposes. Concurrent projects within a collectivity can compete for resources and managerial attention, but they can also be complementary and enhance each other. For example, the teaching and research projects in a university professional school have both competitive and cooperative aspects. Clarity of specific objectives for each of these will help to make this apparent, and enable organizational mutual adjustment of the objectives on a reasoned, rather than just a traditional, purely political, or arbitrary basis.

The importance of specification of the situation for which the responsible professional agent is setting objectives has already been emphasized (pp. 252-3). But each professional agent is, in fact, engaged in a multiplicity of ethically significant projects which may compete or complement each other. The concurrent projects for individual professionals will include personal, family, friendship, and community projects, as well as professional projects. The projects can be very short-term or be running a lifetime; they can relate to individuals or to large collectivities; and they can involve sole responsibility or shared responsibility. Somehow, to achieve and retain a sense of integrity and purpose, the specific objectives of these various projects which together give point and purpose to the professional's life, cannot be too discrepant.

A professional's professional projects can include clients's cases, research projects, professional association concerns, educational development, and one's personal career. Coordinating and balancing the various professional projects is difficult, if not impossible, when a professional is overloaded with professional projects. The mounting concern about the incidence of suicides, family breakdowns, illness, and 'burnout'[1] amongst some groups of professionals indicates that they cannot effectively manage an overload of work projects and their family, friendship and other projects are not providing support, stimulus, and balance in their lives.

All of the projects of ethical significance in which professionals are engaged may be analyzed in terms of the stages of rational action of our model. With so many concurrent responsibilities, professionals need to be as clear as they can be about where each project has reached, their responsibilities in each project, how projects interrelate, and whether they can give adequate attention to each. In each project, coming to a justifiable decision about specific objectives and specifying what ought to be done to achieve them is a vital step.

---

[1] This term has come into common usage, but seems more appropriate for machines than human beings.

10 Professionals in Justifiable Policy Implementation

Feasibility Considerations

Although policy and program phases can merge, the implementation or program phase has its characteristic concerns which call for separate consideration and justification in an examination of appropriate professional conduct. Both at individual and collective levels, it is one thing to decide what ought to be done; it is another to do it. Since morally justifiable 'oughts' must always imply 'can', feasibility questions will already have been considered, at least to some extent, in the policy and program planning stage of a project. The responsible, responding agent is expected to do more than just analyze and discuss the challenging situation. They must decide what is to be done to change the situation for the better, or at least to make it less harmful than it would otherwise be.

Democratic Discussion

In a democratic society, many people can contribute to a discussion of what can, and what ought to be done about the situation in question. A strength claimed for an open, democratic society is that responding, responsible agents are more likely to be better informed about a situation and the action options it presents, when they have the benefit of such discussion. However, the amount of discussion and how much notice is taken of it will obviously vary according to the size and seriousness of the situation, as well as the capacities and values of the responsible agent.

An Example - the Health of the Aboriginal Population in Australia

If, for example, the situation concerns the general well-being of a particular population group, like the Australian Aboriginal people or the American Indians, the well-being of only a small minority of the over-all population is now involved, and their well-being may have relatively little direct impact on

262

the rest of the population. Yet the situation may be viewed as morally serious because they are seen as greatly disadvantaged in comparison with the rest of the population, their indigenous cultural bearings continue to be undermined or destroyed, people of the dominant culture feel guilty about past and/or present treatment of indigenous people, and the situation transgresses international standards of human rights.

In Australia, Aboriginal health in particular has become a bipartisan political issue, with widespread discussion on what ought to be done, and who should be responsible given the evident failure of past policies and programs. Responsibility at the national level has been shifted from the Aboriginal and Torres Straits Islanders Commission, a relatively new general experiment in indigenous responsibility, back to the Commonwealth Department of Health which has been given a coordinating function in relation to all the various parties necessarily involved. At least this may give the Aboriginal population some chance of obtaining reasonable access to modern acute care medicine, but such technical/professional 'solutions' leave untouched the economic and social conditions which give rise to the persistence of ill-health. The health problem, like the problem of Aboriginal deaths in custody, is symptomatic of deep-seated issues of inequality, prejudice and culture conflict, which are clearly not amenable to professional/technological 'fixes'. Such issues can gain a moral commitment from concerned members of the established professions, but they will inevitably be led into political activities and alliances which may strain their professional loyalties.

Professionals' Technical Capacity

We have already seen that professionals play an important role in clarifying feasible policy options in the areas of their expertise. Their technical capacity can, in fact, give them considerable political power as policy makers and consultants in a society which increasingly uses technology to meet its transport, communication, defence, health, education, manufacturing, building, administrative and other requirements. Professionals may leave it to others to pick up the responsibility, having indicated what ought to be done, but field experience often informs professional policy advice and many professionals are, in fact, more heavily engaged in the program phase of projects than in the policy phase.

In this chapter, the focus is on justifiable policy implementation by professionals. A project may have justifiable policies and objectives in terms of human well-being, but unless these are effectively and efficiently implemented, the project has lost its moral point. Unless good intentions lead to effective action, they can, in fact, serve as a protective diversion and can bring into question the actual motivation which is operating. It is in the implementation stage of a project that deliberate action is actually taken to intervene in the lives of people. It is at this stage that the project's potential is fulfilled or not. The questions of justification are no longer just hypothetical, anticipatory, or technical. They relate to actual commitment and action which takes up scarce resources, and impacts on the historical reality of the world. (Already, of course, the earlier stages of the project - the agenda-setting, the determination of appropriate agency, and policy decisions - will have used resources and had their own impacts. Not least of the impacts will have been the raising of expectations that something constructive is going to be done about the ethically challenging situation.)

Professionals as Policy Implementers

The justification of actions of professionals as actual interveners must be embedded in their practice circumstances. There is clearly no one pattern of professional involvement in policy implementation, and each pattern will call for justification relevant to those circumstances. Professionals may be variously involved as policy implementers, with different degrees of control and responsibility. If they have responsibility for all stages of a project, they will be implementing their own policies. The policy and program design decisions which they are implementing may, however, be made by their managers, by governing boards, by professional bodies, by governments, or by professional teams - or by their clients. The professionals may delegate or supervise the implementation of policy and program design, retaining overall responsibility for what is done and for results achieved.

The Interests of Professional Implementers

Whatever is the involvement of professionals in the implementation process, they cannot be viewed merely as a means to the policy ends of the project. Their interests as well as their capacities would need to have been assessed when policy feasibility was considered. A project obviously cannot sustain ethical viability if the interests of the implementers are ignored or neglected, or alternatively, are given exaggerated importance.

The instrumental importance to a project of the knowledge and skills of professionals can help to ensure that their interests are reasonably considered in their conditions of work, including their level of remuneration and degree of professional autonomy. They may, however, be poorly paid and be operating under fairly rigid organizational constraints which place severe limits on their professional autonomy. This, for example, can happen with teachers in large-scale systems of schooling. In other settings, for example professionals working for non-government welfare organizations, professionals may have considerable professional autonomy, but be poorly paid and have limited career prospects if they stay in that setting. 'Professionals' in yet other settings may be willing to forgo professional autonomy in return for substantial remuneration, for example, some lawyers and accountants working for corporations. The reputation of some professionals can give them both high remuneration and considerable autonomy. This can operate both with individuals and with professional collectivities. When the state grants a monopoly for professional practice, the potential for exploitation and giving exaggerated importance to the monopolizers is evident. At the same time, however, the professional practice in question and its level of remuneration are much more likely to come under the scrutiny of democratic governments. And this is especially the case when a government becomes involved as a third party in helping to meet the cost of the professional service.

A Public Service Ethic

As members of professional occupations, professionals claim a public service ethic which cannot easily be reconciled with charging what 'the market' will bear for their services. It has become common amongst economic rationalists to refer to professional education as an economic investment for the individual. While professional knowledge and expertise acquired by an individual is expected to have a reasonable financial return throughout the individual's working life, and while some individuals may choose particular professions because of the expected financial rewards, professional life can never be adequately characterized by economic models. If it is accepted that the primary purpose of professionalism is to make money, business models have been allowed to swamp public service models, and a great deal of professional work does not make sense. It is a macro example of goal displacement, where the end of service to the public through specialized knowledge and expertise has been displaced by economic profitability.

The Professionalism of Managers

Already we have examined the involvement of professionals in ethically justified projects up to the point where objectives have been set and decisions have been taken on how the objectives are to be achieved. A crucial determinant of the size, scope, and effectiveness of the project will be the availability of the means to implement these policy decisions. With human well-being as the prime value, an ethically significant project can be operating within any type and level of social organization - from a couple living together to a world-wide organization. The instrumental importance of formal organizations in the modern world (see pp. 123-4) has given special power, influence and responsibility to those who manage them, and this may be reflected in large, sometimes huge, salaries and fringe benefits which are seen as necessary costs of production paid for by consumers, taxpayers, funders, investors, or members, depending on the type of organization.

Yet modern management is not a professional occupation underpinned by values, knowledge and skills which typify professional practice and which is developed and maintained by educational institutions and professional associations. The education for, and organization of, the occupation is fragmented - perhaps inevitably, because although many management technologies are common in all formal organizations, the purposes and substantive knowledge needed to pursue them is significantly different in different fields of management. (See p. 212.)

Some managers will remain faithful to a profession in which they have been initially educated and socialized, seeing management as a significant method to use the knowledge and skills of the profession to achieve its values, and they may, in fact, have received management education from their profession's educational bodies. For example, management (or administration), along with casework, groupwork, community work, and research, has long been cited as a social work specialty (Patti, 1983: 1-23; Skidmore, 1983: 3-15). Such managers are often employed in organizations where members of their particular profession are a significant part of the work-force - social workers employed as a managers of a social work or a social welfare agency, doctors employed as managers of a medical or health service, lawyers employed as managers of a legal service or a welfare rights centre, engineers employed as managers of an engineering or construction firm, and so on. These arrangements can both reflect and stimulate management as a specialty in each of these professions. Further, they can encourage all professional practitioners in these professions to have a greater understanding and appreciation of their organizational context, and the need for effective and efficient management of their own work.

A single-profession service managed by a member of the profession who has specialized in administration has more likelihood of achieving effective and efficient policy development and policy implementation, than a multi-profession service headed by a manager with a general administrative background, or a manager drawn from just one of the professions. A multi-profession service may be highly desirable from a client viewpoint, but its management can be difficult because of differences in the values, knowledge and skills of the various types of professionals employed.

The Need for Administrative Leadership

Generally, organizations require administrative leadership to keep the structure of the organization effectively related to its purposes, to respond to changing environmental conditions, to deal with internal growth, change, and conflicts, and to achieve as much congruency as possible between individual and organizational purposes (Neugeboren, 1985: 145). The governing board or board of directors of an organization usually appoints a chief executive officer (executive director or manager) to direct and coordinate its internal operations, and to develop and maintain its external relationships. Charts of formal structure typically depict all the divisions and staff of an organization as being accountable to a chief administrator who in turn is accountable to the governing body. In a large organization, the chief administrator heads a hierarchy of administrators - middle managers responsible for divisions of the organization, and supervisors responsible to middle managers for the work of the lower-level workers.

Administrative Power

The ability of an administrator to influence the behaviour of others in the organization depends upon their recognition of the authority of the administrator's position, their response to the administrator's use of sanctions both positive and negative, their respect for the administrator's knowledge and expertise, and their response to the administrator's personality (see Skidmore, 1983: 130-1; Neugeboren, 1985: 147). These various factors explain the extent of a manager's power but do not justify the use of that power. Only argument in terms of the human well-being involved can do that.

Administrative Responsibility

According to lines of formal organizational responsibility, program managers are accountable for program failures, and may, in fact, resign, or be relocated or dismissed, if their program is seen to be inadequate. A governing board may sometimes be forced to act in this way by outside pressure - for example, from discontented shareholders, or from funders of the program. This may, however, be an instance of scapegoating or 'blaming the victim'.

Despite the best efforts of the manager, the program may have been inadequately supported by the governing board; the board's policies for the program may have been anachronistic, too vague, or too detailed; the external environment may have proved non-supportive in its level of funding, its competitive work relations, and in the level of client cooperation achieved; new appropriate staff may not have been able to be recruited; many of the existing staff may not have been appointed by the manager and have not been able to be sufficiently retrained for their responsibilities in the program; and so on. Appointment of a new manager obviously can be expected to make some positive difference to the operations of a failing program, especially when the person has knowledge and experience of both managerial processes and of the field in which the program is operating. Many of the constraints experienced by his or her predecessor may still, however, be experienced.

Administrative Justification

Very generally, managers can justify their activities when the programs for which they are responsible provide worth-while products or services as effectively and efficiently as possible, with due regard to the interests of all the parties involved. Their performance can come under moral challenge when the product or service is trivial, is too costly for the benefits gained, is harmful to third parties, is unnecessarily wasteful of scarce resources, is not in accordance with the objectives of the governing body, does not give adequate consideration to the interests of the staff, the interests of the funders are disregarded, the program's technology is weak and indeterminate, program results are not adequately assessed, and they give priority to their own interests and personal career.

Key Administrative Tasks for Policy Implementation

In a discussion of program management in the implementation stage, Patti identifies three important management tasks (Patti, 1983: 106-54). First, is resource acquisition - obtaining funding and internal organizational support for the program, attracting and maintaining a stable clientele, and developing reciprocal relationships essential to the program - with other organizations and with other units in the host agency (pp. 113-26). Second, is developing an organizational structure, which promotes its efficiency, coordination and accountability (pp. 126-37). Third, is developing and maintaining staff capability through effective recruitment and selection, and staff development (pp.137-49).

Issues in Structuring Organizations

Ever since Weber's classical exposition of bureaucratic organization, organizational structure has been a central topic in organizational theory and in management studies, both because of its significance for the achievement of organizational objectives, and because of its implications for democracy. (See Etzioni, 1964: 50-7; Blau, 1956; 101-18; Pugh et al., 1971: 17-55; Skidmore, 1983; 95-112; Neugeboren, 1985: 55-68; and Patti, 1983: 126-37.)

Patti asserts 'designing the formal structure of an organization or program is likely to be one of the manager's most consequential tasks', affecting morale and job satisfaction, relationships with clients, and efficiency (Patti, 1983: 127). Many authors emphasize the operation of the informal system or structure which diverges from the official one. For example, Blau comments:

> Bureaucracies are not such rigid structures as is popularly assumed. Their organization does not remain fixed according to some formal blueprint, but always evolves into new forms... Some of the practices that emerge in the course of operations further the attainment of organizational objectives, while others hinder it... The administrative problem is how to (discourage the latter and encourage the former). (Blau, 1956: 57.)

Patti, however, confines 'organizational structure' to refer to how activities *should* be orchestrated to achieve desired objectives (Patti, 1983: 127).

Unless an organization is appropriately structured, its work will be ineffective and inefficient. Its flow of work will not be controlled. Individuals will have no performance guidelines. Channels of communication and decision-making will be unclear. People will duplicate work and have no clear jurisdiction. They will not be able to relate and concentrate their various efforts to desired shared goals. Workers will have no path to promotion nor will there be any basis for assessing and paying them. Nor will they have any help or support for their work. (See Carlisle, 1979: 377, quoted in Skidmore, 1983: 96-7.) Too much structuring from above can, however, reduce organizational effectiveness and efficiency, and the job satisfaction of employees. An organization is structured both horizontally and vertically.

Horizontal structuring Work in an organization is departmentalized into related services and functions, which allows for job specialization, particularly in larger organizations. An ethically aware manager will be alive to the disadvantages as well as the advantages of job specialization - for clients, for workers, and for managers concerned with effective and efficient program performance. (See pp. 58-9; and Patti, 129-30.) When attainment of the organizational objectives requires expert knowledge and skills which cannot be successfully reduced to standardized, discrete functions learned on the job and/or in in-service training, organizations employ professionals with the most relevant education, training, and experience. Professionals can, however, prove a troublesome component of an organization's work-force, because of their power derived from their substantive knowledge, and because of their commitment to their profession and its values. As we have observed, the principles of bureaucracy and of professionalism can be seen to be in conflict. In addition to the professionals, technicians may also be employed for highly skilled but circumscribed tasks.

It is evident, then, that a manager's structural decisions about an organization's particular division of labour, and the relations between the various types of labour, will be important determinants of the organization's capacity to attain its objectives.

Often closely related to their decisions about division of labour, managers departmentalize or subdivide their organizations into distinct administrative units. Related functions or services are grouped together, and are placed under middle managers who are directly accountable to the general manager. Each unit allows people with highly interdependent tasks to work together. The form and amount of departmentalization will depend on many factors, including the organization's size, objectives, and strategies. Organizational units may be established on a number of bases - to concentrate expertise (in research, budgeting, planning, training) in support of the whole program, to serve particular types of clients or markets, to tackle a distinctive problem, to separate out different processes or technologies, and/or to cover a particular geographic area. Managers need to weigh the advantages of departmentalization against resources spent on interdepartmental communication, coordination, and conflicts. Also departmental interests may be given priority over organizational interests, and clients may experience discontinuity and fragmentation of service within the organization. (Patti, 1983: 130-1; Skidmore, 1983: 98.)

Vertical structuring Vertical structuring of an organization is required to coordinate and make accountable the horizontal structures. Because a large number of workers cannot all report to one director or supervisor, there must be division and subdivision from top to bottom of an organization. The manager needs to establish clear lines of authority, responsibility, reporting, and supervision. (Skidmore, 1983: 98-9.) Professionals are likely to prefer decentralized or centralized authority structures, depending on their position in the organizational hierarchy. Typically they will seek a reasonable degree of professional autonomy so that they can use their expertise effectively. This can mean considerable decentralized authority when they are providing the direct service of the organization, or centralized authority when they control a program of technical and other services. The relative merits of centralization and decentralization must be related to the organizational functions. Policy decisions are commonly made at the top, with implementation decisions further down. (Neugeboren, 1983: 64-5.)

Because they belong to a peer consultative culture in their professional institutions, professionals in an organization might be expected to favor more participatory management styles. The actual behaviour of managers may, however, be obscured by different language traditions. Business managers may typically use autocratic 'control' language, while managers of so-called human service organizations use participatory-style language. Yet examples of practice can indicate that the former may actually be more participatory and the latter more autocratic than the language would suggest. (Donovan and Jackson, 1991: 61-2.) (There is, of course, the further point, that it seems conceptually odd to distinguish between human service organizations and non-human service organizations if all organizations are expected to justify their activities in terms of human well-being.)

A 'Systems' Approach to Effective Administration

Using an integrating 'systems' approach, Neugeboren suggests that an effective administrator needs to view an organization as consisting of five interdependent, but inevitably conflicting, subsystems, each of which has a different purpose or function. In the production subsystem there is stress on specialization, skill and proficiency, with a potential overemphasis on technique. The maintenance subsystem is concerned with personnel matters with the primary purpose of fostering integration of individual and organizational goals. The purpose of the boundary subsystem is to influence the external environment of the organization - by transacting exchanges with other organizations on which the organization depends, and by obtaining community support and legitimation for the organization. The adaptive subsystem is concerned with research, development and planning. And finally, the managerial subsystem co-ordinates and integrates the other four subsystems to maintain the primary purpose of the organization. The subsystem model is decentralized with each subsystem having authority in its respective area. (Neugeboren, 1983: 73-83.)

There is no question that the activities which are grouped together in this analysis are interdependent, but 'systems' language needs to be used with caution in relation to organizational arrangements. Serious ethical questions are raised if features of physical and biological systems are uncritically applied to social systems. (See Roberts, 1990: 201-20.)

Professional Autonomy

The idea of professional autonomy is complex. The traditional emphasis on professional autonomy may be used to justify private, individual professional practice. Yet what can be achieved by isolated independent practitioners is very limited. By working within organized systems of service, professionals can often achieve far more than they can as isolated practitioners - provided the organization's goals are congruent with those of the professional practitioner. Further, the proximity of their professional peers can encourage greater adherence to professional standards. Professional autonomy can relate either to individual or to collective conduct, but neither makes sense in isolation from the other. The two are, in fact, interdependent.

If autonomous action is intentional, with understanding, and without controlling influences (see Beauchamp and Childress, 1994: 125), policy implementation by professionals (or anyone else) is certainly intentional, that is, it is in accordance with a plan of means and ends. If they are appropriately employed, professionals are likely to have at least a reasonable level of understanding in making their implementation choices, because of their education, training and experience. How much understanding is possible will, of course, vary according to the action arena and what is trying to be achieved. On the third autonomy condition of freedom from constraint, professionals in the real world (like everyone else) only have degrees of freedom. Individuals exercise autonomy when they choose to accept policies made by legitimate authorities - in government, in their profession, and in employing organizations. Autonomy and authority are not necessarily incompatible, although they may be in particular situations. (See Beauchamp and Childress, 1994: 124-5.)

Professionals as Dissidents

Professionals, as individuals, or as collectivities, may challenge the legitimacy of particular authorities, and/or particular policy decisions irrespective of the legitimacy of the authorities. Conflicts between authorities and professionals typically occur when professionals are being expected to implement what they see as intolerable policies. For example, in medicine, when governments expect psychiatrists to control political dissidents, or expect physicians to carry out experiments on human beings without their permission. In these extreme situations, could and should the professionals involved have challenged the authorities and with what effect?

Whenever there is conflict between professionals and the authorities over policy implementation, the justificatory situation cannot be prejudged in favor of one or the other. Either or both parties may, in fact, be more concerned with power considerations, with selfish or sectional considerations, or with genuinely moral considerations trying to consider the well-being of all the people affected.

In recent years, governments and professional bodies have demonstrated increasing concern for the well-being of whistleblowers, who have the courage to 'go public' about policies and practices which they believe are against the public interest. Media interests in encouraging such disloyalty to employers complicates what is often an already ethically complex situation. Effective action within the organization to rectify the offending policies and practices is usually preferable if this can possibly be achieved. How professionalism relates to a propensity to object to organizational policies, to change them when necessary, or to take external action with assistance of one's professional peers, is a large, complex topic.

Because of their knowledge and responsibilities, professionals in policy implementation can be particularly well-placed to observe the effects of policy, and provide feedback to managers, boards of governors, and governments, as well as to their professional peers. Indeed, if they are operating with broad discretionary power, for example in handling complex individual cases, they will be inevitably making policy as well as implementing it. Progressive authorities will encourage, welcome, and take notice of responsible, responsive feedback, and will attempt to recruit professionals who are able and willing to provide it. When authorities are, however, repressive, corrupt, or wrong-headed, they may need the technical services of passive professionals, but do not want any policy critique or feedback. Genuine professionals will obviously try to avoid being employed in such a work context in the first place. If the relevant organization is important for the values of the profession, for example, a government child welfare agency's significance for the social work profession, some professionals may deliberately seek employment in the organization in order to try to reform it from within. If eventually they are unsuccessful, as professionals they are likely to have wider employment options outside than staff with only in-service training. They may, however, find themselves branded as trouble-makers, which will reduce their attractiveness to other employers.

Codes of Ethics and Ethical Justification

As has been observed, a code of conduct, usually called a code of 'ethics', is a typical feature of an occupation organized on professional lines. It is a written declaration by the organized profession of the norms or rules which members of the profession are expected to follow in the course of their professional work. Although any comparative examination of professional codes will indicate considerable variety in their size, format and content, every established profession has one, and often a number of additional ones covering specialties within the profession. They are an essential feature in the professional enterprise, performing political and educational, as well as normative functions, and it is now common to find them in any occupation trying to gain credibility with the public and trying to regulate the conduct of its members. The code of ethics is part of an organized profession's policy response in the professional project, responding to the ethically challenging situation of making a living from the development and use of specialized knowledge and skills in ways that enhance rather than harm human well-being. The code has the political function of giving public reassurance that the occupation is expected to operate 'in the public interest' rather than just for its own sectional advantage. The emerging widespread serious interest in the teaching of ethics in professional education goes far beyond just codes of conduct, as people gain greater understanding of the essential interdependence of values, knowledge and skills in occupational conduct.

The development and application of normative codes can, however, provide significant reference points for members of the occupation, employers, clients, governments, and society in general. If the conduct of a professional is clearly contrary to his or her professional code, questions of justification are likely to be raised by one or more of these interested parties. Alternatively, a professional's conduct may be challenged when a professional is clearly adhering to the code, for example, a journalist refusing to disclose a source given in confidence, and this is not seen as reasonable in the circumstances. Whenever a professional's conduct is being judged, its relationship to his or her occupation's code of ethics is likely to be a relevant consideration. The code is intended to provide *justifiable* standards for the conduct of professionals in deciding what is to be done, what is done, and what has been done. This seems to be the point in describing these as codes of *ethics*.

Assessing the moral status of such codes is, however, complex - not least because of vexed questions about the relationship between the code and the actual conduct of the professionals to whom it is intended to apply. The code may not have been given central importance in the education of a professional, particularly of an earlier generation. Some practitioners, for example in Australian journalism, are not even aware of their code's existence, let alone its content. A code may include aspirational, obligatory, or optional standards, and it is important to know which is which.

Historical study of each code would reveal the part played by leading individual professionals, ethics committees, practitioners, educationalists, ethicists, government officials, clients, notorious cases, and other codes, in the creation of each standard and of the code as a whole. The extent to which a code has been built up from case experience, and the extent it has been concerned with the application of general community norms such as those relating to benevolence, malevolence, justice, autonomy, honesty, promising, and loyalty, would be shown by historical analysis. Historical study would reveal how responsive the code has been to changes in the circumstances of the profession. If the code is to command contemporary respect, it will need to be periodically reviewed so that each standard and the code as a whole have a current rationale.

To serve its general normative purpose, a code would need to cover all the main areas of professional responsibility - education and research activity, as well the main fields of practice, practice in different employment settings (government organizations, not-for-profit organizations, commercial organizations, and private individual practice), relationships with clients, with the families of clients, with employers, with professional peers, with members of other professions, with technicians, with other fellow workers, with government and legal requirements, with the society at large, and with the international community, and the reciprocal relationship between the profession and the individual professional.

A profession is, in fact, likely to develop other policy documents and policy statements which complement the code. To achieve coherence and consistency and moral credibility, a politically active profession must obviously be able to reconcile its policy positions with its code of conduct.

A profession's code will often concentrate on individual practitioner responsibility. Yet the collective responsibility of the profession, for example in relation to the availability of its services, may be of far greater significance for human well-being. Whatever the emphasis, recorded case examples of moral reasoning would seem to be necessary to give substance to a code and for educational purposes.

Codes for professionals need to deal with a variety of issues, such as - conflicting and competing values, the balance between rights and duties, the recognition by others of the rights and duties claimed, the different levels of ethical reasoning (moral theory, values, principles, specific rules, and particular decisions), the level of generality of the code (too detailed, or too vague and general?), questions of personal character, and the recognition of personal, family and citizen responsibilities.

Ethically-conscious professional education would include a systematic introduction to ethical reasoning, so that the concerns reflected in the code will be dealt with pervasively, consistently, and specifically, throughout a professional's education integrating them into the effective socialization of each professional. A profession needs specific arrangements to ensure reasonable levels of recognition of the code - by the profession itself, by employers, by clients, and by members of the public.

Negative sanctions connected with codes can range from exclusion from the profession to reprimands. The complaint procedures connected with a professional code need to be fair, and professionals must be willing to use them against their peers when necessary. Ethics committees can become pre-occupied with handling complaints, to the neglect of their general responsibility to encourage the recognition of a code and the development of moral reasoning in the occupation.

The plethora of codes of conduct coming into existence produced, for example, by employers, by clients, by other professionals, and by subspecialties within the profession in question, may complement or be in conflict with the profession's code. (Sometimes actual wording from other codes is adopted without acknowledgement.)

A professional association can only directly apply its code to its members, but the code may be used more widely. When a profession is registered by the state, the relationship between the profession's standards incorporated in its code and those endorsed by legislation becomes a significant issue.

The use of the word 'code' seems to indicate not only norms written down in the one place, but also that they in some sense constitute a system. The systemic quality of a legal code comes from the notion of legal validity. The system is underpinned by a constitution which prescribes the basic processes for valid law-making and for clarifying the law in cases of dispute. The rules within the legal system are not intended to conflict with each other, and every effort is made to ensure that this does not occur.

It is possible, though difficult, to develop an ethical code, or written system of morally justifiable rules, for a profession, if the profession can agree on its basic values and on principles which derive from those values, and can relate these to the main ongoing role and functions of the occupation in ways that are convincing both to its members and to the society of which it is a part. What gives the 'code' its systemic quality is the general purpose or mission of the occupation combined with the justificatory argument necessary to sustain what ought to be done in the pursuit of the mission. Resort to authority rather than argument does not settle an ethical dispute. A 'code' loses its systemic moral quality when it contains a scatter of detailed specific rules each without any rationale, and/or when the rules are primarily rules of convenience or courtesy.

If the basic value of an occupation is to maximize its power, for example if the main purpose of politicians is to win and retain office, and everything they do is a means to that end, can the occupation develop a viable code of ethics for its members? Provided it clarified what is meant by 'power', it could certainly prescribe a code of conduct likely to maximize its power. Similarly, if the basic code of an occupation - like business, for example - is to maximize financial advantage, or make money, a code of conduct could be devised to achieve this end. In both instances the prescriptions in the code could be 'justified' by the end being sought. However, since concepts of power for occupations include not just technical power but power over other people, and since money gives people power in exchange relationships with others, these end values will provide a final justification for conduct only if other people are of no moral account.

The political system of democratic societies provides the opportunity for such completely self-serving codes to come under ethical challenge. The so-called 'bottom line' can never be the maximization of power or money for a sectional interest if all human beings are of moral worth. With human well-being as the basic value, each occupation can try to establish at least general guidelines for its members so that both individually and collectively their work is enhancing rather than harming human well-being. With this basic value, it can engage in open discourse about its justifiable conduct. This will not, of course, eliminate disagreement, because human well-being is 'a many-splendoured thing', but it will help to clarify the basis for conduct and give substance to the concept of a code of *ethics* because it is grounded in arguments of final justification.

Each professional occupation has its own history bound up with jurisdictional battles with occupational competitors - in the workplace, in the public arena, and in the legislature (Abbott, 1988). Its laying claim to specialized knowledge and skills has been central to successful strategies of development. If these are used, however, with the prime purpose of enhancing the power and/or the wealth of those who possess them, rather than in the service of the human species, it is evident that they have become a tool of exploitation. The next major step in ethical justification will be to take seriously the claims of all sentient creatures, not only humans.

11 Professionals Assessing Ethical Results and Their Attainment

The Ethical Significance of Results

A rational action project with primacy given to human well-being cannot reasonably end with the implementation phase. The project is not complete until the result of the action has been determined and assessed in terms of its impact on human well-being. This is the fifth and final stage in the ethical action cycle. With knowledge of the results, people can decide whether similar patterns of action should be continued, or be modified, or be discontinued. The knowledge may be confined to those directly involved in the project, or it may be disseminated for the enlightenment of others as well. As already indicated (pp. 212-13), however, some people and some organizations may give scant attention to the results stage. This is of ethical concern because of the likely opportunity costs, the possibility of unintentional harm, and their inability to establish the effectiveness and efficiency of their response to the ethically challenging situation which gave rise to the project.

Professionals and Goal Attainment

Professionals in general might be expected to be less neglectful of the results stage than non-professionals for a number of reasons. Their professional education and training has usually been designed to produce effective and efficient practitioners, and notions of effectiveness and efficiency have built into them the idea of goal *attainment*. Professionals study a range of subjects relevant to the content and context of their practice, as well as practice theory which must combine both knowledge and skill elements in the service of the underpinning values of the profession. They have had the opportunity of learning accumulated knowledge seen as relevant to their occupation by those who influence the profession's education, often transmitted in a critical intellectual university environment, and by professional peers. Both university and professional culture are concerned with knowledge-development and transmission.

After many years of learning, the 'good' professional comes to demonstrate relevant values, knowledge and skills in their own professional practice. Such a person might be expected to be results-conscious, for the sake of maintaining their own, and the profession's technical capacity - their capacity to select and use the most appropriate means to achieve a desired result. Much of their credibility and therefore their employment and livelihood depends on this technical capacity. Some allow themselves to be used merely as technicians, if this is the only employment they can obtain or the monetary awards are large enough for them to ignore the professed guiding values of their profession. The good professional, however, insists not only on being technically competent, but being able to use that competence in the service of ethically justifiable goals. This means that results of good practice must be a contribution to human well-being. Assessing results is not, then, just a matter of technical interest. Ethically justifiable results provide the whole point, and the continuing point, of professional education and practice.

The Evaluation Movement

'Evaluation', like the words 'effectiveness' and 'efficiency' to which it is often related has become a popular concept in governmental, industrial, and professional circles. One might have thought that the word would be used for the process of determining the worth or value of something, and further that this would be likely to lead to a process of moral reasoning, the most serious form of justificatory argument. We have observed that the economic or exchange value of goods and services, measured in money terms, has become a dominant feature of valuation in many aspects of a modern, industrial society, but this falls far short of valuation yielded by moral reasoning with human well-being as its prime value.

An Evaluation Profession?

There are now some people engaged occupationally in what is called 'evaluation', and they are aspiring to develop as a new profession. However, a separate professional identity is difficult to establish. Their relations to planners, policy-makers, managers, direct service providers, and to the public are diverse and not settled. Many come from established professional occupations, and in particular the research, education, planning, policy and management arms of those occupations, and may return to them. If they do not have substantive knowledge of the field in which they are acting as evaluators, their credibility is in question. One thing is clear, despite their name, this new occupation is not another instance of ethicists finding practical work opportunities. (See pp. 237-9.) The historical development of 'evaluators' has come primarily from the social sciences and those concerned with empirical verification and not from moral philosophy or ethics.

In her 1972 textbook, Carol Weiss concentrated on the role of evaluation research in judging the merit of social programs designed to improve the lot of people. She wrote:

> In the past decade (in the United States) social programs... have expanded enormously... Decision makers want (and need) to know: How well is this program meeting the purposes for which it was established? Should it be continued, expanded, cut back, changed, or abandoned?... Evaluation research appears well suited to the task of producing the requisite information, and in recent years it has become a growth enterprise... It is viewed... as a way to increase the rationality of policy making. (Weiss, 1972: 2.)

A Need for Reform of Program Evaluation

The movement towards an evaluation profession in the United States gained momentum from the publication in 1980 of a book which argued the need for reform of program evaluation, and that this could only be achieved by the development of a strong evaluation profession. The book was the work of a multi-disciplinary team drawn from the Stanford University Evaluation Consortium. It was written for the various interested parties to help understanding of evaluation as an institution and its possible contribution to their ends. Evaluation's proper mission was 'to facilitate a democratic, pluralistic process by enlightening all participants'. Following Martin Luther's precedent, ninety-five principle points or theses, were set forth to stimulate change - in this case to give clarity and order to thinking about evaluation. (Cronbach and Associates, 1980: x-xi, 1-11.)

Evaluation was taken to mean 'systematic examination of events occurring in and consequent on a contemporary program - an examination conducted to assist in improving the program and other programs having the same general purpose' (p. 14). 'Program' and 'project' were not distinguished. Although the book's examples were mainly drawn from the field of education, its argument was intended to apply to 'the full range of human service programs' (or projects, to use the terminology of our rational action model). The authors claimed that although programs and their political contexts varied, the questions to be considered in planning evaluative work were much the same in all fields. Once evaluators and their customers reached common understanding, evaluations would improve and be better used. (pp. 14-15.)

The sort of evaluative inquiry that the book sought to encourage would 'contribute to enlightened discussion of alternative plans'. It was set up by an agency responsible for a program or by one proposing to meet the same need. Evidence was collected from an existing program or one installed for research, with observations and reasoning documented for others to scrutinize. The evaluator aimed to give a comprehensive and disciplined interpretation intended to impress fair-minded persons. The focus was on how best to bring about improvement, not on accountability and apportioning responsibility for goals attained. Evaluation was seen as an integral part of policy research. 'Policy analysts, like evaluators, have become increasingly thoughtful about their interaction with decision makers and about the need to illuminate emerging questions rather than hand down a verdict on what happened last year'. (pp. 17, 19.)

The major complaint that evaluations were not affecting decisions had three main causes - evaluators rarely came out with strong recommendations and often reported that programs had no measurable effect on clients; negative evaluative findings could be discounted by the backers and operators of a program; and evaluators and policy makers were still learning to engage in evaluations. (pp. 44-7.)

A structural suggestion The authors saw evaluators as contributing to the slow, continuous, cumulative understanding of a problem or an intervention (p. 47). They suggested 'social problem study groups' to weigh, digest and interpret knowledge from diverse sources, including program evaluations. A group would foster needed investigations and make 'the policy-shaping community' aware of what is and is not known. It would 'hear from' those who are conducting evaluations, from academic researchers, from those dealing with the problem in service agencies, and from those with ideas about new policies and interventions. Its members would be diverse in their political sympathies and in their expertise. Two-thirds would be social scientists or members of neighbouring disciplines, and they would be drawn from social research corporations, from government, and from universities. (pp. 372, 10, 373, 379.)

It is clear that such an arrangement would give evaluation activity much broader significance than for just a single program or agency, and could greatly assist in shaping ethical agenda setting as it is perceived in our present discussion. The authors recognize, however, that a critical impediment to the idea is the great number of problems to which social research should be relevant, and the limited amount of time group members could give. (p. 380.)

The professionalization of program evaluation In discussing the need for a strong profession, these authors acknowledged that this could make evaluations worse rather than better - if it served its members rather than its clientele, if it made its training unnecessarily restrictive and prolonged, and if ideals in professional rhetoric did not affect practice. These dangers could only be offset by shaping standards to fit the public interest and by vigour in enforcing them. If individual evaluators remained 'mutually unacquainted, insensitive to their common interests and intellectually fractionated', such standards could not be achieved. The profession had to develop internal agreement on the marks of good practice. It had to press its customers to seek services that were truly beneficial and to use the profession appropriately. Universities had to be persuaded 'to make a place for training in evaluation as a distinctive art, one that could not be compressed within present disciplinary traditions'. A new umbrella professional organization was needed to cope with the same range of topics covered by other modern professional associations. (pp. 352-56.)

The evaluation enterprise itself needed 'penetrating, balanced, extensive inquiry'. Regular peer criticism, in a collegial rather than adversarial spirit, was needed to develop and uphold professional standards. Professional reviews of evaluations were 'sporadic and normally came too late to help either the target evaluation or those who use its findings'. Critics should review the actions of commissioners as well as evaluators. Multiple reviews from different perspectives were needed, but with some attempt at synthesis. The increasingly vigorous reviewing program of the Government Accounting Office was likely to preempt the field and set standards that should be emerging from the profession as a whole. (pp. 356-64.)

Program Evaluation in Australia

Two Australian publications at about the same time indicate an emerging interest in program evaluation - partly arising from Australia's own cycle of events and partly stimulated by the evaluation movement in North America, and, to a lesser extent, in Britain. A national seminar in 1978, led by Rosemary Sarri, an experienced North American evaluator, consisted of a deliberate mix of policy-makers, administrators, researchers and educators, involved in social welfare program evaluation at different levels of government and non-government agencies. The case reports prepared by the participants for the seminar were revised for publication to highlight issues at various stages of the evaluation process. While non-rational elements were recognized in both, a program was conceived as a form of rational action and evaluation as a form of rational inquiry. A social welfare program was conceived as a form of rational action which was social in its auspice and accountability, and had social well-being as its prime purpose. (Sarri and Lawrence, eds, 1980.)

Senator Peter Baume, who chaired the Australian Senate Standing Committee on Social Welfare, was an active participant in this 1978 seminar. At the time his Committee had been asked by the Australian Senate to evaluate the adequacy of Australian health and welfare services, with particular reference to standards of performance and provision, current practice in terms of need and demand, mechanisms for evaluation of effectiveness and efficiency of services, and requirements for ongoing evaluation as an integral part of the development of programs. The Senate Committee's Report (1979) asserted the need for ongoing evaluation in order to achieve an 'efficient, effective, rational and equitable' system. The benefits derived from evaluation include increased accountability of decision -makers, improvement in the decision-making process, more effective use of resources, and enhancement of the capacity of organizations to strengthen their bids for additional resources. The consequences of not evaluating are possible indiscriminate cuts in funds, indiscriminate handing out of funds, continuance of the present ad hoc decision-making process, perpetuation of the present inadequacies in the health and welfare system, and a possible lack of alternative solutions to problems in health and welfare. (*Through a Glass Darkly*, 1979: vol. 1, p. 3.)

Many factors were identified as inhibiting evaluation in Australia - it was threatening especially when the consequences of failure were distressing or costly, there was a lack of national goals, necessary data either did not exist or were not accessible, there was a lack of defined standards for both provision and performance, the present system of funding did not encourage evaluation, neither did the way the Parliament functioned, evaluation required considerable resources, it was not seen as necessary, it was new and relatively unproved, and finally, there were difficulties in converting theory into practice. Despite the difficulties, however, some level of appraisal occurred in most organizations, and some had moved toward formal evaluation. (pp. 105-13.)

Amongst its thirty-five recommendations, the Report included a recommendation 'That all professional groups develop and disseminate comprehensive standards of performance for the guidance of their members and for the protection and information of clients' (p. 78). In addition, the Report noted increasing emphasis on the training of professionals in the necessary evaluative skills (p. 113), but there is no discussion of any need for an evaluation profession.

A Basic Division and Disagreement

In a review of evaluation in the human services in the United States, written for the Australian Senate Committee, Sarri stated that no overarching general synthesis of the varying perspectives in the extensive literature had yet been developed. Two major contrasting approaches were apparent - 'post hoc evaluation for administrative and policy decision-making', relying on social science methodology, and active involvement in the development of effective programs and services. (Sarri, in *Through a Glass Darkly*, 1979: vol. 2, pp. 72-3.)

A roughly similar dichotomy - between 'academically-oriented and 'service-oriented' evaluators - was observed in a 1986 study of members of the Evaluation Network and the Evaluation Research Society as they merged in the American Evaluation Association (AEA). The 31 per cent whose primary professional identity was 'evaluator' were found to be more likely to have a service/stakeholder orientation while those for whom evaluation was a secondary activity within their primary discipline or specialization were more likely to be engaged in academic evaluative research. (The study is referred to by Patton in Alkin, ed., 1990: 203-4.)

An extended published debate between Carol Weiss and Michael Patton (Alkin, ed., 1990), leading protagonists of each of these contrasting orientations gives insight into the tensions within the emerging evaluation profession. They were among ten 'distinguished evaluation professionals' convened to engage in a three-day discussion of evaluation utilization. The free-ranging discussion exposed the differing views on the nature of evaluation held by Weiss and Patton in particular.

Weiss's 1987 plenary address to the American Evaluation Association was titled 'Evaluation for Decisions: Is Anybody There? Does Anybody Care?' (republished in Alkin, ed., 1990). In it she 'intended to illustrate the many and varied ways in which evaluation results influence programming even when program decision makers did not implement results immediately and directly'. Yet in a subsequent address, Patton took exception to her report on 'the dismal state of evaluation utilization'. He argued that her view of 'indifferent success' in specific evaluation contributions to program improvement might apply to national policy research, but it did not apply to program evaluation which was focused on 'intended use by intended users to improve programs directly'. He acknowledged that he and Weiss typically operated in different arenas and were involved in evaluation in different ways, but he believed they had 'fundamentally different views of evaluation as a field of practice'. Hers was an academic research perspective and his an action research and stakeholder-oriented approach, described in his book on 'utilization-focused evaluation' (Patton, 1986). As the AEA President, Patton claimed, however, that he wanted to facilitate open discussion and debate about alternative visions of evaluation practice, not just advocate one view. (Alkin, ed, 1990: 186-8, 204-6.)

In response, Weiss agreed that evaluators could encourage greater attention to their findings, but she doubted that evaluators could ever persuade stakeholders to make evaluation results the overriding consideration in program decisions. 'Program people know a lot more about their programs than simply the things the evaluator tells them'. To ask program managers and planners to embrace evaluation findings fully was to ask them to abdicate their responsibility in favor of an evaluator who inevitably had only a partial view. Evaluators should illuminate the range of options and likely effects. Evaluation should be continuing education for program managers, planners, and policy makers. She went on to note many reasons why program people did not always pay close attention to evaluation results. Self-interest, organizational protection, and the quest for advantage were program realities which Patton's world of rational arguments for program improvement seemed to ignore. (Weiss, in Alkin, ed., 1990: 210-12.)

Weiss said that as practitioners of evaluation, it was important to believe in the worth of the enterprise (of evaluation), but as *evaluators*, 'we are obligated to examine the evidence'. The connections between evaluators' recommendations and the data needed to be closely examined. In some cases, evaluators had expert knowledge of the program field. More often they did not and had to rely on developing a logical model of the program in their mind, and base their recommendations on their layperson's understanding. (pp. 216-17.)

Weiss was particularly troubled by the notion that if it was acknowledged that evaluation did not routinely lead to program improvement, evaluators could not get clients. It was very wrong, she said, to mislead clients and potential clients about what an evaluation could offer them just to get their custom. She insisted that although she taught at a university, she was 'as committed to use of evaluation results as any person alive'. (pp. 219-20.)

A Conceptual Overview of Program Evaluation

From the early 1980s, proceedings of the Australasian Evaluation Society indicated a steady growth in the 'relatively new discipline' of program evaluation, encouraged by small groups of academics. One of these, John Owen, produced a 1993 text using Australian examples. It was highly conceptual and inclusive insisting on the contribution of evaluation to *all* phases of program development, and not just program outcomes. Evaluation activities were seen as complementary to and supportive of program development and provision. Evaluation was 'a process of providing information designed to assist decision-making about what was being evaluated'. The most likely objects of an evaluation were: planning, programs, policies, organizations, products, and individuals. (Owen, 1993: 2-14.) A program evaluation could be carried out for one or more reasons - enlightenment, accountability, program improvement, program clarification, and/or program development. (pp. 14-18.)

Owen also mentioned symbolic evaluation which was not done for any of these reasons, but to give the appearance of evaluation. [In 1968, Suchman had distinguished six forms of 'pseudo-evaluation' or 'evaluative abuse': when attention was limited to favorable aspects, when objective appraisal was avoided, when evaluation was designed to eliminate a program, when the objective and scientific pose was adopted without such substance, when action was delayed while awaiting needless evaluation, and when failure in an essential program activity was disguised by shifting attention to a less relevant but more defensible program aspect (quoted in Thompson, 1975: 15-16.)]

The Different Forms of Evaluation

Owen differentiated five forms of genuine evaluation with a chapter devoted to each (Owen, 1993: pp. 19-30, 86-166). It was suggested that the forms could be used by interested parties and evaluators as a basis for deciding on the most appropriate type of evaluation for a given program at a given time. Each form consisted of five dimensions - an *orientation* or ultimate reason for the evaluation; the (developmental) *state* of the program to be evaluated ranging from one not yet in existence to one that was 'settled'; the *focus* or program component(s) upon which the evaluation was concentrated, context, design, delivery, and/or outcomes; the *timing* or temporal links between the evaluation and program delivery; and the *evaluation approach(es)* appropriate to the form.

Impact evaluation was used to assess at some logical end point the impact of a settled program, to determine its merit or worth. Its typical approaches included 'the extent and level of attainment of specified objectives, the level of performance on simple outcome indicators, or the compilation of both intended and unintended outcomes'. This 'summative' evaluation might also require a review of a program's implementation.

Evaluation in program management was appropriate for a well established, ongoing program where there needed to be some indication of the success or otherwise of the program or one of its components, for accountability and/or funding purposes. This might involve the development of a system of regular monitoring with performance information rapidly available.

These first two forms of evaluation were more likely to be addressed to managers and funders. *Process evaluation*, however, was aimed at those responsible for implementing an operating program at the local or site level. Here the purpose was to collect information that would improve the program during its formative stages, that would improve the practice of those delivering the service, and that would help those associated with a program to understand how and why it operated as it did.

Design evaluation was focused on clarification of the logic of the program. This was appropriate when an operating program did not have a clear underlying structure and rationale, or reflected conflicts over aspects of its design, or there was confusion about program implementation.

Evaluation for development was the name given by Owen to evaluations which occurred before a program was designed, to assist planners to make decisions about the type of program that was needed. [This is, of course, the first stage of our model.] Needs assessment, research synthesis, and review of exemplary practice were three approaches appropriate to this form of evaluation which was largely concerned with the social, political, and economic context in which the program would develop.

Owen commented that, until recently, evaluation was rarely seen as having a role in decisions about the creation or clarification of programs (p. 20).

The Key Players

Key players in an evaluation included those who provided resources for it, those for whom its findings were intended, and those who carried it out - commissioners, audience, and evaluators. Owen stated that their relationships, their contributions, and their information needs had to be clarified when an evaluation was being planned. The most likely situation was one where the commissioning agent was the primary audience for the evaluator, although self-evaluation could occur, for example, as part of the practice of a professional, or by a department within an organization. Different configurations of players, including whether they were seen as insiders or outsiders, influenced the style of evaluation. (pp. 31-41.)

Standards of Professional Practice

Whether or not evaluators were insiders or outsiders, there was a need for evaluators 'to conduct themselves in ways which are a credit to the profession of evaluation'. Although in practice there could be conflict between some of the standards, the existence of standards and adherence to them by evaluators were essential aspects of 'the professionalization of evaluation as a discipline'. Owen quoted in full the set of standards for educational evaluation produced in 1981 in the United States, referred to current American refinement of these, and mentioned work in the Australasian Evaluation Society to develop a set of standards for its members. (pp. 41-6.)

The thirty standards quoted by Owen were grouped into four areas. The *utility* standards were intended to help in planning evaluations that were informative, timely and influential. The *feasibility* standards recognized that evaluations were generally conducted in natural settings, and they had to be realistic, diplomatic and financially well managed. The *propriety* standards aimed at ensuring that the rights of people influenced by the program and its evaluation will be protected. And the *accuracy* standards were concerned with the production of valid and reliable knowledge about the evaluation and the object under review.

Limits to the Professionalization of Evaluation

It is fascinating to observe the way in which the evaluation movement which gathered momentum especially from the government programs of the 1960s, has begun to be professionalized. Seen in the context of our framework or model of ethical rational action, this new group of aspiring professionals concentrated initially on the results stage of other people's projects. They are clearly located at the bottom of the parallel assessment function (see pp. 40, 51-2). Although they are called evaluators, the special expertise which justified their employment in other people's affairs was their measurement skills, and their knowledge production about results of past actions. They could reasonably make recommendations and judgments about these descriptive matters, but decisions about how to utilize the knowledge for human well-being, or some more limited, or other purpose, required commitment and moral reasoning to justify it.

A thoughtful assessment of results, both intended and unintended, must lead back into an inquiry of what has produced the 'results'. In other words, impact evaluation encourages assessment of the earlier stages of the rational action model. Increasingly 'evaluators' have become concerned about the program management, process, design, and development evaluations sketched by Owen. These are roughly the equivalent of the program, policy, and agenda phases of our model. The slower involvement of the emerging evaluation 'profession' in design and development evaluation has, however, been noted. One obvious reason for this could be that politicians and policy makers who tend to be the commissioners of evaluations may not wish to place their own agenda and priority setting functions under too close a scrutiny or limitation. Yet more and more in the complex world in which they live and function, they need to be educated by the sort of help that development and design evaluations can give them - provided the final value choices still remain with them, otherwise the technocrats have taken over.

The Stanford Evaluation Consortium perceived evaluation as a novel political institution (Cronbach and Associates, 1980: x), and the political nature of evaluation has been recognized in more recent years (Sarri, in Sarri and Lawrence, 1980: 7-8). A variety of interests inevitably are at stake and are contending for recognition. Researchers can expose the interests and the likely effects of different courses of action on the interests, but to evaluate a situation for action or policy purposes is to do more than describe it. It is to take a position about what ought to be done. In this sense, evaluators appropriately described, are engaged in political decision-making, whether they recognize it or not. There is, as yet, no evaluation profession, in any significant sense of the term, at least partly because the main underlying values of its members have not been clarified, and its educational underpinning is weak and ambiguous.

Like the related concepts of planning and management, evaluation relates to a general process within the rational action model. It is only when the purposes or values are specified, for example, health, legal justice, or education, that it is possible to give substance to ideas of planning, management, or evaluation, and to know what kind of planning, management, or evaluation, is relevant. Then an occupation organized on professional lines can develop on the basis of these selected values, and the knowledge and skills relevant to their attainment, and can argue a moral case for its particular contribution to human well-being, if that is the prime value for justificatory argument. The evaluation literature inevitably overlaps and interweaves with the policy, planning, and management literature, but strangely not very much with the literature which deals with moral reasoning.

Evaluation in the form of assessing the effectiveness and efficiency of human action obviously must occur to some extent at every stage in the primary decision-making of the rational action cycle and not only in the parallel assessment stage. Indeed, this is where the actual decision-making and value commitments are being made and demonstrated. People called 'evaluators' (management or planning consultants) may be used to make the decision-makers better informed about future possibilities but the evaluators are not responsible for the valuations demonstrated in actual decision-making. If any of these consultants become the decision-makers they have taken over from the previous decision-makers and are no longer consultants.

The Reach of the Evaluation Movement

As has been made clear in the agenda-setting chapters of our rational action model where ethically challenging situations for government and non-government collectivities were considered (Chapters 6 and 7), the effects of all human projects should come under moral scrutiny, not just those that are said to be social programs. The above sketch of the evaluation movement has concentrated on 'social' programs. It has been evident, even here, that the motivation is often mixed, and in recent times has been as much concerned with cutbacks and increased social control as with providing improved service which will enhance people's lives. The evaluation movement has also extended to most, if not all, government programs, at least partly as a managerial tool. Its extension to the private entrepreneurial sector is less certain, although commonly the good manager is still described as one who maximizes profits, irrespective of the social impact of the organization. As firms undertake social and environmental impact studies, both prospective and retrospective, and develop a capacity for genuine moral reasoning to justify their various operations, they will provide a more acceptable work environment for their professional and other staff, and can contribute to a socially-minded evaluation movement. If, however, their critera for evaluation remain narrowly focused, managerial 'success' can cause considerable damage, leaving families and social agencies to deal with it.

The Role of Secondary Assessors

As we have already discussed, 'ethicists' are being increasingly employed in various settings, presumably to strengthen the moral reasoning of the actual decision-making. It will be remembered, however, that the employment of ethicists can be just as problematic as the employment of evaluators, if human well-being is the prime value. Neither has direct responsibility for decision-making, and the analysis of neither is likely to be complete for decision-making, because the ethicist's analysis is likely to be stronger in its value components than in its empirical or factual components, while the strengths and weaknesses of the evaluator are likely to be in the opposite direction. Neither is actually making the decision about what ought to be done, all things considered. Only genuinely justificatory argument by the actual decision-maker can do this, and in this it is the value and factual arguments which count, not the claimed professional authority of an ethics consultant and/or evaluator. The well-educated primary decision-maker is able to understand the data and arguments of consultants of various kinds including ethicists and evaluators, without losing their own sense of responsibility and direction. Consultants can have an important educative role when performing the parallel assessment function in our model.

Although professionals value their autonomy, they are accustomed to learning from the criticism of their peers - in case discussions, in their professional literature, and in supervision from more experienced practitioners. They, in turn, are expected to operate constructively in the parallel assessment function as well as in primary decision-making, otherwise peer review and professional education could not operate.

When the parallel assessment function is performed not by sympathetic colleagues, but by professional competitors, or by people who do not have their knowledge and skills, or by people who do not share their values, the parallel assessment function can distract and sometimes destroy the primary decision-making of the professionals. It is evident that the assessment function itself needs to be critiqued using the model of rational ethical action. (See p. 52.)

Some of the most rewarding and controversial contributions to human well-being are made by people who work in the fields of the performing and creative arts. The profession of journalism has developed its art critics, its music critics, its theatre critics, its literature critics, and so on. The critics often have not been accomplished practitioners of the art in question, and may not have any interest, in any case, in constructive or fair criticism, provided their own journalistic career flourishes. Their self-appointed, or editor-appointed task is to pass judgment in the limited formats of the modern press, or television, on the work of people trying to make a living as performing or creative artists. This is obviously not peer review, and it is more than just another viewer, listener, or reviewer, saying what they like and dislike. Good or bad reviews by critics can influence public opinion and make or break particular artists or performers. The ethics of public criticism is rarely discussed by the critics. Every human activity can, of course, be improved by a tradition of constructive criticism, but this would seem to require more frequent collective discussion of the relevant criteria than has been achieved by the journalist critics, and greater respect for critics by the practitioner groups. Critics, like those whose work they critique, are, however, often fiercely independent.

The words 'critic', 'criticism', and 'criterion' all relate to the notion of judgment ('krites' in Greek means 'judge'), but curiously the first two are often used only for negative judgment. Ethically justifiable judgment cannot reasonably concentrate only on negative aspects of what is being judged. Criteria for judgment obviously should differ for works of fiction, and works that claim to portray reality. The blurring of the categories has serious moral implications, particularly when it is done covertly and for monetary gain.

One form of judgment in which professionals are centrally involved is the form of judgment found in the law courts. We have already seen that lawyers' attempted appropriation of the concept of justice needs to be understood for what it is (p. 147). A legal judgment must pay regard to legal criteria for judgment but these do not necessarily coincide with morally justifiable criteria. Legal judgments are about other people's judgments. They constitute a special, powerful, and often expensive instance of the parallel assessment function, this time by a professional monopoly in the name of the state. Legal advice is not a legal judgment; it is an attempt to anticipate what one would be, if the matter were brought to court. The effects of the legal system on many aspects of human well-being, especially in societies with large numbers of legal practitioners who encourage litigation and 'rights' talk is a topic which democratic governments might be expected to take seriously - provided they in turn are not too dominated by members of the legal profession.

We have already argued (pp. 51-2) that when the process of rational ethical conduct necessarily involves the well-being of people, any stage of the process or the whole process can come under separate ethical scrutiny and assessment - by those involved reflecting on their own conduct, or by others. The others may be formally appointed for the task, like the evaluation 'professionals', or committees of inquiry, or they may have some special interest or general interest in the adequacy of the primary project.

The assessment function, especially when it is separate and formally organized, has a life of its own, which in turn calls for ethical assessment. It itself is a rational action project whose terms of reference, use of resources, policies, procedures, and findings, may affect not only the interests of people connected with the project which gave rise to it, but the interests of its sponsors, and the assessors themselves. If the primary project has great ethical significance, it may come under multiple assessment, both near the time of the original decision-making and later when the longer-term effects have been experienced and become more apparent. Decisions which shape the well-being of a whole nation, for example, establishing a national constitution, declarations of war, international treaties, population policies, and major social and economic policies, are likely to come under periodic assessment, not only by professional historians, but by policy analysts and others, concerned about their contemporary significance.

Individual Conscience

One of the most pervasive examples of the parallel assessment function is self-evaluation at the individual level by an individual's conscience. Owen mentioned the possibility of self-evaluation as part of the practice of a professional (see p. 292). If professional socialization has been effective, professionals will be self-critical and will welcome critiques of their work especially by their peers, not least because this can provide a safeguard against self-deception. These are the habits of a conscientious professional. According to Beauchamp and Childress, 'roughly speaking, an individual acts conscientiously if he or she has tried with due diligence to determine what is right, intends to do what is right, exerts an appropriate level of effort, and is motivated to do what is right because it is right'. It is a virtue that is significant for both ordinary morality and moral ideals. (Beauchamp and Childress, 1994: 475-83.)

Conscientious professionals will apply this standard both in their primary decision-making and in their parallel reflective assessments. They are acting in accordance with what might be called their professional conscience. Since their profession's standards have become their own, their violation will undermine the professional's sense of integrity and feelings of guilt or remorse can ensue. The person will experience a bad professional conscience. The violation may occur because other professional situations, or other non-professional situations have been given priority, or the professional's work environment makes the maintenance of professional standards impossible. But the violation of standards caused by these will not be experienced as a matter of conscience if these are not the professional's own personal standards. The conscience-stricken professional may seek to renegotiate the working situation, or may move to a situation that does not violate his or her sense of professional integrity.

Professionals, like others, can appeal to a 'conscientious objection', if they do not wish to violate their conscience. However, a person's conscience can take as many forms as there are internalized personal standards. The one person can experience a conflict of conscience when different and sometimes conflicting courses of action seem to be required by a person's internalized standards. A person can have a work conscience (professional work can produce a particularly strong work conscience), a family conscience (which can be sorely tested by work commitments), a religious conscience (which can vary greatly in its scope and strength), and a community conscience (which again can vary greatly in its scope and strength). These may be reconciled by compromise and careful specification and weighting, to maintain some sense of personal integrity. Without a form of conscience that can do this, the person can become fragmented and guilt-ridden.

The standard appeal to conscience when exploring or justifying an action or a refusal to act may merely claim that a person's sense of integrity is seen to be at stake. If, however, that integrity is achieved at the expense of others or is used to harm others, the appeal to conscience which maintains this sort of integrity is not ethically justifiable. The only appeal to conscience that has moral justification is a conscience grounded in rational argument relating to the attainment of human well-being, if that is the accepted prime value.

12 Concluding Comments and a Proposal

It will be remembered that a basic assumption that sets in train a project is that something constructive can be done about an ethically challenging situation. The course of the subsequent project and its result and assessment indicate whether the initial assumption was warranted. With the help of a model of rational action for human well-being, it is possible to consider the ethical significance of any human activity - provided, of course, that the basic values of rationality and human well-being are accepted. As we have seen there is plenty of room for disagreement within the model, both about ends and means, but at least these basic values provide a shared framework within which the disagreements can be pursued and possibly resolved by argument rather than coercion. We have noted that the model can be extended to cover the well-being of all sentient creatures, and not just humans, and increasing numbers of people are arguing for this broader moral framework. The different stages of the action model and the subsequent parallel assessment help to keep the justificatory argument focused on the task in hand, without losing sight of the overall process. It can give more general point and purpose to the immediate participants, and give them a greater sense of involvement in an ethically justified enterprise.

In the second section of the book, we have used the model of rational action for human well-being to consider the ethical significance of a particular form of human activity, professional conduct. Our historical and analytic examination of this concept in earlier chapters revealed that although the topic is complex and controversial, it is still possible to develop a meaningful descriptive model which has utility in at least Anglo-American societies, and in any society concerned about the responsible use of specialized knowledge to make a living. While 'professional' is obviously used in a variety of ways - to refer to working for money, to refer to high standards in any sort of performance, or to membership of any organized occupation - our professional model is derived from those occupations which are built upon the development and use of specialized knowledge and skills for socially desirable purposes, and not just to make a living. To achieve this, the occupation has characteristic social structures. Its work organization allows sufficient autonomy for professional practice; educational institutions or professional schools develop and transmit the occupation's values, knowledge and skills to recruits to the occupation; and professional associations perform educational, industrial, and social policy functions.

The level of collective and individual autonomy and social status associated with this professional model has made it attractive for large numbers of modern occupations, although achieving effective professional structures in a changing, competitive, modern environment, is a constant struggle. As has been indicated by Abbott, professional occupations and aspiring ones come and go.

Professional conduct has become of particular ethical interest in modern society, not only because this is the way considerable numbers of the 'better-educated' members of society earn their living and find personal and collective fulfillment, but because the great growth of professional expertise has opened up enormous potential for both good and evil, in terms of human well-being.

Proposal for a Standing Commission on the Professions

The ethical rational action model can be fruitfully applied to each occupation organized on professional lines. This will see the occupation itself as an occupational project, to be assessed periodically in terms of its contribution to human well-being. Ideally, this calls for independent assessment, in addition to self-assessment. A democratic government could consider the establishment of a Standing Commission on the Professions. The Commission could assist in a periodic, systematic, ethical assessment of each profession, and of the professions as occupational groupings in major areas of societal functioning. This could help to ensure that each occupation and each group of occupations organized on professional lines is responding to an appropriate ethical agenda, is accepting appropriate responsibilities for its capacities and purposes, is using ethically justifiable criteria in determining policies and strategies, is implementing these in ethically acceptable ways, and is assessing results and how they were attained. The development of adequate information and knowledge about the professions (see pp. 98-9) would be essential to the Commission's work.

The Commission would have to proceed through argument, education and persuasion, but it could in the longer term produce a much more ethically justified 'professional system', to use Abbott's term, than the present one which is based so much on the competitive strength and traditions of different occupations, and their often chance cooperation around matters of common interest. We have commented in passing on the absence of a professionalized occupation in a variety of areas important for human well-being, for example, the absence of work professionals (p. 182). The Standing Commission on the Professions could identify these areas and encourage initiatives to develop new professions, or extend the coverage of existing ones. It could help existing professions to be better informed about the professional system as a whole and their place in it, and about community and governmental developments relevant to their functioning. It could also encourage cooperative strategies when appropriate. If such a Commission did not command the respect and cooperation of the professionals themselves, it could not operate effectively. There is the obvious danger that its work could become highly politicized. For example, it could be dominated by government interests, or by powerful traditional professions, or by politically active aspiring professions, or by professional bureaucrats. Yet it does seem that the overview, coordinating, and data collection functions that such a body could perform cannot be achieved at present, no matter how ethically aware any one profession becomes.

The Commission could be set up as an independent statutory body, with a mandate to serve the general interest without fear or favour. Its members would need to be appointed for reasonably long renewable terms, so that they could come to grips with the responsibilities of the Commission. Some members may have no particular professional background, but most would be drawn from across the spectrum of professional fields, although not seen as representing any field or profession.

All members would be distinguished by the quality of their moral reasoning, in relating the professional system as a whole to society, as well as in the affairs of particular professions and groups of professions. Both the exploitative and service potentials of professionalism would be well understood. The Commission would, however, need to make an assumption of goodwill, unless experience and evidence in particular cases proved this to be mistaken. If the Commission were to demonstrate an assumptive cynicism about professional motivation, this would undermine the possibility of having constructive relations with professionals, not least because many professionals and others would see it as unreasonable.

The Commission would be staffed by people with substantive knowledge of the various professional fields, understanding of occupational sociology, social research skills, and an appreciation of the professional ethos operating in the different professions.

Occupations would become affiliated with the Commission on a voluntary basis, but they would need to meet criteria set by the Commission. The policy decision about the criteria would shape the size and much of the substance and politics of the Commission's work. Unless the Commission grasps the definitional nettle, occupational self-selection could lead to a complete fragmentation of ideas of professional identity, and make the Commission's mandate virtually impossible to fulfill.

The Commission would produce regular public reports on the scope, achievements, and problems of professionalism, as it operates nationally, and to the extent possible, internationally. As a statutory body, the Commission would report annually to the Congress or the Parliament, where democratically elected representatives and the government of the day will decide how well the Commission is serving its general public interest mandate, and what financial resources it should receive for its work. If the Standing Commission on the Professions does not in fact improve the contribution of professional occupations to human well-being, it should be discontinued - like any other initiative which demonstrably does not make a contribution to human well-being.

Professional occupations may themselves establish a Professional Council, or an Association of Professions, for discussion of mutual concerns, but these are much more likely to be mutual benefit cooperatives safeguarding members' interests and their autonomy than critical arenas for ethical assessment in a societal frame of reference. Professions are obviously much too ethically significant to be left just to their own collective devices. A statutory Commission funded by taxpayers is likely to have greater societal legitimacy and resources, provided it can work cooperatively with the professions without undermining their sense of responsibility.

Bibliography

Abbott, A. (1988), *The System of the Professions: an Essay on the Division of Expert Labor*, The University of Chicago Press, Chicago.

Abel, R. L. (1989), *American Lawyers*, Oxford University Press, New York.

Abramovitz, M. (1988), *Regulating the Lives of Women: Social Policy from Colonial Times to the Present*, South End, Boston, Massachusetts.

Acton, H. B. (1971), *The Morals of Markets: An Ethical Exploration*, Longman, London.

Alexander, I. (1981), 'Post-War Metropolitan Planning: Goals and Realities', in P. N. Troy (ed.), *Equity in the City*, George Allen and Unwin, Sydney, pp. 145-71.

Alkin, M. C. (ed.) (1990), *Debates on Evaluation*, Sage, Newbury Park, California.

Annas, G. J. (1994), 'Will the Real Bioethics (Commission) Please Stand Up?', *Hastings Center Report*, 24, no. 1, pp.19-21.

Atwan, R., Orton, B., and Vesterman, W. (eds) (1986), *American Mass Media: Industries and Issues* (3rd ed.), Random House, New York.

Australian Institute of Family Studies (1994), *Annual Report 1993-94*, Commonwealth of Australia, Melbourne.

Baier, K. (1987), 'The Moral Point of View' in G. Sher (ed.), *Moral Philosophy: Selected Readings*, Harcourt Brace Jovanovich, San Diego, pp. 332-449.

Bailey, J. (1980), *Ideas and Intervention: Social Theory for Practice*, Routledge and Kegan Paul, London.

Barnsley, J. H. (1972), *The Social Reality of Ethics: the Comparative Analysis of Moral Codes*, Routledge and Kegan Paul, London.

Barrow, R. (1982), *Injustice, Inequality and Ethics*, Barnes and Noble, Totowa, New Jersey.

Bates, E., and Lapsley, H. (1987), *The Health Machine: The Impact of Medical Technology*, Penguin Books, Ringwood, Victoria.

Bayles, M. (1989), *Professional Ethics* (2nd ed.), Wadsworth, Belmont, California.

Beauchamp, T. L. et al. (1982), *Ethical Issues in Social Science Research*, The Johns Hopkins University Press, Baltimore.

Beauchamp, T. L., and Childress, J. F. (1989, 1994), *Principles of Biomedical Ethics* (3rd ed., 4th ed.), Oxford University Press, New York.

Bell, D. (1973), *The Coming of Post-Industrial Society*, Basic Books, New York.

Benn, S. I., and Peters, R. S. (1959), *Social Principles and the Democratic State*, George Allen and Unwin, London.

Bennet, G. (1987), *The Wound and the Doctor: Healing, Technology and Power in Modern Medicine,* Secker and Warburg, London.

Berger, P. L., and Luckmann, T. (1966), *The Social Construction of Reality: A Treatise in the Sociology of Knowledge*, Doubleday, New York.

Berger, P. L. (1986), 'Epilogue', in J. D. Hunter and S. C. Ainlay (eds), *Making Sense of Modern Times: Peter Berger and the Vision of Interpretive Sociology*, Routledge and Kegan Paul, London, pp. 221-5.

Blau, J. R. (1984), *Architects and Firms: A Sociological Perspective on Architectural Practice*, The Massachusetts Institute of Technology Press, Cambridge, Massachusetts.

Blau, P. M. (1956), *Bureaucracy in Modern Society*, Random House, New York.

Bledstein, B. J. (1976), *The Culture of Professionalism: the Middle Class and the Development of Higher Education in America*, W. W. Norton and Co., New York.

Bliss, C. (1987), 'Economics', in J. Kuper (ed.), *Key Topics of Study*, Routledge and Kegan Paul, London, pp. 44-56.

Blustein, J. (1982), *Parents and Children: The Ethics of the Family*, Oxford University Press, New York.

Bok, D. (1982), *Beyond the Ivory Tower: Social Responsibilities of the Modern University*, Harvard University Press, Cambridge, Massachusetts.

Boreham, P., Pemberton, A., and Wilson, P. (ed.) (1976), *The Professions in Australia: a Critical Appraisal*, University of Queensland Press, St. Lucia.

Briggs, A. (1965), 'The Welfare State in Historical Perspective', in M. N. Zald (ed.), *Social Welfare Institutions*, John Wiley and Sons, New York, pp. 37-70.

Bucher, R., and Strauss, A. (1961, 1966), 'Professions in Process', in H. M. Vollmer and D. L. Mills (eds), *Professionalization*, Prentice-Hall, Englewood Cliffs, New Jersey, pp. 186-95.

Burns, E. M. (1956), *Social Security and Public Policy*, McGraw-Hill, New York.

Burnup, C. (1993), '"Beyond Compliance" - A Corporate Response to Environmental Ethics', in C. A. J. Coady and C. J. G. Sampford (eds), *Business, Ethics and The Law*, The Federation Press, Annandale, New South Wales, pp. 172-86.

Callahan, D. (1986), 'International Bioethics', *Hastings Center Report* 16, no. 5, p. i.

Callahan, D. (1993), 'Why America Accepted Bioethics', in A. R. Jonsen (ed.), "The Birth of Bioethics", Special Supplement, *Hastings Center Report* 23, no. 6, pp. S8-S9.

Callahan, D. (1994), 'Bioethics: Private Choice and Common Good', *The Hastings Center Report*, 24, no. 3, pp. 28-31.

Callahan, D., and Bok, S. (eds) (1980a), *Ethics Teaching in Higher Education*, The Hastings Center, Hastings-on-Hudson.

Callahan, D., and Bok, S. (eds) (1980b), *The Teaching of Ethics in Higher Education*, The Hastings Center, Hastings-on-Hudson.

Callahan, J. C. (ed.) (1988), *Ethical Issues in Professional Life*, Oxford University Press, New York.

Caplan, J. (1977), 'Lawyers and Litigants: A Cult Reviewed', in I. Illich (ed.), *Disabling Professions*, Marion Boyars, London, pp. 93-109.

Caplow, T. (1954, 1966), 'The Sociology of Work', in H. M. Vollmer and D. M. Mills (eds), *Professionalization*, Prentice-Hall, Engelwood Cliffs, New Jersey, pp. 20-1.

Carr-Saunders, A. M. (1928, 1966), 'Professions: Their Organization and Place in Society', in H. M. Vollmer and D. L. Mills (eds), *Professionalization*, Prentice-Hall, Engelwood Cliffs, New Jersey, pp. 3-9.

Carr-Saunders, A. M., and Wilson, P. A. (1933), *The Professions*, Oxford University Press, London.

Charlesworth, M. (1993), 'Ethical Reflection and Business Practice', in C. A. J. Coady and C. J. G. Sampford (eds), *Business, Ethics and the Law*, The Federation Press, Annandale, New South Wales, pp. 187-205.

Cohen, S. (1987), 'Criminology', in J. Kuper (ed.), *Key Topics of Study*, Routledge and Kegan Paul, London, pp. 28-33.

Coleman, M. (1976), 'An Idea Before Its Time', in A. Graycar (ed.) (1978), *Perspectives in Australian Social Policy: A Book of Readings*, Macmillan, Melbourne.

Cooper, J. D. (1974), 'Dimensions of Parenthood' in *The Family in Society: Dimensions of Parenthood*, Her Majesty's Stationery Office, London.

Costigan, F. (1993), 'Conflict of Interest - Chinese Walls and Bamboo Curtains', in C. A. J. Coady and C. J. G. Sampford (eds), *Business, Ethics and The Law*, The Federation Press, Annandale, New South Wales, pp. 113-26.

Cranford, R. E., and Doudera, A. E. (eds) (1984), *Institutional Ethics Committees and Health Care Decision Making*, Health Administration Press, Ann Arbor, Michigan.

Cronbach, L. J., and Associates (1980), *Toward Reform of Program Evaluation*, Jossey-Bass, San Francisco.

Cuff, D. (1991), *Architecture: The Story of Practice*, The Massachusetts Institute of Technology Press, Cambridge, Massachusetts.

Dale, J., and Foster, P. (1986), *Feminists and State Welfare*, Routledge and Kegan Paul, London.

Daniels, A. K. (1973), 'How Free Should Professionals Be?', in E. Freidson (ed.), *The Professions and Their Prospects*, Sage Publications, Beverly Hills/ London, pp. 39-57.

Diener, E. and Crandall, R. (1978), *Ethics in Social and Behavioural Research*, University of Chicago Press, Chicago.

Dingwall, R. (1976), 'Accomplishing Profession', *The Sociological Review*, vol. 24, no. 2, pp. 31-49.

Dingwall, R., and Lewis, P. (eds) (1983), *The Sociology of the Professions*, St. Martin's Press, New York.

Donnison, D. V. (1965), 'The Development of Social Administration', in D. V. Donnison and V. Chapman (eds), *Social Policy and Administration*, George Allen and Unwin, London, pp. 15-30.

Donovan, F., and Jackson, A. C. (1991), *Managing Human Service Organisations*, Prentice-Hall, New York.

Downie, R. S., and Telfer, E. (1969), *Respect for Persons*, George Allen and Unwin, London.

Dunham, A. (1958), *Community Welfare Organization: Principles and Practice*, Thomas Y. Crowell Company, New York.

Durkheim, E. (1947), 'Preface to the Second Edition 1902', in *Division of Labor in Society*, The Free Press, Glencoe, Illinois.

Eban, A. (1983), *The New Diplomacy: International Affairs in the Modern Age*, Random House, New York.

Ehrenreich, B. and J. (1979), 'The Professional-Managerial Class', in Pat Walker (ed.), *Between Labor and Capital*, South End Press, Boston, pp. 5-45.

Elliott, P. (1972), *The Sociology of the Professions*, Herder and Herder, New York.

Elliston, F. A., and Feldberg, M. (eds) (1985), *Moral Issues in Police Work*, Rowman and Allanheld, Totowa, New Jersey.

Engel, G. V., and Hall, R. H. (1973), 'The Growing Industrialization of the Professions' in E. Freidson (ed.), *The Professions and Their Prospects*, Sage Publications, Beverly Hills / London, pp. 75-87.

Ericson, R. V., Baranek, P. M. and Chan, J. B. L. (1989), *Negotiating Control: A Study of News Sources*, Open University Press, Milton Keynes.

Etzioni, A. (1964), *Modern Organizations*, Prentice-Hall, Engelwood Cliffs, New Jersey.

Etzioni, A. (ed.) (1969), *The Semi-Professions and Their Organization*, The Free Press, New York.

Evans, G. S. (1977), *Preserving the Person: a Look at the Human Sciences*, Inter Varsity Press, Downers Grove, Illinois.

Feather, N. T. (1975), *Values in Education and Society*, The Free Press, New York.

Feldman, F. (1978), *Introductory Ethics*, Prentice-Hall, Englewood Cliffs, New Jersey.

Fell, C. (1991), *Engineering in Australia*, Working group paper to Prime Minister's Science Council, Australian Government Publishing Service, Canberra.

Fisher, D. (1985), *Morality and the Bomb: An Ethical Assessment of Nuclear Deterrence*, Croom Helm, London.

Flexner, A. (1915), 'Is Social Work a Profession?' in *Proceedings of the National Conference of Charities and Correction*, Hildmann Printing Co., Chicago, pp. 576-90.

Fotion, N. (1968), *Moral Situations*, The Antioch Press, Yellow Springs, Ohio.

Fotion, N., and Elfstrom, G. (1986), *Military Ethics: Guidelines For Peace And War*, Routledge and Kegan Paul, Boston.

Francis, W. (1990), 'Evolving Systems of Project Business', in *The Quest for Quality: An Engineer's View on Responsibility and Liability*, American Society of Civil Engineers, New York, pp. 35-40.

Frankena, W. K. (1973), *Ethics* (2nd ed.), Prentice-Hall, Engelwood Cliffs, New Jersey.

Freidson, E. (1973a), 'Professions and the Occupational Principle', in E. Freidson (ed.), *The Professions and Their Prospects*, Sage Publications, Beverly Hills / London, pp. 19-38.

Freidson, E. (ed.) (1973b), *The Professions and Their Prospects,* Sage Publications, Beverly Hills / London.

Freidson, E. (1983), 'The Theory of Professions: State of the Art', in R. Dingwall and P. Lewis (eds), *The Sociology of the Professions*, St. Martin's Press, New York.

Freidson, E. (1986), *Professional Powers: a Study of the Institutionalization of Formal Knowledge*. The Chicago University Press, Chicago.

Friedman, M. and Friedman R. (1980), *Free to Choose*, Secker and Warburg, London.

Fromm, E. (1942, 1984), *The Fear of Freedom*, Ark Paperbacks, London.

Gans, H. J. (1972), *People and Plans: Essays on Urban Problems and Solutions*, Penguin Books, Harmondsworth, Middlesex.

Geison, G. L. (ed.) (1983), *Professions and Professional Ideologies in America*, The University of North Carolina Press, Chapel Hill.

Gewirth, A. (1987), *Reason and Morality*, The University of Chicago Press, Chicago.

Gilbert, N. (1983), *Capitalism and The Welfare State: Dilemmas of Social Benevolence*, Yale University Press, New Haven.

Gilbert, N., and Specht, H. (1974), *Dimensions of Social Welfare Policy*, Prentice-Hall, Englewood Cliffs, New Jersey.

Gioseffi, D. (ed.) (1993*)*, *On Prejudice: A Global Perspective*, Anchor Books, Doubleday, New York.

Goldman, A. (1980), *The Moral Foundation of Professional Ethics*, Roman and Littlefield, Totowa, New Jersey.

Goode, W. (1961, 1966), 'The Librarian: From Occupation to Profession', in H. M. Vollmer and D. L. Mills (eds), *Professionalization*, Prentice-Hall, Englewood Cliffs, New Jersey, pp. 34-43.

Goode, W. J. (1957), 'Community Within a Community: the Professions', *American Sociological Review*, vol. 22, no. 2 , pp. 194-200.

Goode, W. J. (1969), 'The Theoretical Limits of Professionalization', in A. Etzioni (ed.), *The Semi-Professions and Their Organization*, The Free Press, New York, pp. 266-313.

Goode, W. J. (1982), *The Family* (2nd ed.), Prentice-Hall, Engelwood Cliffs, New Jersey.

Goodwin, H. E. (1987), *Groping for Ethics in Journalism* (2nd ed.), Iowa State University Press, Ames, Iowa.

Grace, D., and Cohen, S. (1995), *Business Ethics*, Oxford University Press, South Melbourne.

Greenwood, E. (1957), 'Attributes of a Profession', *Social Work*, vol. 2, no.3, pp. 44-55.

Green, F., and Sutcliffe, B. (1987), *The Profit System: The Economics of Capitalism*, Penguin Books, Harmondsworth, Middlesex.

Gross, R., and Osterman, P. (eds) (1972), *The New Professionals*, Simon and Schuster, New York.

Grunebaum, H. (1985), 'Family Therapy', in A. and J. Kuper (eds), *The Social Science Encyclopedia*, Routledge and Kegan Paul, London, p. 293.

Gummer, B. (1987), 'Competing Perspectives on the Concept of "Effectiveness" in the Analysis of Social Services', in R. J. Patti, et al. (eds), *Managing for Service Effectiveness in Social Welfare Organizations*, The Haworth Press, New York, pp. 257-70.

Gunningham, N. (1993), 'Beyond Command and Control: Towards Flexible and Cost-effective Business Regulation', in C. A. J. Coady and C. J. G. Sampford (eds), *Business, Ethics and The Law*, The Federation Press, Annandale, New South Wales, pp. 93-112.

Hall, P. (1976), *Reforming the Welfare: The Politics of Change in the Personal Social Services*, Heinemann, London.

Halmos, P. (1970), *The Personal Service Society*, Shocken Books, New York.

Halmos, P. (ed.) (1973a), *Professionalization and Social Change*, The Sociological Review Monograph 20.

Halmos, P. (1973b), 'Sociology and the Personal Service Professions', in E. Freidson (ed.), *The Professions and Their Prospects*, Sage Publications, Beverly Hills / London, pp. 291-305.

Hare, R. M. (1981), *Moral Thinking, its Level, Method and Point*, Clarendon Press, Oxford.

Harris, C. C. (1985), 'The Family', in A. and J. Kuper (eds), *The Social Science Encyclopedia* (pp. 289-91), London: Routledge and Kegan Paul.

Haug, M. R., and Sussman, M. B. (1973), 'Professionalization and Unionism: A Jurisdictional Dispute?', in E. Freidson (ed.), *The Professions and Their Prospects*, Sage Publications, Beverly Hills / London, pp. 89-103.

Heilbroner, R. L. (1980), *The Worldly Philosophers* (5th ed.), Simon and Schuster, New York.

Held, V. (1984), *Rights and Goods: Justifying Social Action*, The Free Press, New York.

Horsburgh, M. (1980), 'Relationships between Government and Voluntary Organizations in Social Welfare', in F. Pavlin et al. (eds), *Perspectives in Australian Social Work*, PIT Publishing, Bundoora, Victoria, pp. 17-34.

Howard, D. S. (1969), *Social Welfare: Values, Means and Ends*, Random House, New York.

Hudson, S. D. (1986), *Human Character and Morality: Reflections from the History of Ideas*, Routledge and Kegan Paul, Boston.

Hughes, E. (1960, 1966), 'The Professions in Society', in H. M. Vollmer and D. L. Mills (eds), *Professionalization*, Prentice-Hall, Englewood Cliffs, New Jersey, pp. 64-70.

Hughes, R. (1993), *Culture of Complaint: The Fraying of America*, Oxford University Press, New York.

Huntington, J. (1981), *Social Work and General Medical Practice: Collaboration or Conflict?*, George Allen and Unwin, London.

Hurst, J., and White, S. A. (1994), *Ethics and the Australian News Media*, Macmillan, South Melbourne.

Illich, I. (ed.) (1977), *Disabling Professions*, Marion Boyars, London.

Industry Commission (1995), *Charitable Organizations in Australia*, Report no. 45, June 1995, Australian Government Publishing Service, Melbourne.

International Federation of Social Workers (IFSW) (1994), The Ethical Instruments of the IFSW.

Jackson, J. A. (ed.) (1970), *Professions and Professionalization*, Cambridge University Press, London.

Johnson, T. J. (1972), *Professions and Power*, Macmillan, London.

Jones, K., et al. (1983), *Issues in Social Policy* (2nd ed.), Routledge and Kegan Paul, London.

Kahn, A. (1969), *Theory and Practice of Social Planning*, Russell Sage Foundation, New York.

Kent, R. A. (1981), *A History of British Empirical Sociology*, Gower, Aldershot.

Keyfitz, N. (1987), 'Demography', in J. Kuper (ed.), *Key Topics of Study*, London, Routledge and Kegan Paul, pp. 34-40.

Kirby, M. (1983), *Reform the Law: Essays on the renewal of the Australian legal system*, Oxford University Press, Melbourne.

Kluckhohn, F. R., and Strodbeck, F. L. (1961), *Variations in Value Orientations*, Row Peterson, New York.

Kramer, R. (1981), *Voluntary Agencies in the Welfare State*, University of California Press, Berkeley.

Kultgen, J. (1988), *Ethics and Professionalism*, University of Pennsylvania Press, Philadelphia.

Kumar, K. (1985), 'Post-Industrial Society', in A. and J. Kuper (eds), *The Social Science Encyclopedia*, Routledge and Kegan Paul, London, 633-4.

Ladd, J. (1978), 'Ethics: the Task of Ethics', in *Encyclopedia of Bioethics*, The Free Press, New York, pp. 400-7.

Langan, J. (1993), 'The Ethics of Business and the Role of Religion', in C. A. J. Coady and C. J. G. Sampford (eds), *Business Ethics and the Law*, The Federation Press, Annandale, New South Wales, pp. 52-66.

Larmore, C. E. (1987), *Patterns of Moral Complexity*, Cambridge University Press, Cambridge.

Larson, M. S. (1977), *The Rise of Professionalism: a Sociological Analysis*, University of California Press, Berkeley.

Lasch, C. (1979), *The Culture of Narcissism*, W. W. Norton, New York.

Laski, H. (1931), *Limitations of the Expert*, Fabian Tract, London.

Laski, H. (1935), 'The Decline of the Professions', *Harpers Monthly Magazine*, November, 656-7.

Lawrence, J. (1983), The Relevance of Moral Philosophy for Professional Education, Prepared for a Rutgers University Committee on the Professions Colloquium.

Lawrence, J. (1984), 'Human Survival and Development: Our Urgent Need for a Reflective Universal Morality' - Younghusband Memorial Lecture, in B.Schlesinger and R. C. Nann (eds), *22nd International Congress, International Association of Schools of Social Work*, International Association of Schools of Social Work, Montreal, pp. 3-23.

Lawrence, R. J. (1966), 'Organizational Issues in Social Welfare', in R. J. Lawrence (ed.), *Community Service: Citizens and Social Welfare Organizations*, F. W. Cheshire, Melbourne, pp. 29-50.

Lawrence, R. J. (1968), 'A Social Transaction Model for the Analysis of Social Welfare', *The Australian Journal of Social Issues*, vol. 3, no. 4, pp. 51-72.

Lawrence, R. J. (1978), 'Human Well-Being and Human Rights', in *Human Well-Being: the Challenge of Continuity and Change - 50th Anniversary Publication*, International Council on Social Welfare, Jerusalem, pp. 101-10.

Lewis, H. (1987), 'Ethics and the Managing of Service Effectiveness in Social Welfare', in R. J. Patti, et al. (eds), *Managing for Service Effectiveness in Social Welfare Organizations*, The Haworth Press, New York, pp. 271-84.

Lewis, J. (1994), 'Shoddy Teachers Face Lawsuits', *Sydney Morning Herald*, 30 August, p. 1.

Lewis, R., and Maude, A. (1953), *Professional People in England*, Harvard University Press, Cambridge, Massachusetts.

Lieberman, J. K. (1970), *The Tyranny of the Experts*, Walker and Co., New York.

Lyon, D. (1988), *The Information Society: Issues and Illusions*, Polity Press, Cambridge.

MacIntyre, A. (1967), *A Short History of Ethics*, London, Routledge and Kegan Paul.

MacIntyre, A. (1981), *After Virtue: a Study in Moral Theory*, Duckworth, London.

MacIver, R. (1966, 1922, 1955), 'The Social Significance of Professional Ethics', in H. M. Vollmer and D. L. Mills (eds), *Professionalization*, Prentice-Hall, Englewood Cliffs, New Jersey, pp. 50-5.

Marshall, T. H. (1939), 'The Recent History of Professionalism in Relation to Social Structure and Social Policy', *The Canadian Journal of Economics and Political Science*, vol. 5, no. 3, pp. 325-40.

Mayo (1986), *The Philosophy of Right and Wrong*, Routledge and Kegan Paul, London.

McKnight, D. (1994), *Australia's Spies and Their Secrets*, Allen and Unwin, Sydney.

McKnight, J. (1977), 'Professionalized Service and Disabling Help', in I. Illich (ed.), *Disabling Professions*, Marion Boyars, London, pp. 69-91.

Midgley, J. (1981), *Professional Imperialism: Social Work in the Third World*. Heinemann, London.

Midgley, J. (1984), 'Fields of Practice and Professional Roles for Social Planners: an Overview', in J. Midgley and D. Piachaud (eds), *The Fields and Methods of Social Planning*, Heinemann, London.

Millerson, G. (1964), *The Qualifying Associations: a Study in Professionalization*. Routledge and Kegan Paul, London.

Milligan, V. et al. (eds) (1984), *Non-Government Welfare Organizations in Australia: A National Classification*, Social Welfare Research Centre Reports and Proceedings no. 51, Social Welfare Research Centre, The University of New South Wales, Kensington, New South Wales.

Mishra, R. (1981), *Social Theory and Social Policy: Theories and Practice of Welfare* (2nd ed.), Macmillan, London.

Mishra, R. (1984), *The Welfare State in Crisis: Social Thought and Social Change*, Wheatsheaf Books, Brighton, Sussex.

Mok, A. L. (1973), 'Professional Innovation in Post-Industrial Society', in E. Freidson (ed.), *The Professions and Their Prospects*, Sage Publications, Beverly Hills / London, pp. 105-15.

Moore, W. E. (1970), *The Professions: Roles and Rules*, Russell Sage Foundation, New York.

Morris, L. (1994), 'Fear of Murder is Rife, Survey Reports', *Sydney Morning Herald*, 17 November.

Mount, E. Jr (1990), *Professional Ethics in Context: Institutions, Images, and Empathy*, Westminster / John Knox Press, Louiseville, Kentucky.

Munson, R. (1988), *Intervention and Reflection: Basic Issues in Medical Ethics* (3rd ed.), Wadsworth, Belmont, California.

Murphy, M. J. (1977), 'Financing Social Welfare: Voluntary Organizations', in J. B. Turner (ed.), *Encyclopedia of Social Work*, 17th Issue, vol. 1, National Association of Social Workers, Washington, D.C., pp. 478-84.

National Education Association (1976), *Values Concepts and Techniques*, National Education Association, Washington, D.C..

Nelson, H. L. (1993), 'The Newest Profession', *Hastings Center Report* 23, no. 4, p.2.

Neugeboren, B. (1985), *Organization, Policy, and Practice in the Human Services*, Longman, New York.

O'Connell, R. L. (1989), *Of Arms and Men: A History of War, Weapons, and Aggression*, Oxford University Press, New York.

Owen, J. M. (1993), *Program Evaluation: Forms and Approaches*, Allen and Unwin, St. Leonards, New South Wales.

Palca, J. (1995), 'Society's Choices', *Hastings Center Report* 25, no. 3, p. 7.

Palmer, G. R. and Short, S. D. (1989), *Health Care and Public Policy: An Australian Analysis*, Macmillan, South Melbourne.

Parker, R. S. (1972), 'Planning and Politics', in R. S. Parker and P. N. Troy (eds), *The Politics of Urban Growth*, Australian National University Press, Canberra, pp. 24-36.

Parsons, T. (1968), 'Professions', in D. L. Sills (ed.), *Encyclopedia of the Social Sciences*, The Macmillan Co. and the Free Press, New York, pp. 536-47.

Patti, R. J. (1983), *Social Welfare Administration: Managing Social Programs in a Developmental Context*, Prentice-Hall, Engelwood Cliffs, New Jersey.

Patti, R. J., et al. (eds) (1987), *Managing for Service Effectiveness in Social Welfare Organizations*, Special double issue of *Administration in Social Work*, vol. 11, nos 3/4, The Haworth Press, New York.

Patti, R. J. (1987), 'Managing for Service Effectiveness in Social Welfare: Toward a Performance Model', in R. J. Patti, et al. (eds), *Managing for Service Effectiveness in Social Welfare Organizations*, The Haworth Press, New York, pp. 7-21.

Patton, M. Q. (1986), *Utilization-focused Evaluation* (2nd ed.), Sage, Beverly Hills, California.

Peccei, A. (1982), *One Hundred Pages for the Future: Reflections of the President of the Club of Rome*, Futura Publications, London.

Perkin, H. (1989), *The Rise of Professional Society: England since 1880*, London, Routledge.

Perrow, C. (1986), *Complex Organizations: A Critical Essay* (3rd edit.), Random House, New York.

Phillips, D. L. (1973), 'Sociologists and Their Knowledge: Some Critical Remarks on a Profession', in E. Freidson (ed.), *The Professions and Their Prospects*, Sage Publications, Beverly Hills / London, pp. 307-26.

Piven, F. F., and Cloward, R. A. (1971), *Regulating the Poor: the Functions of Public Welfare*, Pantheon Books, New York.

Pixley, J. (1993), *Citizenship and Employment: Investigating Post-Industrial Options*, Cambridge University Press, Cambridge.

Poirot, J. W. (1990), 'Defining Quality, Responsibility and Liability', in *The Quest for Quality: An Engineer's View of Responsibility and Liability*, American Society of Civil Engineers, New York, pp. 10-19.

Popper, K. R. (1950), *The Open Society and its Enemies*, Princeton University Press, Princeton.

Prest, W. (ed.) (1987), *The Professions in Early Modern England*, Croom Helm, London.

Pugh, D. S., Hickson, D. J., and Hinings, C. R. (1971), *Writers on Organizations* (2nd ed.), Penguin Education, Harmondsworth, Middlesex.

Pusey, M. (1991), *Economic Rationalism in Canberra: A Nation-Building State Changes Its Mind*, Cambridge University Press, Cambridge.

Rachels, J. (1986), *The Elements of Moral Philosophy*, Temple University Press, Philadelphia.

Rapp, C. A., and Poertner, J. (1987), 'Moving Clients Center Stage Through the Use of Client Outcomes', in R. J. Patti, et al. (eds), *Managing for Service Effectiveness in Social Welfare Organizations*, The Haworth Press, New York, pp. 23-38.

Rawls, J. (1972), *A Theory of Justice*, Oxford University Press, London.

Reamer, F. G. (1995), 'Ethics Consultation in Social Work', *Social Thought*, vol. 18, no. 1, pp. 3-16.

Reich, B., and Adcock, C. (1976), *Values, Attitudes and Behaviour Change,* London, Methuen.

Rein, M. (1970), *Social Policy*, Random House, New York.

Report of the Objectives Committee (1981), Benevolent Society of New South Wales, Sydney.

Report to the Secretary-General by a Group of Consultant Experts (1983), *Economic and Social Consequences of the Arms Race and of Military Expenditures*, United Nations, New York.

Rescher, N. (1969), *Introduction to Value Theory*, Prentice-Hall, Engelwood Cliffs, New Jersey.

Revay, S. G. (1990), 'Quality, Responsibility and Liability', in *The Quest for Quality: An Engineer's View on Responsibility and Liability*, American Society of Civil Engineers New York, pp. 1-9.

Ritzer, G. (1973), 'Professionalism and the Individual', in E. Freidson (ed.), *The Professions and their Prospects*, Sage Publications, Beverly Hills / London, pp. 59-73.

Roberts, R. (1990), *Lessons From the Past: Issues for Social Work Theory*, Tavistock / Routledge, London.

Rokeach, M. (1973), *The Nature of Human Values*, The Free Press, New York.

Rueschemeyer, D. (1983), 'Professional Autonomy and the Social Control of Expertise', in R. Dingwall and P. Lewis (eds), *The Sociology of the Professions*, St. Martin's Press, New York, pp. 38-58.

Rueschemeyer, D. (1986), *Power and the Division of Labour*, Polity Press, Cambridge.

Ryan, W. (1971), *Blaming the Victim*, Pantheon, New York.

Sampford, C., and Wood, D. (1993), 'The Future of Business Ethics: Legal Regulation, Ethical Standard Setting and Institutional Design', in C. A. J. Coady and C. J. G. Sampford (eds), *Business, Ethics and The Law*, The Federation Press, Annandale, New South Wales, pp. 2-23.

Sandercock, L. (1977), *Cities for Sale: Property, Politics and Urban Planning in Australia*, Melbourne University Press, Carlton, Victoria.

Sarri, R. C. (1979), 'History and Development of Evaluation in the Human Services: a View from the United States', in *Through a Glass Darkly*, vol. 2, Australian Government Publishing Service, Canberra, pp. 61-75.

Sarri, R. C. (1982), 'Management Trends in the Human Services in the 1980s', in *Administration in Social Work*, vol. 6, nos 2/3, 19-30.

Sarri, R. C., and Lawrence, R. J. (eds) (1980), *Issues in the Evaluation of Social Welfare Programs: Australian Case Illustrations*, New South Wales University Press Ltd., Kensington, New South Wales.

Sax, S. (1984), *A Strife of Interests: Politics and Policies in Australian Health Services*, George Allen and Unwin, Sydney.

Scott, D. (1981), *'Don't mourn for me - organize...'* George Allen and Unwin, Sydney.

Seebohm Report (1968), *Report of The Committee on Local Authority and Allied Personal Social Services*, Her Majesty's Stationery Office, London.

Seldon, A. (1987), *Law and Lawyers in Perspective*, Penguin Books, Harmondsworth, Middlesex.

Sexton, M., and Maher, L. W. (1982), *The Legal Mystique: The Role of Lawyers in Australian Society*, Angus and Robertson, London.

Shils, E. (1987), 'Sociology', in J. Kuper (ed.), *Key Topics of Study*, Routledge and Kegan Paul, London, pp. 210-32.

Shonfield, A., and Shaw, S. (1972), *Social Indicators and Social Policy*, Heinemann, London.

Simpson, R. L., and Simpson, I. H. (1969), 'Women and Bureaucracy in the Semi-Professions', in A. Etzioni (eds), *The Semi-Professions and Their Organization*, The Free Press, New York, pp. 196-265.

Sinclair, A. (1993), 'Improving Ethics Through Organisational Culture: A Comparison of Two Approaches', in C. A. J. Coady and C. J. G. Sampford (eds), *Business, Ethics and The Law*, The Federation Press, Annandale, New South Wales, pp. 128-48.

Singer, P. (1977), *Animal Liberation*, Avon Books, New York.

Singer, P. (1979), 'Equality for Animals?', in *Practical Ethics*, Cambridge University Press, Cambridge, pp. 48-71.

Singer, P. (1981), *The Expanding Circle: Ethics and Sociobiology*, Farrar, Sraus and Giroux, New York.

Skidmore, R. A. (1983), *Social Work Administration: Dynamic Management and Human Relationships*, Prentice-Hall, Englewood Cliffs, New Jersey.

Smart, J. J. C. (1984), *Ethics, Persuasion and Truth*, Routledge and Kegan Paul, London.

Society's Choices: Social and Ethical Decision Making in Biomedicine (1995), National Academy Press, Washington, D.C..

Solomon, W. D. (1978), 'Ethics: Rules and Principles', in W. T. Reich (ed.), *Encyclopedia of Ethics*, The Free Press, New York, pp. 407-12.

Starr, P. (1982), *The Social Transformation of American Medicine*, Basic Books, New York.

Stein, H. D. (1962), 'The Study of Organizational Effectiveness', in D. Fanshel (ed.), *Research in Social Welfare Administration*, National Association of Social Workers, New York, pp. 22-4.

Strauss, A. L. (1975), *Professions, Work and Careers*, Transaction Books, New Brunswick, New Jersey.

Stonehouse, B. (ed.) (1987), *Philip's Illustrated Atlas of the World*, George Philip Ltd..

Sussman, M. B. (1977), 'Family', in *Encyclopedia of Social Work*, vol. 1, National Association of Social Workers, Washington, D. C., pp. 357-68.

Sutherland, S. (1994), *Irrationality: The Enemy Within*, Penguin Books, London.

Svensson, N. L. (1990), *Introduction to Engineering Design*, New South Wales University Press, Kensington, New South Wales.

Sydney Morning Herald, Editorial (1994), 'Kirby's Law For NSW Teachers?' 31 August, p. 18.

Tawney, R. H. (1961, 1921), *The Acquisitive Society*, Fontana.

The Family in Society: Preparation for Parenthood (1974), Her Majesty's Stationery Office, London.

*The Family in Society: Dimensions of Parenth*ood (1974), Her Majesty's Stationery Office, London.

Thiroux, J. P. (1980), *Ethics: Theory and Practice* (2nd ed.), Glencoe, Encino, California.

Thompson, M. S. (1975), *Evaluation for Decision in Social Programmes*, Lexington Books, Lexington, Massachusetts.

Through a Glass Darkly: Evaluation in Australian Health and Welfare Services (1979), Report from the Senate Standing Committee on Social Welfare, vols.1 and 2, Australian Government Publishing Service, Canberra.

Titmuss, R. (1963), 'The Social Division of Welfare: Some Reflections on the Search for Equity', in *Essays on 'The Welfare State'*, George Allen and Unwin, London, pp. 34-55.

Titmuss, R. (1968), *Commitment to Welfare*, Pantheon Books, New York.

Tonnies, F. (1957), *Community and Society: Gemeinschaft and Gesellschaft*, Translated and with an introduction by C. P. Loomis, Harper and Row, New York.

Toohey, B. (1994), *Tumbling Dice: The Story of Modern Economic Policy*, William Heinemann, Port Melbourne.

Totaro, P. (1994), 'Facts not Allowed to Get in the Way of the Politics of Fear', *Sydney Morning Herald*, 23 November.

Toyne, P. (1994), *The Reluctant Nation: Environment, law and politics in Australia*, ABC Books, Sydney.

Tropman, J. E., and E. J. (1977), 'Community Welfare Councils', in J. B. Turner (ed.), *Encyclopedia of Social Work*, 17th Issue, vol. 1, National Association of Social Workers, Washington, D. C., 187-93.

Troy, P. N. (ed.) (1981), *Equity in the City*, George Allen and Unwin, Sydney.

Turner, C., and Hodge, M. N. (1970), 'Occupations and Professions', in J. A. Jackson (ed.), *Professions and Professionalization*, Cambridge University Press, London, pp. 19-50.

United Nations (1948), *Universal Declaration of Human Rights*, UN, New York.

United Nations (1976), *The International 'Bill of Human Rights'*, UN, New York.

United Nations (1978), *The International Bill of Human Rights*, UN, New York.

United Nations (1983), *Human Rights International Instruments*, UN, New York.

United Nations Department of Public Information for Economic and Social Information (1980), *Towards a World Economy That Works*, UN, New York.

Veatch, R. M. (1993), 'From Forgoing Life Support to Aid-in-Dying', in A. R. Jonsen (ed.), "The Birth of Bioethics" Special Supplement, *Hastings Center Report* 23, no. 6, pp. S7-S8.

Vollmer, H. M., and Mills, D. L. (eds) (1966), *Professionalization*, Prentice-Hall, Englewood Cliffs, New Jersey.

Warnock, G. J. (1971), *The Object of Morality*, Methuen, London.

Warnock, M. (1966), *Ethics Since 1900* (2nd ed.), Oxford University Press, London.

Watson, T. (1987), *Sociology, Work and Industry* (2nd ed.), Routledge and Kegan Paul, London.

Weiner, T. (1994), 'Spy Case Reveals Heavy Damage to CIA', *Sydney Morning Herald*, 26 September.

Weiss, C. H. (1972), *Evaluation Research: Methods of Assessing Program Effectiveness*, Prentice-Hall, Englewood Cliffs, New Jersey.

Wells, C. C. (1986), *Social Work Ethics Day to Day: Guidelines for Professional Practice*, Longman, New York.

White House Domestic Policy Council (1993), *Health Security: The President's Report to the American People*, Simon and Schuster, New York.

Wilensky, H. (1964), 'The Professionalization of Everyone?' *American Journal of Sociology*, vol. 70 (September), pp. 142-6.

Wilensky, H. L., and Lebeaux, C. N. (1965), *Industrial Society and Social Welfare* (2nd ed.), The Free Press, New York.

Williams, B. (1973), 'The Idea of Equality', in *Problems of the Self: Philosophical Papers 1956-72*, Cambridge University Press, Cambridge, pp. 232-5.

Williams, B. (1985), *Ethics and the Limits of Philosophy*, Harvard University Press, Cambridge, Massachusetts.

Williams, R. (1960), *American Society: a Sociological Interpretation* (2nd ed.), Knopf, New York.

Willis, E. (1989), *Medical Dominance: The division of labour in Australian health care*, Allen and Unwin, Sydney.

Windschuttle, K. (1988), *The Media: A New Analysis of the Press, Television, Radio, and Advertising in Australia*, Penguin Books, Ringwood, Victoria.

Wolf, S. (1987), 'The Deflation of Moral Philosophy', *Ethics*, vol. 97 (July), pp. 821-33.

Wolfenden Committee Report (1978), *The Future of Voluntary Organizations*, Croom Helm, London.

Wong, D. (1984), *Moral Relativity*, University of California Press, Berkeley.

Wright, P. (1987), *Spycatcher*, William Heinemann, Richmond, Victoria.

Wright, T., and Seccombe, M. (1994), 'Traitor in ASIO Told All, Says KGB General', *Sydney Morning Herald*, 4 November.

Year Book of Labour Statistics (1986).

Zola, I. (1977), 'Healthism and Disabling Medicalization', in I. Illich (ed.), *Disabling Professions*, Marion Boyars, London, pp. 41-67.

Index

Abbott, A.76, 81, 85-6, 95-6, 99, 227, 228
Abel, R. 99, 143
Acton, H. 195
Alexander, I. 171
altruism 37, 43, 87, 91, 108, 115, 221-2
animals, moral claims 34, 174, 278
Australian Senate Standing Committee On Social Welfare 284-5
authority 17, 59, 73,74, 89, 93, 94, 238, 277
autonomy 22, 36-7,39, 42, 44, 46, 59, 87, 92, 111-12, 132-4, 153, 175, 191, 209, 213, 358

Baier, K. 14-15
Bailey, J. 141, 142
Barrow, R. 35
Bates, E. and Lapsley, H. 153, 154, 156-7, 161
Baume, P. 284
Bayles, M. 26-7, 228-31
Beauchamp, T. and Childress, J. 226, 231, 256-7, 295
Bell, D. 55
Benn, S. and Peters, R. 5, 11-12, 15, 33, 34, 35, 36, 38, 124-5, 198
Berger, P. 142
biological determinism 39, 54
blame 22
Blau, P. 269
Bledstein, B. 88-9
Bliss, C. 140
Blustein, J. 190
Bucher, R. and Strauss, A.78, 82, 87-8

Callahan, D. 240-1
Callahan, D. and Bok, S. 24
Caplow, T. 89
Carr-Saunders, A. 81
Carr-Saunders, A. and Wilson, P. 67-72, 77, 81-2, 87
causality 38
Christians 224, 225
change in economic, political and social climate 31
Charlesworth, M. 194-5, 196-7
civil and political rights 44
class 32, 34, 65, 67, 92-3, 95, 96-7, 98
comparative policy studies 30
conscientious moral agent 17
consensus 17-18, 23, 42, 44, 82, 87-8
consequences, *see* evaluation, model of ethical conduct - result
consumers in the modern economy 90
convention
    values 7-8, 12-13, 38-9, 41, 44, 45, 53-4
        concepts and characteristics 7-8; conflicts 8; operational 8
    rules 8-13
        existence 9-10; four rule systems 11-12; principles, policies, regulations 9; rights and duties 12; sanctions 10, 73; scope 11; systems 11, 277
Cooper, J. 189-90
Costigan, F. 198
critical moral thinking 16
Cronbach, L. and Associates 31, 281-3
cultural diversity 12-13, 20-1, 54

315